BRITISH BUILT AIRCRAFT

AIRCRAFT

VOLUME 2

South West & Central
Southern England

BRITISH BUILT AIRCRAFT

VOLUME 2
South West & Central Southern England

Ron Smith

The History Press

Other books by Ron Smith:

British Built Aircraft (volume 1) – Greater London
British Built Aircraft (volume 3) – South East England
British Built Aircraft (volume 4) – Central & Eastern England
British Built Aircraft (volume 5) – Northern England, Scotland,
Wales & Northern Ireland

First published 2003
Reprinted 2010
The History Press
The Mill, Brimscombe Port
Stroud, Gloucestershire, GL5 2QG
www.thehistorypress.co.uk

British Library Cataloguing in Publication Data.
A catalogue record for this book is available from the British Library.

ISBN 978 0 7524 2785 0
Typesetting and origination by The History Press
Printed in Great Britain
Manufacturing managed by Jellyfish Print Solutions Ltd

Contents

Introduction

This volume is the second in a series, which, when completed, will provide a complete record of aircraft construction in Britain. Each volume of this work focuses on a different regional area, documenting activity over the whole period from 1908 until the present day, keyed to the places where this enterprise was actually performed. The objective of the whole work is to pay tribute to the heritage of the British aircraft industry, and to create and preserve a record of its lost endeavours. Perhaps the major new element presented in this work is to shed some light on the sheer scale of the effort involved in the construction of aircraft during the First World War.

As soon as one starts to examine the history of the aircraft industry, it becomes clear that it has developed through a number of distinct phases. These phases can be characterised as the pioneers (1908 to 1914), First World War mass production (1914 to 1918), collapse and re-birth between the wars (1919 to 1939), Second World War mass production (1939 to 1945), post-war (1945 to 1960), and modern times. A discussion of the evolution of the industry covering these six main periods of activity can be found in Section One. The aim of this review of the evolution of the industry is to place the remainder of the work within the overall context, whilst highlighting developments that are specific to the area of South West and Central Southern England.

Some twenty-five years ago, on the formation of British Aerospace (BAe), the American magazine *Aviation Week and Space Technology* wryly commented that the final phase of development of the Society of British Aircraft Constructors (SBAC) had now taken place. Whereas previously the numerous members of the SBAC had reflected the vigour, diversity and inventive spirit of the British industry, it had, following restructuring in 1960, been reduced to the 'Society of Both Aircraft Companies' (i.e. the British Aircraft Corporation and Hawker Siddeley Aviation Ltd). The formation of BAe was the final act in the process, with the once great industry reduced to the 'Single British Aerospace Company'.

This light-hearted comment contains an important message. British aircraft industry names, which were once well known to the public, have disappeared from the day to day business of manufacturing aeroplanes. Indeed, in many instances, their operating sites have even disappeared from the map. At first sight it seems as if the once vibrant British aircraft industry has contracted virtually to the point of extinction since the Second World War. The entire industry has been reduced to the firms of BAE SYSTEMS, AgustaWestland, Slingsby and Britten-Norman (surviving, as I write, in its latest manifestation: B-N Group), together with sundry microlight and home-built aircraft suppliers.

Hornet Moth G-AELO is seen here at Pocklington prior to the 1994 Dawn to Dusk competition flight by Colin Dodds and the author. (Author)

Many British aircraft manufacturers have disappeared altogether and this has provided the inspiration for this survey of the industry. Pondering on the demise (in this area alone) of such company names as Airspeed, Supermarine, Folland, Gloster, Parnall, Saunders-Roe, Bristol and Vickers-Armstrongs, the idea grew that an effort should be made to record something of Britain's aircraft construction history and heritage. This area has also seen the closure of many airfields; the increasing pressure for housing is reflected in the loss of Christchurch, Portsmouth and Yate, whilst Tarrant Rushton, Chilbolton and Moreton Valence have returned to agriculture. Industrial development has claimed Hucclecote and South Marston.

The first outcome of this desire to document the past achievements of the British aircraft industry was a successful entry in the 1994 Pooley's International Dawn to Dusk Flying Competition by the author, with his colleague Colin Dodds. The entry, under the title *Lost Names in British Aviation*, consisted of the record of a flight made on a single day (between dawn and dusk) in a 1936 de Havilland Hornet Moth, over sites in Britain where aircraft had once been built, by companies that no longer exist. The research carried out in support of that competition entry has been greatly extended to provide the basis for this record of British achievement, innovation, failure and success.

Content

This series of books, of which South West and Central Southern England is the second, records British aircraft manufacture in nearly all its manifestations, in the form of a regional survey of the UK. The scope of the work is deliberately wide, including as many locations as possible where aircraft have been built, whether by their original designers or by contractors. Exclusions are limited to balloons, the majority of gliders and microlight aircraft, and home-built aircraft of foreign design, unless substantially modified in the form flown in the UK.

Being centred on the various manufacturing sites, the book allows a wider scope than a mere litany of product histories, allowing additional discussion of people, places and events. As a result, the major players of the industry are recorded alongside the wealth of early activity, light aircraft and one-off designs that provide a rich background to the main scene. Such is the scope of this record that the space that can be allocated to any individual firm is necessarily limited. This mainly has the effect of producing a somewhat condensed view of some of the largest and best known companies. This limitation is, hopefully, compensated for by some of the fascinating but unfamiliar material presented, covering many companies which are likely to be unfamiliar to the reader.

Those interested in the detailed history of the major manufacturers will be able to find many excellent books with which to fill in the detail if they wish. The same cannot be said for companies such as The Bournemouth Aviation Co. Ltd, Bath Aircraft Ltd, Motor Mac's Ltd, Oddie, Bradbury & Cull Ltd, Gosport Aircraft Co., and a number of other lesser known companies from South West and Central Southern England that are included here.

Structure

These introductory remarks are followed by a discussion of the evolution of the aircraft industry, highlighting the activities that characterise each of the main periods identified above, and tailored to the specific region covered by this volume. The contraction through successive mergers that has given rise to the present shape of the industry is presented, together with a family tree of British Aerospace (which contains all of the aircraft heritage of the present BAE SYSTEMS) and of the helicopter manufacturer AgustaWestland.

The main content of the volume follows in Section Two; this volume being a survey of aircraft manufacture in South West and Central Southern England, as defined by the following counties: Cornwall, Devon, Somerset, Dorset, Gloucestershire, Wiltshire, Hampshire, the Isle of Wight and the Channel Islands. The presentation structure is alphabetical by county, and then alphabetical by location. For most locations, individual manufacturers are then presented alphabetically in sequence.

Where activity at a single site has only involved one firm at any time, or where the evolution of a single major firm has dominated a particular site, the presentation is chronological, rather than alphabetical. Filton and Yeovil are examples of such a variation. Where there is a concentration of activity in a single vicinity, the entries are also grouped. Two instances apply in this volume: the Bristol area, and the Southampton area.

When the series is complete it will provide a comprehensive geographic and product history of UK aircraft construction. I have attempted to cover all sites where aircraft manufacture took place, and to select photographs which provide a balanced mix of example products, locations as they are now and as they were during their heyday, or combinations of these. A number of the photographs are of the sites as taken from the air during the 1994 Dawn to Dusk competition.

Information Sources and Acknowledgements

A number of major reference sources were used to create this survey of the British aircraft industry. Chief among these were magazines such as *Flight, The Aeroplane*, and *Aeroplane Monthly*, and the following books and publications, which provide particularly useful material across the whole spectrum of the industry: Terence Boughton's excellent *History of the British Light Aeroplane*; A.J. Jackson's *British Civil Aircraft since 1919*; the individual company histories published by Putnam; Ken Ellis' *British Homebuilt Aircraft Since 1920*; R. Dallas Brett's *History of British Aviation 1909-14*; Arthur Ord-Hume's encyclopaedic *British Light Aeroplanes – Their Evolution, Development and Perfection 1920-40*; the equally outstanding *British Aircraft Before The Great War* by Michael H. Goodall and Albert E. Tagg; many editions of *Jane's All the World's Aircraft*; a wide range of test pilot autobiographies; and numerous other sources.

In setting out to document the British aircraft industry I wish to give a flavour of the breadth of the endeavour in terms of the diversity of both products and places used for aircraft manufacture. It is not my intention to provide a definitive record of every aircraft built, nor an encyclopaedia of production quantities. In some cases, I have found the latter aspect clouded with uncertainty; unless clearly definitive data is available, I have used Bruce Robertson's *British Military Aircraft Serials 1878-1987* as a guide when indicating production quantities. I have not hesitated to highlight areas where conflicting information may be found in readily available references. It is for others to research and clarify these issues.

Particular thanks are due to my colleague Rob Preece for the loan of his original unbound copies of *Flight* covering the period 1911 to 1923, and to Liz and Peter Curtis for access to a complete collection of *Aeroplane Monthly* magazines. Thanks are also due to Chris Ilett for the loan of *Flight* magazines from 1929 and 1930. A further acknowledgement must be made to the Royal Aeronautical Society library; not only are their early copies of *The Aeroplane* bound complete with their advertising pages, but here I also found a copy of R. Borlase Matthews' *Aviation Pocket-Book 1919-1920* whose Gazetteer of the industry put me on the track of many unfamiliar companies. I am most grateful for the assistance provided by George Jenks (AVRO Heritage Centre) and the late Barry Abraham (Airfield Research Group). Dave Fagan has provided helpful comments in respect of the content for Hampshire, Dorset and the Isle of Wight.

Acknowledgement is due to those companies still extant (and not today associated with the aircraft industry) who answered my correspondence. Mention must also be made of the information and photographs supplied for this series by Ken Ellis, and by Mr A.H. Fraser-Mitchell (Handley Page Association), the late Fred Ballam (Westland), Olivia Johnston (Bombardier Aerospace, Belfast), Sarah Beazley (Marshall Aerospace plc), Chris Hodson (Folland Aircraft Ltd) and Del Hoyland (Martin-Baker Aircraft Co. Ltd). I must further acknowledge the access provided to photographic material by my present employer, BAE SYSTEMS. In making this acknowledgement, I should also stress that all opinions expressed herein are entirely my own. I also acknowledge the permission received from BAE SYSTEMS plc, which enables me to reproduce a number of advertisements from BAE SYSTEMS legacy companies in this volume. Every effort has been made to provide the correct attribution for the illustrations used. Please inform the publisher should any errors or omissions have been made, and these will be rectified at the earliest opportunity.

Finally, as indicated earlier, the research for this book was triggered by the successful entry in the 1994 Pooley's International Dawn to Dusk competition. This could not have been made without the support, encouragement, experience and competence of my colleague Colin Dodds who flew the aircraft and the generosity of David Wells who made his aircraft, G-AELO, available for the competition flight.

Not Yet Found (and Imperfect Knowledge Disclaimer)

In a work of this scope, it is inevitable that mistakes and omissions will be made; for these I apologise, throwing myself upon the mercies of a hopefully sympathetic readership. Any additions and corrections made known to me will be most welcome and will be incorporated in any further edition that the publisher sees fit to print.

Whilst the original intention was to list companies that built complete aircraft, lack of information about the actual products of some companies means that (particularly in the First World War) the content has certainly strayed into the component supply industry. Although this may stretch the scope of the menu beyond the taste of some, it does at least add richness to the feast.

Some firms which sound like aircraft factories may have only built parts (for example, The Worms Aircraft Construction Co., and Bath Aircraft Ltd); others, which entered the industry to build parts ended up building complete machines (for example, H.H. Martyn & Co. which spawned The Gloucestershire Aircraft Co. Ltd); finally there are those which might have done almost anything (for example, the United Aircraft Co.). Once again, I must trust that any blurring of definitions as to what to include or exclude will be forgiven.

In the modern era I have also chosen to include the contributions of a number of companies that specialise in aircraft restoration and replica construction. The scope, quality and complexity of the work undertaken by these firms exceeds, in many cases, the difficulty of the original manufacturing task. Furthermore, I wish to draw specific attention to the contribution of these organisations to the preservation of Britain;s aviation heritage.

Mention must also be made of aircraft and companies which are definitely known to have existed, but for which I have been quite unable to establish a location. At the time of writing, these are:

The **Buckle** parasol monoplane. Illegally flown, unregistered, in 1929, the Buckle monoplane was constructed by Mr S.L. Buckle for the princely sum of £17. Sopwith Snipe wings, ailerons, rudder, elevator and tailplane were used. A simple rectangular section fuselage was built, and power was supplied by a 45hp six-cylinder Anzani radial. The propeller was obtained from a shed at Brooklands and cut down until the Anzani provided a satisfactory rpm. (Source: *Aeroplane Monthly*, April 1979.)

The **Newport Aircraft Co.** A question was asked in Parliament in November 1918 in relation to unpaid wages and bonuses at this company.

In addition, the following companies whose addresses are unknown: **Cambrian Aircraft Constructors Ltd**, and **Northwold Aircraft Co. Ltd**.

Finally, for clarity, should any reader feel that I have adopted an inconsistent approach to the spelling of Mr Pemberton Billing's name, and/or the title of his company, the gentleman's name was not hyphenated, unlike the name of the company that he formed.

The Evolution of
the British Aircraft Industry

This section presents a summary of the overall development of the aircraft industry in Britain, highlighting specifically (in this volume) activities in South West and Central Southern England. Although, perhaps, not the most active of Britain's regions in terms of pioneer flying, South West and Central Southern England is notable for the activities of a number of important companies. Chief among these are The British & Colonial Aeroplane Co. Ltd and its successors, Westland Aircraft Works, The Supermarine Aviation Works and the Gloster Aircraft Co. (in their respective various guises). To these major firms one can add S.E. Saunders Ltd/Saunders-Roe Ltd, Airspeed Ltd, Folland Aircraft Ltd and Britten-Norman Ltd, together with the Hamble operations of A.V. Roe & Co. Ltd and Sir W.G. Armstrong Whitworth Aircraft Ltd.

This volume was first published in March 2003. In the light of a number of significant anniversaries across the industry during 2010, the publishers have taken the decision to issue a reprint of this volume to coincide with the celebrations of the centenary of the founding of the British & Colonial Aeroplane Company (and the Bristol Aeroplane Co. Ltd) by Sir George White. These companies were both founded on 19 February 1910, although the company initially traded only under the British & Colonial name.

The legacy of the Bristol Company stretches from the contribution of its training schools during the pioneer period through the Bristol Fighter of the First World War; the classic inter-war Bulldog biplane fighter; the Blenheim and Beaufighter of the Second World War; its post-war helicopters – the Sycamore and Belvedere; and finally to its civil transports, the Bristol Freighter and the Britannia turbo-prop – the 'whispering giant'. Integration within the British Aircraft Corporation saw the company make ground-breaking contributions to the supersonic Anglo-French Concorde programme, before becoming a centre of excellence within the Airbus programme.

Since initial publication of this work, there have been a number of changes within the British aircraft industry that should be borne in mind when reading this reprinted edition:

Concorde: Concorde was withdrawn from service with Air France and British Airways in 2003, the last BA service being flown on 24 October 2003, its last positioning flight taking place on 26 November the same year.

AgustaWestland: On 26 May 2004, GKN announced the sale of its 50% share in AgustaWestland to Finmeccanica, the company then becoming 100% Italian-owned. Since this volume first went to print, the AgustaWestland EH101 has been sucessful in winning significant orders from both Japan and India. The type was also down-selected as the new VIP helicopter for the US President (as the VH-71), but this order was cancelled in 2009 following the election of President Obama.

Airbus: On 6 April 2006, BAE SYSTEMS announced its intention to sell its 20% shareholding to EADS. This sale was completed on 13 October 2006, this move seeing BAE SYSTEMS' final exit from the manufacture of commercial aircraft. The Airbus A380 has now entered full passenger service on the long-range routes of a number of airlines and the Airbus A400M has entered its flight test progamme.

1
Pioneers
(1908-1914)

Flying in Europe began in France in 1906, with the flights of Santos Dumont in October and November of that year. By 1908, practical machines were being flown in France by such pioneers as Farman, Voisin and Blériot. The Wright brothers astounded their audiences with the performance and controllability of their craft when it was publicly displayed at Le Mans in the autumn of 1908. The time was now right for Britain's pioneers to take to the air.

A.V. Roe had been experimenting for some time at Brooklands, but his short flights of 8 June 1908 failed to achieve official recognition. S.F. Cody flew at Farnborough in October 1908, J.T.C. Moore-Brabazon flew at Eastchurch at the end of April 1909, and by July 1909 A.V. Roe's triplane was performing well at Lea Marshes. In February 1909, the Short brothers took a licence to manufacture Wright biplanes for the Aero Club, setting up a factory at Leysdown on the Isle of Sheppey. Britain now possessed an aircraft industry.

The pioneering period prior to the First World War was marked by adventure, experiment and innovation – the techniques of building and flying aeroplanes were not yet understood. There was no right or wrong solution to any aspect of design, and consequently almost every possible configuration was attempted and many blind alleys were explored. Potentially good designs were let down by poor detail design, inadequate control arrangements, or heavy, inefficient and unreliable engines.

The pioneer aircraft that have been included in this volume are, in the main, those which are known to have flown successfully. In some cases, where the fact of flight is not entirely certain, aircraft have been included which at least have the appearance that they might have flown successfully (e.g. Fritz Monoplane, Brooklands 1911). Known freaks have been excluded (e.g. the Aerial Wheel Monoplane which was entered in the 1912 Military Trials at Larkhill). Hamble River, Luke & Co. at Hamble, and The Aeronautical Syndicate Ltd (at Larkhill and Hendon) made short-lived contributions to aircraft production, but had come and gone before the First World War.

The main flying locations prior to the First World War were Brooklands, Eastchurch, Hendon and Shoreham, with Hendon being second only to Brooklands in importance. In South West and Central Southern England, Filton was the pre-eminent manufacturing site; the British & Colonial Aeroplane Co. Ltd also having important flying schools at Larkhill and Brooklands.

The remaining significant pioneer activity in this area is summarised below:

- S.F. Cody, J.W. Dunne, Geoffrey de Havilland and the Royal Aircraft Factory at Farnborough.
- Geoffrey de Havilland at Whitway.
- The Aeronautical Syndicate Ltd and the 1912 Military Trials at Larkhill.
- McArdle & Drexel in Bournemouth and the New Forest.
- Messrs Moon and Eggleton in the Southampton area, followed by Mr Pemberton Billing.
- Hamble River, Luke & Co. and Sopwith flying from Southampton Water.
- J. Samuel White on the Isle of Wight.

(Copyright: BAE SYSTEMS plc)

Enthusiasm for flying resulted in the establishment of a number of flying schools, notably at Brooklands, Larkhill and Hendon. The schools necessarily became adept at the repair, modification and re-building of aeroplanes. As a result, even where their school machines were initially of standard types, many were later modified, adapted, re-engined, etc. to become new variants. A number of schools then branched out to design their own machines based on the experience gained in school flying.

In all the excitement of this period, with its many bizarre and unsuccessful designs, the seeds of today's configurations, and of the future aircraft industry, were sown. Great fruit was to be harvested once these seeds found the fertile ground of warfare.

2
First World War Mass Production (1914-1918)

The First World War saw an exponential growth in aircraft production, which is reflected in this survey of aircraft production in South West and Central Southern England. The importance of the aeroplane during the First World War, and the reasons for the rapid growth in production demand are therefore discussed in some detail below.

The Aircraft as a Machine of War

At the outbreak of the First World War, the utility of the aeroplane had only just begun to be appreciated by the Services. It was then slow, fragile and unarmed; moreover, very few were available. Thus the Royal Flying Corps (RFC) had a total of only sixty-three first line aeroplanes, with a further thirty-nine landplanes and fifty-two seaplanes available to the Royal Naval Air Service (RNAS).

The war developed into static trench warfare, with major actions or 'pushes' preceded by artillery barrages. An early use was found in reconnaissance and artillery observation, and this role became the cornerstone of military aviation. General von Below is quoted by Maurice Baring, in *Flying Corps Headquarters 1914-1918*, as stating in a memorandum: 'The main object of fighting in the air is to enable our photographic registration and photographic reconnaissance to be carried out, and at the same time to prevent that of the enemy.' The use of fighters to prevent reconnaissance operations was therefore a natural development, followed by the application of the aeroplane to bombing operations, anti-submarine patrols and operations against airships.

Changing operational roles and the rapid development of aircraft and armament meant that existing in-service types were rapidly rendered obsolete. New designs were essential, and had to be rushed into large-scale production. Aircraft were flown intensively, and losses were high through both enemy action and accidents. A large-scale training activity was required to maintain a supply of pilots to the operational squadrons, giving rise to its own losses of both men and machines.

All of this required a rapid expansion of production of all types, a process hampered by the fact that many of the potential workforce were enlisting in the Services. This problem could only be solved by bringing into the production effort industrial enterprises that had no prior experience of aircraft manufacture; the furniture and motor trades were both critical in this respect. Similarly, the workforce needed to be augmented, and many women entered the production lines of the munitions factories (including the aircraft industry) for the first time.

The types that were most widely contracted out included the designs of the Royal Aircraft Factory (such as the BE2, BE12, RE8, FE2 and SE5A), training aircraft (notably the Avro 504 and DH6), Felixstowe-designed flying boats, patrol seaplanes (Short 184), and successful combat aircraft (Sopwith Pup, Camel, 1½ Strutter and Snipe, Bristol F.2B Fighter, AIRCO DH4, DH9, DH9A). Toward the end of the First World War significant orders were placed for the contract manufacture of long-range bomber types, such as the Handley Page O/400 and Vickers Vimy. Many of these orders were cancelled following the Armistice.

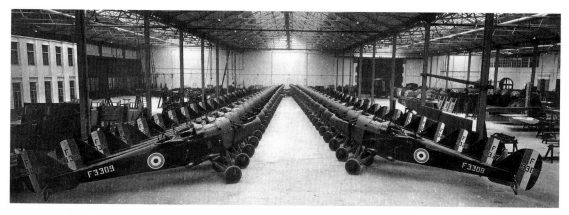

An example of the contract production of Royal Aircraft Factory designs is provided by this large quantity of RE8 aircraft at The Siddeley-Deasy Motor Car Co. Ltd. (Terry Treadwell & Alan C. Wood)

Loss Rates

The expansion of production during the First World War was, in truth, an enormous enterprise. Because of its significance, it is worth reflecting on some of the facts and figures associated with this accelerated production programme. As background, one needs to appreciate the intensity of air operations, and the high rate of loss and material consumption involved, as indicated by the following contemporary data:

> *The average life of an aeroplane at the battlefront is not more than two months. To keep 5,000 aircraft in active commission for one year it is necessary to furnish 30,000. Each machine in the period of its activity will use at least two motors, so that 60,000 motors will be required.*
> (M. Flaudin, head of the Allied Air Board, quoted in the American magazine *Flying*, September 1917)

These figures seem extraordinary, but closely match the levels actually achieved by the end of the conflict.

Aircraft losses in late 1918 were running at some 200 per month. In fact, aircraft destroyed by the enemy, and in training accidents, together with those that had to be scrapped as being obsolete, represented some 60% of the total constructed during the war. Sadly, training exacted a heavy toll. A question in Parliament during the 1918 Air Estimates debate revealed that during 1917 more men were lost at the training schools than were lost flying on all fronts. Winston Churchill also spoke in Parliament on 4 April 1917 on the subject of the heavy losses being suffered by the RFC during training.

Data published in 1919 (in *Flight* and elsewhere) indicates that the total aircrew casualties over the whole period of the war were 6,166 killed, 7,245 wounded and 3,128 missing. 330 British airmen lost their lives in April 1917, the so-called 'Bloody April'. At this time, the expected operational life of an RFC pilot was no more than 17½ flying hours. Peter King in *Knights of the Air* indicates that losses in every month of 1918 were equal to the entire strength of the RFC at the start of the First World War.

The demands imposed by these short service lives and high attrition were considerable; how were the resultant production needs to be met?

Expansion of the Production Programme

Production at existing aircraft companies was rapidly expanded, and contracts were placed with established industrial concerns, particularly in the motor car and furniture trades, to boost supply. Many new companies were also founded specifically to meet this growing demand, and to provide a sub-contract infrastructure. The resultant explosion of industrial activity was truly amazing, and has been inadequately recorded.

In May 1917, less than three years after the outbreak of the First World War, the position was summarised by the 'British Comptroller of Aeronautic Supplies' in a statement to the Board of Governors of the Aero Club of America. He stated: 'There are 958 firms in England engaged on work for the British Directorate of Aeronautic Supplies, 301 of which are direct contractors and 657 are sub-contractors.' The report further states that 'The total number of hands employed by the fifty firms of most prominence is 66,700. [...] The present British budget for aeronautics in the present year totals \$575,000,000' (reported in *Flying*, June 1917). These are impressive figures by any standard.

The *Aviation Pocket-Book of 1919-1920* listed 148 aeroplane manufacturers and many other suppliers, and commented on the adequacy of its Gazetteer thus:

> *It does not pretend to include the names of all who are accustomed to making aeroplane parts, for many firms were doing so for the period of the war only – in fact there is hardly a motor car or motor car accessory or wood-working firm that was not fully occupied with aviation work at the time of the Armistice [...] Possibly, however, some names are not included that ought to be, since it is not an easy task, when compiling a directory of this nature, to ensure its being absolutely complete.*

The author must echo these sentiments in respect of the present work.

Manufacture was split between aircraft manufacturers, with their own design teams, capable of producing original designs; contractors, who built established designs to order; and component suppliers. Within the area covered by this volume, the most significant aircraft manufacturing concerns were: The British & Colonial Aeroplane Co. Ltd at Filton and Larkhill; Parnall & Sons Ltd in Bristol; The Gloucestershire Aircraft Co. Ltd at Cheltenham; The Royal Aircraft Factory at Farnborough; the test-flying activities of A.V. Roe & Co. Ltd and The Fairey Aviation Co. Ltd at Hamble; Pemberton-Billing Ltd/The Supermarine Aviation Works Ltd at Southampton; S.E. Saunders Ltd and J. Samuel White & Co. Ltd on the Isle of Wight; and Westland Aircraft Works (Branch of Petters Ltd) at Yeovil.

Lesser known companies included:

- Poole Aviation Co., 24 West Quay Road, Poole.
- Worms Aircraft Construction Co., Rutland Road, Bournemouth.
- Redcliffe Aircraft Ltd, Harford Street, Bristol.
- The United Aircraft Co. Ltd of Gosport, Hants.
- The Canute Airplane Co., Royal Pier Gate, Southampton.
- Bath Aircraft Ltd, Flight Works, Lower Bristol Road, Bath.

Production Quantities

The achievements of the rapidly expanding industry were remarkable. This is illustrated rather graphically by the following statement made by Winston Churchill, Minister of Munitions, speaking in Parliament on 25 April 1918, when presenting the Estimates of the Ministry of Munitions:

We are now making in a single week more aeroplanes than were made in the whole of 1914, in a single month more than were made in the whole of 1915, and in a single quarter more than were made in the whole of 1916.

The total British production during the First World War is widely reported as 55,093 airframes (other figures are also quoted, see below), with an additional 3,051 purchased abroad. Very significant production was also undertaken in France and the USA, with American production running at around 12,000 aircraft per year by the end of the war. Data published after the First World War (as a Parliamentary Paper on 24 April 1919) gave the following figures for British production.

First World War Aircraft Production

Period	Duration (months)	Aircraft built	Aircraft per month
Aug 1914 – May 1915	10	530	53
June 1915 – Feb 1917	21	7,137	340
March 1917 – Dec 1917	10	13,521	1,352
Jan 1918 – Oct 1918	10	26,685	2,669

(Note: This gives a total of 47,873, some 7,200 less than is given by more recent sources.)

The expansion in production is also reflected in the numbers of aircraft on charge with the RFC and RNAS, as follows: August 1914, 272; January 1917, 5,496; January 1918, 11,091; October 1918 (RAF) 22,171. These figures, from the same source as the production numbers, show that in four years the aircraft establishment of the flying services had been increased more than eighty fold, with the production rate increasing more than fifty fold. To provide a comparison with UK production, one should acknowledge that this enormous acceleration in the field of aviation was evident among all combatants.

As an inevitable consequence of the fighting, a large number of wrecked, damaged and unserviceable aircraft congregated at the operational and training bases. A significant reconstruction activity used cannibalised parts to produce new aircraft to return to operations. Serial blocks were allocated to as many as 500 such aircraft at a time (rebuilt from depots in France, for example). To illustrate the scale of this effort, some examples of units within the repair organization, and activities down to squadron level, are provided in the table below (which is by no means comprehensive):

Organisation	Location	Example Output
No.1 (Southern) Aircraft Repair Depot	Farnborough	700 aircraft covering at least eighteen types
No.2 (Northern) Aircraft Repair Depot	Coal Aston	Reservations for some 500 aircraft including FK8, RE8, FE2B, BE2E, etc.
No.3 (Western) Aircraft Repair Depot	Yate	At least 200 aircraft including Camel, RE8, SE5A, Avro 504, Bristol F.2B, BE2E
No.5 (Eastern) Aircraft Repair Depot	Henlow	Fifty allocations including F.2B, Avro 504, Camel, DH4, DH9A
6 Wing Aircraft Repair Station	Dover	Nine Pup, three Camel, DH5, BE2C, DH4, Avro 504, 1½ Strutter
19 Repair Station	Northolt	DH2 from spares A5211
18 Repair Station	Montrose	Twelve BE2C and a Bristol Scout from spares

Organisation	Location	Example Output
3 Training Depot Station	Lopcombe Corner	Three Camel
43 Training Depot Station	Chattis Hill	Seven Camel, two as two-seaters
23 Training Wing Aircraft Repair Station	South Carlton	Avro 504 and two-seat Camel
26 Wing Aircraft Repair Station	Thetford	Small numbers of BE2E, Pup, Avro 504, Farman S.11, DH6, RE8, etc.
7 Wing Aircraft 504, Repair Station	Norwich	Small numbers of Pup, Avro DH6, Shorthorn, DH4, BE2D/E, RE8, FK3
RAF Ascot	Ascot	Twenty-five DH9A built up from spares
Central Flying School	Upavon	Four Sopwith Camel
63 Training Squadron	Joyce Green	Sopwith Pup B9440

There were a number of Aircraft Depots in France (for example at St Omer and Candas), together with mobile Aircraft Parks to assist in maintaining supplies and spare parts.

Production Difficulties

Significant production difficulties were encountered (and re-encountered in the Second World War) due to the difficulty of building up production among a large number of dispersed and sometimes inexperienced sub-contractors. The requirement to accelerate production was hampered by the steady depletion of the workforce as more and more were called up for service in France. Near continuous industrial unrest resulted due to the heavy demands on the individual, and the Defence of the Realm Act was much used to maintain stability in the munitions industries.

Engine suppliers had great difficulty maintaining pace with airframe manufacture. Early in 1915 a serious shortage of 90hp RAF engines occurred leaving Armstrong Whitworth with no less than 100 engineless BE2 machines hanging three or four deep from the ceiling. Similarly, in January 1918, no less than 400 SE5As were waiting for engines. The lower than expected performance of the Siddeley Puma proved to be a problem for the DH4. Martinsyde F3 production was reduced because of the need for Rolls-Royce Falcon engines to power the Bristol Fighter. The lack of availability of Falcon engines resulted in the Bristol Fighter being flown (with variable success) with 300hp Hispano-Suiza, Siddeley Puma and Sunbeam Arab engines. Production of the FE2D was also constrained by the shortage of supply of its Rolls-Royce Eagle engine. The 200hp Hispano-Suiza engine fitted to the Sopwith Dolphin suffered from frequent connecting-rod failures. The supply of engines was further hampered by the need to create a new industry to supply magnetos, the manufacture of which, until the outbreak of the First World War, had been the almost exclusive province of German industry.

At the end of the First World War, engine orders were running at around 65,000 per year, more than 8,500 of these orders being for the disastrous ABC Dragonfly. F. Warren Merriam comments: 'There is no doubt that at this late stage in the War, our aero engines were becoming less and less reliable.' Shortages affected nearly every type. Standardisation was absent; in early 1918, Mr Pemberton Billing pointed out that forty-four different types of engine were in use. Ironically, the attempt to standardise on the Dragonfly also was an ignominious failure. In 1918, with vast numbers of engines on order from thirteen contractors, the Dragonfly was achieving a typical engine life of only 2½ hours before failure.

Scarcity of Resources

The needs of aircraft production resulted in a tremendous drain on resources, and even had an impact on the agricultural landscape, through the demand for flax to supply the need for aircraft linen. In July 1917, Dr Addison, Minister of Munitions, gave a specific indication of the strategic requirements of the aircraft industry, as follows:

> *The fact that no fewer than 1,000 factories are engaged on some process or other connected with the construction and equipment of the flying machine proves the magnitude of the work we have in hand. The needs of the aeroplane programme are enormous, almost passing belief. For our present programme of construction, more spruce is required than the present annual output of the United States, more mahogany than Honduras can supply – and Honduras is accustomed to supply the requirements of the World. Besides this, all the linen of the type required made in Ireland, the home of the linen industry, and the whole of the alloyed steel that England can produce can be used. As for flax, the Government has actually to provide the seed from which to grow the plant essential for its purposes.*

Flax seed was supplied free to growers, who were further encouraged with significant subsidies and guaranteed prices. The scheme was administered by the Flax Production Branch of the Board of Agriculture. Further financial assistance to growers was offered in July 1918 as a result of the Flax Companies (Financial Assistance) Bill. So successful were these measures that by the time of the Armistice, production of aircraft fabric was running at 7 million yards (nearly 4,000 miles) per month. By April 1919, the Ministry of Munitions had in stock and available for disposal no less than 31,970,725 yards of linen. In mid-1919, the total surplus (by now 40 million yards, or nearly 23,000 miles of fabric, in sixteen varieties and widths of 25-72ins) was sold to one individual, Mr J.L. Martin, for about £4 million.

The Government requested in late 1917 that farmers carry out a census of ash trees, where potential supply problems were causing some concern. In supporting this request it was stated that: 'The Government requirements for the next twelve months [i.e. 1918] are expected to exceed 200,000 trees.' In all, about one third of the volume of timber standing at the outbreak of war was felled, much being used in aircraft manufacture.

Overall, perhaps the most striking feature of the First World War mass production effort was that the entire enterprise, involving more than a thousand companies, was created within ten years of the construction of Britain's first aeroplane.

Foundation of the SBAC

On 23 March 1916, the main constructing firms came together to form an interest group through which to voice their common concerns. This was the Society of British Aircraft Constructors (SBAC), an organisation that continues to be a spokesman for the industry. The founder members include a significant number of firms that are less than familiar today. The initial list of forty founder members, as published in April 1916, was as follows:

Aircraft Manufacturing Co. Ltd
Airships Ltd
The Austin Motor Co. (1914) Ltd
Wm Beardmore & Co. Ltd
The Blackburn Aeroplane & Motor Co. Ltd
Boulton & Paul Ltd
The Brush Electrical Engineering Co. Ltd
The Coventry Ordnance Works Ltd
The Daimler Co. Ltd

Darracq Motor Engineering Co. Ltd
Wm Denny & Brothers
The Dudbridge Iron Works Ltd
Fred^k Sage & Co. Ltd
G. & J. Weir Ltd
The Grahame-White Aviation Co. Ltd
Handley Page Ltd
Hewlett & Blondeau Ltd
Jouques Aviation Works
Mann, Egerton & Co. Ltd
Mann & Grimmer
Martinsyde Ltd
D. Napier & Son, Ltd
The Norman Thompson Flight Co. Ltd
Parnall & Sons
Phoenix Dynamo Manufacturing Co. Ltd
Robey & Co. Ltd
A.V. Roe & Co. Ltd
Ruston, Proctor & Co. Ltd
S.E. Saunders Ltd
Short Bros.
The Siddeley-Deasy Motor Car Co. Ltd
The Sopwith Aviation Co. Ltd
The Standard Motor Co. Ltd
The Sunbeam Motor Car Co. Ltd
Vickers Ltd
Wells Aviation Co. Ltd
Westland Aircraft Works
J. Samuel White & Co. Ltd
Whitehead Aircraft Co. Ltd
Wolseley Motors Ltd

This group of companies, plus a few others which joined the SBAC shortly thereafter (such as Sir W.G. Armstrong, Whitworth & Co. Ltd), made up the aircraft industry at the end of the First World War. Not one survives today as a wholly British aircraft manufacturer, although Shorts (as a subsidiary of Bombardier) and AgustaWestland are honourable near-survivors.

3
Collapse and Re-birth
Between the Wars (1919-1939)

The inter-war period was marked by the near-complete collapse of the military aircraft market and the return of the majority of contractors to their original products and markets. The larger companies were restructured in the immediate post-war period to avoid Excess Profit Duty, and they all faced competition from their own products, now being marketed by The Aircraft Disposal Co. Military sales were very limited in number, although, within this region, the Bristol Aeroplane Co. Ltd (with its long-lived Bristol Fighter followed by the Bulldog) and Westland Aircraft Works (with the DH9A and Wapiti) were cushioned from the worst of these problems. In the 1930s, the light aircraft movement resulted in expansion of civil production, and many new concerns were established, only to be cut off at the start of the Second World War. Re-armament began in 1935, and provided a lifeline for the main manufacturers.

Post-war Collapse

What brought about the collapse? Quite simply, the need for aircraft evaporated virtually overnight. Once the war stopped, the country had neither the resources, nor the need, to sustain the aircraft production juggernaut. Many orders were cancelled, and the enormous stock of war surplus aircraft was sold on favourable terms to The Aircraft Disposal Co. at Croydon. In consequence, any firm attempting a new aircraft venture during the immediate post-war period inevitably found itself competing with its own, or its competitors', second-hand products. When this difficulty was combined with the effects of Excess Profits Duty, it is not surprising that wholesale re-organisation took place. Most of the sub-contractors either went into liquidation or returned to their former trades. The prime contractors also re-organised, slimmed down, or went into liquidation; many flirted with the motor trade and other

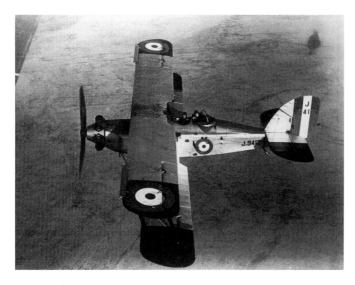

The successful Wapiti provided sustained production for Westland Aircraft Works during the bleak inter-war years. (Ken Ellis Collection)

The Bristol Bulldog was one of the classic fighters of its day. Its all-metal construction was much advertised by Bristol, and the type helped to ensure the company's survival through a difficult period for the industry. (Ken Ellis Collection)

forms of diversification. Examples in this area include Westland building pianos, and The Gloucestershire Aircraft Co. Ltd producing the Unibus motor scooter. A number of those that entered voluntary liquidation emerged in new, fitter guises to carry on in the aircraft business. The survivors drew the protective cloak of the SBAC tightly around themselves.

The scale of the contraction after the Armistice was incredible. On 11 November 1918, 25,000 aircraft were on order. The Air Ministry sought to shut down production of all obsolete types immediately, and only accept delivery of those contracts from which they positively could not extricate themselves. Those obsolete types that could not be cancelled would be sent directly to store. By cancellation of these orders, the number of aircraft that the Ministry was obliged to accept was reduced to 13,432. Scrapping for the recovery of useful parts proved not to be very economic, and it was recommended that greater savings would be made if the engine were to be removed and the rest of the machine burned.

Hilary St George Saunders in *Per Ardua – The Rise of British Air Power* indicates an establishment at the end of the First World War of ninety-five squadrons and seven flights in France, Belgium and the Rhineland, together with thirty-four squadrons and eight flights in other theatres, and a Home establishment of fifty-five operational and no less than 199 training squadrons, for a grand total of 383 squadrons and fifteen flights. Within eighteen months, this was reduced to eighteen squadrons overseas, eight in India and seven in the Middle East, plus only two Home squadrons. Manpower was correspondingly reduced to some 10% of the numbers engaged at the time of the Armistice.

By the end of 1920, AIRCO, British & Colonial Aeroplane Co. Ltd, Nieuport, Martinsyde, Central Aircraft, Grahame-White and Sopwith had variously closed, entered receivership, or re-organised. By June 1922 only ninety-seven British civil aircraft had Certificates of Airworthiness, down from 240 in 1920. By the mid-1920s, the industry had reduced to sixteen major manufacturers: Sir W.G. Armstrong Whitworth Aircraft Ltd; A.V. Roe & Co. Ltd; The Blackburn Aeroplane & Motor Co. Ltd; Boulton & Paul Ltd; The Bristol Aeroplane Co. Ltd; The de Havilland Aircraft Co. Ltd; Fairey Aviation Ltd; George Parnall & Co. Ltd; S.E. Saunders Ltd; Short Brothers (Rochester & Bedford) Ltd; The Supermarine Aviation Works Ltd; Vickers Ltd and Westland Aircraft Works (Branch of Petters Ltd).

Military Production in the 1920s and 1930s

From this point onwards, military aircraft manufacture was virtually reduced to the modification and development of the existing in-service types and the development of a smattering of prototypes. The prototype activity was spread across the industry and just about sustained the industrial base. The lack of active operations meant that only small production volumes of largely obsolescent aircraft were required to fulfil the needs of the RAF. Shorts, for example, built less than forty aircraft during the whole of the 1920s.

Fairey Aviation was a significant exception to this bleak scene: the Fairey IIIF, Gordon, Seal, Fawn, Flycatcher, Swordfish and Battle ensuring continuous production through this difficult period. Another successful military manufacturer was Hawker at Kingston upon Thames, which, after a period of limited production in the early 1920s, found production success and stability with the Hawker Hart, and its subsequent long line of variants, eventually leading to the Fury and the Hurricane.

As indicated earlier, The Bristol Aeroplane Co. Ltd and Westland Aircraft Works also fared comparatively well during this period. The Gloster Aircraft Co. Ltd (as it was known from late 1926) survived on a combination of prototypes and Hawker sub-contracts, together with the manufacture of its single-seat fighters: the Grebe, Gamecock, Gauntlet and Gladiator. The Supermarine Aviation Works Ltd (in its various guises) and Saunders-Roe Ltd were also reduced to relatively modest production quantities, but survived until their production fortunes changed with mass production contracts for the Spitfire, Walrus and Sea Otter.

One measure of the desperation of the industry was that key military requirements, likely to lead to significant production contracts, would lead to a rash of official and private venture prototypes being produced. A good example is provided by requirement N.21/26

The Hawker Hart family was a mainstay for Hawker. Production of the Hart family was also extensively contracted out across the industry, represented here by Hector production at Westland, who also built forty-three Hawker Audax. (Westland)

for a single-seat fleet fighter to replace the Fairey Flycatcher. Ten designs were produced to compete for this single contract, with competing prototypes as follows:

- Armstrong Whitworth Starling (private venture, A-1)
- Armstrong Whitworth AW XVI (private venture S1591)
- Fairey Firefly III (private venture, F1137 later S1592)
- Fairey Flycatcher II (N216)
- Gloster Gnatsnapper (N227)
- Hawker Hoopoe (N237)
- Hawker N.21/26 (private venture, later officially adopted as the Nimrod, becoming S1577)
- Parnall Pipit (N232, N233)
- Vickers 141 (private venture, ex G-EBNQ)
- Vickers 177 (private venture based on Type 143, no markings)

The military market remained stagnant until, during the late 1930s, tension rose within Europe leading to progressive re-armament from 1935. From this point onward, the military manufacturers saw increasing orders and the start of sub-contract/dispersed production to increase capacity. This is discussed in Chapter 4.

Civil Production and the Light Aeroplane Movement

Immediately after the First World War, there were limited attempts to generate an air transport market, with A.V. Roe & Co. Ltd (Avro Transport Service), Blackburn (North Sea Aerial Navigation Co. Ltd), Handley Page (Handley Page Transport Ltd) and AIRCO (Aircraft Transport & Travel Ltd) all starting airline services, mainly using converted military aircraft. These efforts were unsuccessful and, although small numbers of commercial aircraft were sold to independent airlines, there was no real demand for air travel. Even after the formation of Imperial Airways, airliner production in Britain was restricted to modest production runs from Armstrong Whitworth, de Havilland, Handley Page and Shorts. The appearance of the de Havilland Dragon (1932), and Dragon Rapide (1934) saw production quantities increase. It is fair to say, however, that with the exception of de Havilland, and Empire flying boat production at Shorts, military aircraft production dominated the affairs of most companies. One exception was Airspeed Ltd, whose Envoy flew in 1934. Eighty-two were built, and the type was developed into the Oxford trainer.

Whilst the Lympne Light Aircraft Competitions generated much publicity for the potential of privately owned aircraft, the competing aircraft themselves were not a great success. The appearance of the de Havilland Moth, and the availability of subsidies for flying schools, radically changed this picture. New companies emerged and prospered, including the famous names of Airspeed, de Havilland, General Aircraft, Percival, and Miles (then as Phillips & Powis Aircraft Ltd). Much of this activity was concentrated in, and near, London, as flying gathered popularity as a fashionable activity.

A new phenomenon also arose in the form of the craze for the Flying Flea, sparked by the design of the tandem wing *Pou de Ciel* by Henri Mignet. Although ultimately (and in some cases tragically) unsuccessful, the Flea served to legitimise the eccentric British habit of constructing home-built aircraft. This had originated in the pioneering period by the enthusiasm of the likes of Mr Jezzi at Eastchurch, being continued after the First World War by such characters as F.H. Lowe at Heaton, and the Blake brothers at Winchester. This tradition has been carried on to this day in Britain by individuals such as John Isaacs, John Taylor, Ivan Shaw and many others, now under the very professional administration of the Popular Flying Association.

4
Second World War Mass Production (1939-1945)

Rearmament and the Shadow Factory Scheme

The expansion of the aircraft production programme against the threat of war built up gradually from 1935. It is inseparably linked to the Second World War aircraft production effort. Whilst to many eyes the move to re-arm Britain's forces came perilously late, moves began some five years before the Second World War broke out. The first step was the adoption of an expansion plan in July 1934, known as Scheme A, to increase the size of the Royal Air Force. Under this scheme the Metropolitan Air Force was intended to grow to 1,252 operational aircraft by the spring of 1939.

Hitler had become Chancellor in January 1933, but his repudiation of the Treaty of Versailles, reoccupation of the Rhineland, the Austrian Anschluss, the annexation of Czechoslovakia and the Nazi-Soviet Pact were still years ahead. It is clear, therefore, that some early positive decisions were made and, as a result, the armaments industry began to grow. The real difficulty lay in the lack of investment in modern designs and technology, combined with the drastic reduction in production capacity caused by the lean years of the 1920s and early 1930s.

The pace of re-armament in the aircraft industry quickened with Scheme C, which was instituted in May 1935 and which brought about further significant increases in both the size of the RAF and the production of new aircraft types. From October 1936 the need for increased production led to the formation of the 'shadow factory' scheme. New factories were constructed using public funds, owned by the Government, but run by private industry to boost the production of (initially) aero engine components, where the shortfall in production capacity was even more marked than in the airframe industry. The contractual complexities of the shadow factory scheme introduce uncertainty in some instances over the precise responsibility for site management and aircraft production/assembly at particular sites. This is an area that would benefit from further research.

In addition to Bristol (whose engines were to be produced), the five companies initially involved in the shadow factory scheme were The Austin Motor Co. Ltd, The Rover Co. Ltd, The Daimler Co. Ltd, Rootes Securities Ltd (Humber), and The Standard Motor Co. Ltd. In February 1937 the scheme was extended to allow Austin and Rootes to construct airframes as well as engines. Despite this early recognition that engine availability was critical to the acceleration of airframe production, there were periods, as in the First World War, when engineless airframes were in plentiful supply.

The early expansion schemes favoured light day bombers such as the Fairey Battle and Vickers Wellesley. Unfortunately, the concept of the light day bomber proved to be a blind alley, with the Battle, in particular, suffering from high operational losses whilst trying to stem the Blitzkrieg across the Low Countries during 1940. (Fairey Battle losses between 10 May and 14 May 1940 were sixty aircraft, out of the 108 deployed operationally, during attacks against troop concentrations and the Albert Canal bridges.) From 1936 onward types such as the Blenheim, Wellington, Hurricane and Spitfire began to be ordered in quantity through parent and shadow factories. Later on, the focus switched to heavy bomber production (particularly the Halifax and Lancaster), anticipating the need for a bomber offensive against Germany.

Wartime saw an enormous increase in activity across South West and Central Southern England associated with the Spitfire, Seafire, Beaufighter, Hurricane and Typhoon, together with dispersed production of the Miles Master and Short Stirling at South Marston, and assembly of the Albemarle at No.2 factory, Brockworth. The period closed to the sound of jet engines from Gloster.

Production Difficulties

Large-scale orders were one thing; production proved to be quite another problem. Production difficulties were encountered with the accelerating demands placed on both airframe and engine manufacturers, particularly as the British industry was only just accommodating retractable undercarriages, variable pitch propellers and all-metal stressed skin monoplanes. In contemporary reports one finds reference to:

- Poorly organised initial production by Supermarine at Woolston, with mismatched wing and fuselage production rates.
- Similar problems at Filton with the Blenheim, with thirty-two fuselages produced before any wings appeared.
- The initial inability of the Morris-run Castle Bromwich shadow factory to get the Spitfire into production.
- Production levels in 1937–1938 running at around one-third of those planned for the Battle and Blenheim, and virtually zero for the Spitfire.
- Miles Master development and production dictated by availability of particular engine types.
- Master, Oxford and Tiger Moth airframes dispersed into storage to await their engines.
- Fairey's problems of excessive dispersal of its factories, including delays to the Albacore due to problems with its Taurus engine. The delay to Albacore production led to a delay of about a year in establishing Firefly production. A delay of two years to the Barracuda was attributed to priority being given to other types in production by Fairey at Heaton Chapel and Errwood Park. Sir Stafford Cripps intervened to introduce new personnel and re-organise project management at Fairey Aviation.
- Bristol's engineless Beaufighters towed by road from the factory at Filton to Whitchurch to await completion.

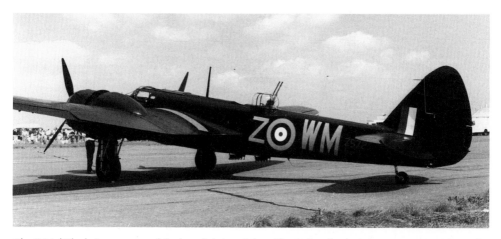

The Bristol Blenheim was one of the beneficiaries of the military aircraft expansion programme prior to the outbreak of the Second World War. (Author)

As the Spitfire transferred to full production, delays were encountered in wing manufacture. The complexity of the wing structure is revealed by this photograph of a de-skinned wing at the Warbirds of GB Ltd facility at Blackbushe. (Nick Blackman)

- Slow production build up for the Halifax by the London Aircraft Production Group, delaying output from the assembly line at Leavesden.
- Dozens of Typhoons at Brockworth without engines being ferried to maintenance units using 'slave' engines. The engines were then removed, sent back to the Gloster factory, and refitted to the next aircraft for its delivery.

The setting up of the shadow factory scheme was a drain on the resources of the parent firms due to their need to produce additional drawings and tooling, and to provide oversight of the expansion factories. One should not, however, forget the scale of the task, and the depleted production resource initially available for the effort.

Production Quantities and Standardisation

Despite all these difficulties, expansion in the immediate pre-war period was more successful than has been widely acknowledged. In 1935, 893 military aircraft were produced. This figure was more than doubled in 1936, and by 1939 reached 7,940, a nearly nine-fold increase in only five years. In 1941, the figure was more than 20,000, and by 1944 it exceeded 26,000.

The main production effort during the Second World War was split between the following organisations:

- The main design firms of A.V. Roe & Co. Ltd; Sir W.G. Armstrong Whitworth Aircraft Ltd; Blackburn Aircraft Ltd; Bristol Aeroplane Co. Ltd; The de Havilland Aircraft Co. Ltd; The Fairey Aviation Co. Ltd; Gloster Aircraft Co. Ltd; Handley Page Ltd; Hawker Aircraft Ltd; Short Brothers (Rochester & Bedford) Ltd; Vickers-Armstrongs Ltd and Westland Aircraft Ltd.
- Shadow and dispersed factories controlled either by aircraft industry parent firms, or by the motor industry (Rootes Securities Ltd; the Austin Motor Co. Ltd; Morris Motors Ltd; Standard Motor Co. Ltd, etc.), mainly in the Midlands and the north west of England. This activity includes contract production by The English Electric Co. Ltd at Preston and Samlesbury (Hampden, Halifax and Vampire), and Short & Harland Ltd in Belfast (Bombay, Hereford, Sunderland and Stirling).
- Smaller companies such as Airspeed (1934) Ltd; Cunliffe-Owen Aircraft Ltd; Folland

Aircraft Ltd; Heston Aircraft Ltd; Phillips & Powis Aircraft Ltd/Miles Aircraft Ltd; Percival Aircraft Ltd and Taylorcraft Aeroplanes (England) Ltd.
- Firms within the Civilian Repair Organisations such as AST at Hamble; manufacturer's Repair Organisations such as SEBRO at Cambridge; and RAF Maintenance Units such as Henlow and Kemble. Many aircraft that were nominally repaired and returned to service were substantially new airframes by the time that 'repair' had been completed.

The risk of bomb damage to main factory sites led every firm to set up dispersed operations. As in the First World War, large numbers of firms were involved and, as early as mid-1939, some 1,200 companies were involved in sub-contract aircraft production. Peak production in the Second World War reached 2,715 aircraft per month (March 1944) with, in addition, more than 500 aircraft per month returned to service after repair.

Unlike the First World War, there was a general policy of limiting the number of types in production. The increased efficiency and production volume that resulted offset the loss of some potentially outstanding designs (such as the Martin-Baker MB5), the production of which was blocked. As production gathered momentum, a number of companies were diverted from building their own types, in favour of the standardised designs. This is typified by Westland production of the Seafire, and Gloster taking over the primary responsibility for the Typhoon.

A major plank of this effort was to secure Spitfire production, this being achieved by a combination of dispersed and shadow factory production under the control of the parent company, with additional production by Westland Aircraft Ltd. Bristol Aeroplane Co. Ltd types were also produced under contract, including the Blenheim (by A.V. Roe & Co. Ltd and Rootes Securities Ltd), the Bombay (Short & Harland Ltd), the Beaufighter (Fairey Aviation Ltd and Rootes Securities Ltd), and the Bolingbroke (A.V. Roe & Co. Ltd and Rootes Securities Ltd, plus 676 in Canada).

The Civilian Repair Organisation made an important contribution to the war effort. Here Gloster-built Hawker Typhoons receive a near-complete rebuild by Marshalls of Cambridge. (Marshall Aerospace Ltd)

The main Second World War production types are summarised in the following table:

Main Second World War Production Types

Fighter	Bomber	Trainer/Liaison	Other
Defiant	Hampden	Tiger Moth	Swordfish
Hurricane	Battle	Oxford	Sunderland
Spitfire	Blenheim	Master	Firefly
Typhoon	Wellington	Magister	Seafire
Tempest	Stirling	Anson	Walrus
Beaufighter	Halifax	Auster	Lysander
	Lancaster	Proctor	Beaufort
	Mosquito	Dominie	Barracuda

By about 1941, most of the production capacity for front-line machines had been grouped on the Stirling, Halifax and Lancaster bombers, the Beaufighter, the Mosquito, the Spitfire and the Barracuda. The reduced number of types produced reflects the technical maturity of the industry; it was no longer possible for the enemy to produce a new design that would completely change the balance of air power overnight. The Messerschmitt Me262

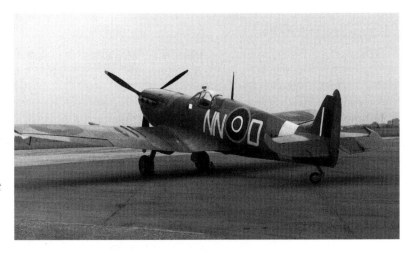

Dispersal of Supermarine Spitfire production was a significant feature across South West and Central Southern England. This example – Mk VB AR510 – was built by Westland Aircraft Ltd, and is seen here at its Yeovil birthplace. (Author)

The Beaufighter was one of the standardised types selected for mass production, this example having been built in the shadow factory managed by Bristol Aeroplane Co. Ltd at Weston-super-Mare. (H.E. North)

*The Second World War saw the return of the female population to aircraft
production, as shown by this classic propaganda photograph of
Halifax production by the London Aircraft Production Group.*
(Handley Page Association)

might have had such an effect, had it been available earlier and in larger numbers, but in general it was found that progressive improvement of existing designs could keep pace with new enemy designs. Thus, the Spitfire was able to maintain its operational utility, through progressive engine, carburation and airframe developments, in the face of the Focke Wulf Fw190 and its developments.

Figures released at the end of the war by the Ministry of Aircraft Production stated that wartime production totalled some 125,000 complete aircraft, largest numbers being (in sequence) Spitfire, Hurricane, Wellington, Anson, Lancaster, Mosquito, Halifax, Beaufighter, Blenheim and Oxford (all 5,000 aircraft or more). (Note that the published list does not include non-operational types such as the Tiger Moth, more than 8,800 of which were built.)

It is also worth noting, in the light of the post-war domination of the industry by the USA, that although starting later, the US industrial machine outstripped UK production by a comfortable margin. The US built some 360,000 aircraft in the Second World War, nearly 96,000 of them in 1944 alone.

5
Post-war
(1945-1960)

When peace came, the various shadow factories were no longer required and were closed, or converted for car and engine manufacture. The aircraft industry set about meeting the challenges that it faced. These included the relatively unfamiliar demands of the commercial market and the race to exploit the new technologies of war as tensions mounted between the West and the Soviet Bloc. The industry's efforts were made more difficult by the weakness of Britain's war-shattered economy.

Commercial Aircraft Developments

A key decision, which has shaped the post-war commercial aircraft industry, was that wartime transport aircraft production was allocated to the USA. As a result, the excellent C-47 Dakota or DC-3 was immediately available for opening up the post-war air routes, with longer range services provided by the DC-4 (C-54 Skymaster), the later DC-6 and the Lockheed Constellation. Not only were these excellent aircraft in their own right, but they also proved capable of development into a line of successful derivative aircraft.

What then of Britain? New aircraft types were needed; Britain's pre-war airliners had, after all, not exactly led the world in their performance or technology. Despite the strain on the economy, an attempt was made, through the Brabazon Committee, to identify and develop a fleet of new aircraft covering a wide range of commercial applications. Unfortunately, these designs could not be created overnight and, in the short-term, stop-gap designs and converted bombers were all that was available to compete for airline markets. Worse was to follow, as when the new types appeared, they were (with a couple of notable exceptions) not well suited to the prevailing market conditions. One common fault seems to have been the specification of too few passenger seats. Perhaps this reflected the view that few people could afford to fly, and those that could, would expect a suitably civilised environment!

To modern eyes, and admittedly with the benefit of hindsight, the first post-war commercial offerings from the British industry seem brave but, in many cases, doomed from the outset. Among these were:

- The hurriedly converted bombers – the Lancastrian, Halton and Stirling V.
- Britain's only true transport of the war, the Avro York – itself a development of the Lancaster bomber.
- The Sunderland flying boat conversions and developments – the Hythe, Sandringham and Solent.
- Non-starters – Armstrong Whitworth Apollo, Bristol Brabazon, Cunliffe-Owen Concordia, Portsmouth Aerocar, Percival Merganser and Saunders-Roe Princess.
- The honourable exceptions – the new designs which reached production. These were the Airspeed Ambassador, Avro Tudor, Bristol Freighter, Bristol Britannia, de Havilland Comet, de Havilland Dove, Handley Page Hermes, Handley Page (Reading) Marathon, Vickers Viking and Vickers Viscount.

Sadly, the vast majority could not compete with the operational economics of the American designs, nor the economies of scale afforded by the US industrial machine. Of British

The elegant Airspeed Ambassador was one of the Brabazon Committee types to enter production, but only twenty-three were built. (Rolls-Royce via Ken Ellis)

The Short Solent represents, perhaps, the peak of development of the passenger flying boat in the UK. Southampton and Southampton Water will long remain associated with these services. (Bombardier Aerospace, Belfast)

The ten-engine Princess was a design that was overtaken by events and never had the opportunity to demonstrate its potential. The prototype is seen here undergoing a trial launch on 19 August 1952. (SARO via Ken Ellis)

Britain's aviation heritage is epitomised by this evocative photograph of the prototype Comet 1, G-ALVG, banking over the Bristol Brabazon 1, G-AGPW. (BAE SYSTEMS plc)

One successful design of the immediate post-war years was the utilitarian Bristol Freighter, 214 of which were built for a diverse mix of civil and military customers. (J.S. Smith)

This evocative photograph, taken at Gatwick, shows Vickers' successful Viscount with a British United Airlines Bristol Britannia. (Via Author)

commercial aircraft in the immediate post-war period, only the de Havilland Dove and the Vickers Viscount were unqualified successes. It is indeed tragic that the Comet, which could have achieved a generation of British leadership in the skies, proved to be unexpectedly flawed. Although redesign of the Comet eventually produced a robust and successful aircraft, the moment had been lost as far as British domination of the commercial air transport market was concerned.

Military Aircraft Programmes

On the military side, the defeat of Germany and Japan brought peace, but no reduction in tension, because of the development of the 'Cold War' with the Soviet Union. The end of the war had seen the development of long-range surface-to-surface rockets, jet and rocket-propelled aircraft, and the atomic bomb. German technical progress with the development of the thin swept wing had also opened the door to much higher speeds and the prospect of supersonic flight. Britain, and indeed the whole developed world, therefore plunged into a race to develop and exploit these technologies in the military field.

Britain's brilliant lead in jet engine technology saw operational fruit with the Meteor and Vampire, but was rapidly surpassed by the pace of development in both the USA and the USSR. In these nations, the significance of German swept wing developments was better understood and acted upon, resulting in the superlative North American F-86 Sabre and Mikoyan & Guryevich MiG 15/17. Despite 'super-priority' programmes, Britain was unable to bring its own Swift or the Hunter quickly into service, and had to suffer the indignity of the interim operation of the F-86 Sabre in order to preserve a credible operational capability.

In the field of bombers, the superb Canberra was flown in 1949 and continues in RAF service in 2003, more than fifty years later. The Canberra was followed by the challenging V Bomber programme, which demonstrated that Britain could indeed produce world-class designs. How extraordinary, however, that after all its deprivations in the Second World War, the country could actually afford to carry all three V-Bombers – the Valiant, Victor and Vulcan – into production in the face of the Cold War threat. Transport and training aircraft progammes also delivered some long-serving types, including the Valetta and Varsity, Hastings, Beverley, Devon, Pembroke, Prentice, Provost and Chipmunk.

Westland transitioned to the manufacture of helicopters based upon the licence-built construction of Sikorsky designs, initially in the form of the WS-51 Dragonfly and the WS-55 Whirlwind. A wider rotorcraft industry developed with a range of home-grown designs from Bristol (Sycamore and Belvedere), Fairey (Ultra-Light, Gyrodyne and Rotodyne) and Saunders-Roe (Skeeter and P.531).

Manufacture by Westland of the WS-51 Dragonfly under licence from Sikorsky proved to be a decisive step for Westland Aircraft Ltd. Brand new civilian Dragonfly G-AMRE is seen here during test-flying from Yeovil. (Westland)

An immaculate Westland WS-55 Srs 1 – BEA Sir Arthur Class Sir Kay – equipped with amphibious floats. (Westland)

The TSR2 programme proved to be a major catalyst for the enforced rationalisation of the aircraft industry. (J.S. Smith)

Re-structuring of the Industry

As the 1950s came to a close, it was clear that an industry where every company built every type of aircraft could not be sustained. The Government recognised that this situation was unacceptable, and applied great pressure on the industry to produce rationalisation.

Duncan Sandys' Defence White Paper of 4 April 1957, *Outline of Future Policy*, has become somewhat notorious for its suggestion that missile technology was now maturing at such a rate that it would supplant the manned aircraft in many roles. It stated that in view of 'the good progress made towards the replacement of the manned aircraft of RAF Fighter Command with a ground to air missile system, the RAF are unlikely to have a requirement for fighter aircraft of types more advanced than the supersonic P1, and work on such projects will stop'. Development of a supersonic manned bomber was not to be started, emphasis being switched to atomic weapons and guided missiles.

Clearly great changes in the aircraft industry were becoming inevitable. The first step was the formation of the British Aircraft Corporation Ltd in January 1960, the Government having indicated that it would only support the TSR.2 programme if it were to be produced by a single company. This resulted in the aviation interests of Vickers, Bristol and English Electric joining forces, with Hunting Aircraft following shortly afterwards. In parallel, the companies in the Hawker Siddeley Group – Armstrong Whitworth, A.V. Roe & Co. Ltd, Blackburn, Gloster and Hawker – found themselves being progressively joined by new bedfellows. These consisted of Folland (in 1959), de Havilland and its Airspeed Division (in 1960), and Blackburn (also in 1960). In July 1963, this group was further reorganised to generate Hawker Siddeley Aviation Ltd.

Thus was created what *Aviation Week* has called the 'Society of Both Aircraft Companies'. This was something of an exaggeration, as Short Brothers & Harland continued in Belfast, as did Scottish Aviation Ltd at Prestwick, Handley Page Ltd at Radlett and Auster at Rearsby. The helicopter industry was the subject of a similar Government-dictated rationalisation, in which Westland acquired the helicopter interests of its competitors: Saunders-Roe Ltd (in 1959); Bristol (in 1960); and Fairey Aviation (also in 1960).

6
Rationalisation:
The BAC and Hawker Siddeley Years
(1960-1977)

Market Trends – Commercial and General Aviation

BAC and Hawker Siddeley inherited a civil market that was struggling to break out from American domination. It is unfortunate that during the initial post-war period, a unique British ability to market the wrong products had resulted in the commercial market for piston-engined aircraft being dominated by the USA. It was doubly unfortunate then that, despite the success of the Viscount, the Comet disasters opened the door to the Boeing 707 and DC-8.

If possible, worse was to follow. Myopic specifications from Britain's nationalised airlines (BEA and BOAC) and political indifference to the commercial aircraft industry undermined the potential of the Vanguard and VC-10, BAC One-Eleven and Trident. The technically brilliant Concorde was economically, politically and environmentally flawed, particularly after the oil price shock of the 1970s, and the on-off-on development of the HS146 (later the BAe 146 and Avro RJ family) appeared to be driven by pure politics.

In a significant move for the future, the Hatfield Division of Hawker Siddeley entered into an agreement to develop wings for the new European consortium Airbus Industrie. This followed inter-governmental agreement to support Airbus project definition, signed in September 1967. From May 1969, the UK government withdrew from further project funding, but Hawker Siddeley took the decision to continue in the project on a purely commercial basis.

In the field of general aviation, the 1960s scene seemed more positive; Beagle (British Executive & General Aviation Ltd) was set up in October 1960, drawing upon the creative

The BAC One-Eleven was moderately successful in the commercial market, with more than 230 aircraft sold. G-CBIA was photographed on its approach to land at London Gatwick Airport. (Author)

G-ATCT was the first prototype of Britten-Norman's classic utility aircraft, the Islander. (Britten-Norman via Ken Ellis)

abilities of Auster at Rearsby and F.G. Miles at Shoreham. New designs emerged in the shape of the Beagle Pup, the twin engine Beagle 206 and the Bulldog military trainer. De Havilland had seen the value of the executive jet market and designed their DH125, initially known as the Jet Dragon, which was taken up and marketed by Hawker Siddeley as the HS125 with great success worldwide.

At Bembridge, Isle of Wight, John Britten and Desmond Norman had, through their operation of agricultural aircraft in some of the more basic areas of the world, identified the need for a simple robust utility aircraft capable of operation from short airstrips in all climates. The design that resulted, the Islander, fulfilled the designers' concept in every respect. On a larger scale, Shorts were also successful in bringing the utilitarian Skyvan into production for both civilian and military users.

In the helicopter arena, Westland Helicopters Ltd built a solid base from its manufacture of Sikorsky products under licence. The Whirlwind and Wessex attracted large-scale orders, and the Saunders-Roe P.531 was developed successfully into the Scout and Wasp. Westland boomed in the 1970s as the Anglo-French helicopter deal came to fruition, with WHL building its own Lynx, and the Aérospatiale-designed Puma and Gazelle. Simultaneously, the company secured large national and export orders for the Sea King helicopter, which it built under licence from Sikorsky in the USA.

Commercial Casualties

Handley Page Ltd, having achieved only modest sales with the Herald, conceived a twin turboprop feeder liner, the Jetstream. The Jetstream was greeted with enormous enthusiasm in the marketplace, with significant sales achieved before its first flight. This sales success was in large measure dependent upon the aircraft delivering its declared performance, within its FAA certification limited maximum weight of 12,500lb. In the event, this could not be achieved.

Handley Page Ltd had invested in tools and facilities for large-scale production, and were now faced with a difficult and expensive development programme, whilst bearing the costs of their unfulfilled production expectations. The company proved unable to withstand the financial pressures and entered voluntary liquidation in August 1969, ceasing to trade in June 1970. The subsequent development of the aircraft by British Aerospace shows that this was, regrettably, another case of that British trait, most familiar in the field of sport, of defeat snatched from the jaws of victory.

Similar difficulties were encountered at Beagle. Here, despite the sale of nearly 400 Pup aircraft, the Government withdrew financial support to the company in December 1969.

The Wessex was developed by Westland as a turbine derivative of the Sikorsky S-58. The type saw long and valuable service with the British armed services, not least in the search and rescue role. (Ken Ellis Collection)

The Sea King was subject to extensive development by Westland Helicopters Ltd, resulting in a long production life and significant export sales. Qatar Sea King Mk 74 QA30/G-17-16 banks away from the camera, showing clearly its Exocet armament. (Westland)

Beagle eventually produced 152 Pup aircraft and eighty-five Beagle 206. Even the hugely popular Islander suffered from the problems brought about by sales success. Although the aircraft survived and remains in limited production, the company suffered a series of financial crises, including a number of periods in receivership.

Military Developments and Collaborative Ventures

In the military field, an almost mortal blow was struck when BAC, having been drawn together to produce the TSR.2, saw it cancelled by Dennis Healey in April 1965. BAC military efforts were then concentrated on the completion of Lightning production, supplemented by export Canberra refurbishment and the development of the pressurised Jet Provost T. Mk 5, and the BAC167 Strikemaster. BAC then moved on to the collaborative development of the Jaguar.

In the late 1960s, the RAF identified the requirement to reduce its number of front line types, whilst achieving the following aims:

- The progressive replacement, from the late 1970s, of the Canberra and the V-bomber fleet.
- To establish the capability to carry out the low-level penetration roles that were to have been the province of the TSR.2.
- In the longer term, to phase out the Lightning and Phantom from their air defence roles.
- Also in the longer term, to replace the Buccaneer in its low-level strike, reconnaissance and maritime strike roles.

With all these objectives in mind, a further collaborative project emerged known as the Multi-Role Combat Aircraft, or MRCA – later named Tornado. BAC joined with MBB and Aeritalia to form Panavia to produce the Tornado, which first flew in 1974.

Hawker Siddeley faced their own political traumas, with the cancellation of the supersonic V/STOL P.1154 project, the Royal Navy variant being cancelled by Peter Thorneycroft in February 1964. The RAF version followed under the Healey axe of 1965, which also saw the

The tri-national Panavia Tornado has succeeded in its initial programme objectives and is a true multi-role combat aircraft. This GR. Mk 4A was photographed at the 2002 SBAC Show. (Author)

cancellation of the HS.681 V/STOL transport. Despite these difficulties, Hawker Siddeley prospered on the strength of the products that it had inherited from its parent companies. Of particular note were the Harrier from Hawker, the HS748 from A.V. Roe & Co. Ltd, and the HS125 from de Havilland. Other work included the Buccaneer (ex-Blackburn), the Nimrod maritime patrol aircraft, Hunter refurbishment and production of the Trident.

During this period Hawker Siddeley designed what may prove to be Britain's last purely home-grown military aircraft, the HS.1182 Hawk trainer, which first flew in 1974 and continues to be one of the world's most successful trainer aircraft. In 1977, the next major stage in the development of the British Aircraft industry took place: the creation of British Aerospace – the 'Single British Aircraft Company'.

Beagle's instant classic: Beagle Pup 150 G-OPUP shows the clean lines of a thoroughbred. (Author)

Blackburn's NA39 was developed into the Hawker Siddeley Buccaneer and saw service with both the Fleet Air Arm and the Royal Air Force. This example has been modified for use as an avionics development aircraft in support of the Tornado programme. (Marshall Aerospace Ltd)

7
Modern Times

The Nationalisation and Privatisation of British Aerospace

British Aerospace (BAe) was formed as a nationalised corporation in April 1977 as a result of the Aircraft and Shipbuilding Industries Act 1977. In January 1981, BAe converted from a nationalised corporation to a public limited company (plc) in preparation for privatisation. The UK Government sold 51.57% of its shares in February 1981, and all but a single £1 'golden share' in May 1985.

When BAe was founded, it employed some 50,000 people on eighteen sites – Bitteswell, Brough, Chadderton, Chester, Christchurch, Dunsfold, Filton, Hamble, Hatfield, Holme-on-Spalding Moor, Hurn, Kingston, Preston, Prestwick, Samlesbury, Warton, Weybridge and Woodford.

Throughout its existence, BAe (now BAE SYSTEMS) has developed an ever more inter-national flavour. The BAC collaboration on Jaguar was followed by the tri-national Tornado programme. Tornado production for Saudi Arabia has now ended, and BAE SYSTEMS has started production of Eurofighter, in partnership with Spain, Italy and Germany.

Something of a defining moment for the industry came on 24 December 1998 when new-build Sea Harrier FA.2 NB18 was 'bought off' by the Royal Navy customer. The completion of this aircraft was said by BAe to mark the last delivery of an all-British fighter aircraft to the UK armed services. February 2002 saw the announcement of the plan to withdraw the Sea Harrier FA.2 from service by 2006. One national programme, the Hawk, continues to go from strength to strength. Private venture developments of the Hawk 100 and Hawk 200 have allowed the type to remain effective, and it continues to be selected as the preferred training and light attack aircraft of many armed forces around the world.

By the time of the merger of British Aerospace with Marconi Electronic Systems to form BAE SYSTEMS on 30 November 1999, the number of sites manufacturing aircraft compo-nents was down to eight – Brough, Chester, Chadderton, Filton, Prestwick, Samlesbury, Warton and Woodford – less than half the number of sites taken over in 1977. By this time,

The troubled Handley Page Jetstream was successfully developed by British Aerospace at Prestwick as the Jetstream 31. (Author)

Commercial aircraft success for BAE SYSTEMS has come through its stake in the Airbus programme; more than 3,000 Airbus aircraft had been sold by Autumn 1998. (Author)

only Filton and Yeovil remained as major sites of aircraft and helicopter manufacture in South West and Central Southern England, with components still being produced at Cowes, Weston-super-Mare and Hamble.

Further ahead is the JSF programme, with BAE SYSTEMS teamed with Lockheed Martin to produce the supersonic CTOL/ASTOVL F-35 multi-role strike fighter for the USAF, US Navy, US Marine Corps and the RAF. Other transatlantic military co-operations include the T-45 Goshawk for the US Navy, and the AV-8B Harrier II and II Plus with McDonnell Douglas (now Boeing). Work is underway on an extensively developed Nimrod, the MRA.4, (with new wings and engines) to preserve Britain's maritime patrol capability.

BAe/BAE SYSTEMS Commercial Programmes

In the civil field, the establishment of the Airbus consortium has at last introduced a note of success into Britain's involvement in commercial aviation. Much against many observers' expectations, Airbus has proved to be a worthy rival to Boeing, achieving initial market penetration with the A300 and A310. These types have been followed up by the smaller, and hugely successful, A320 family, and the A330 and A340 long-haul transports. Airbus has now launched its super-wide body project, the A380, and is also the nominated project management organisation for a joint European military transport project, the Future Large Aircraft A400M.

Elsewhere, the civil market has not proved a happy experience for British Aerospace/BAE SYSTEMS. Corporate jet activity was continued with production of the BAe125 (previously HS125, previously DH125). The aircraft has been extensively developed throughout its production life, the final BAe production versions being the Hawker 800 and Hawker 1000. BAe sold its corporate jet business to the Raytheon Corporation in June 1993.

BAe's regional turboprop products were the Jetstream and the Advanced Turbo-Prop, or ATP, a stretched and re-engined development of the Avro/HS 748. The ATP was manufactured at Woodford until October 1992, when production was transferred to Prestwick, and the aircraft re-launched under the designation Jetstream 61. At Prestwick, meanwhile, a growth version of the Jetstream, the Jetstream 41, was launched. Market conditions proved initially unfavourable due to production over-capacity in this sector. BAe responded by forming an alliance with Aérospatiale and Alenia known as Aero International (Regional), AI(R), with a view to rationalising product lines. An early casualty was the ATP/Jetstream 61, which, together with the original Jetstream 31, was not taken up by the AI(R) consortium. BAe continued with the Jetstream 41, but announced in May 1997 that the production line would close by the end of 1997. The AI(R) consortium was, itself, disbanded in 1998.

In the regional jet market, BAe produced the 146, taken over from Hawker Siddeley. Although produced in significant numbers (219 aircraft), initially at Hatfield and then at Woodford, the 146 was not a financial success for BAe. Production costs were high and many aircraft were leased on terms that ultimately proved unprofitable to BAe. The aircraft was re-launched as a family of types known as the Avro RJ (Regional Jet) series.

Unfortunately, the terrorist attack on the New York World Trade Center on 11 September 2001 sounded the death knell for the RJ/RJX programme. On 27 November 2001, BAE SYSTEMS announced that it would be withdrawing from the construction of commercial aircraft at Woodford and would close the RJ and RJX programmes, with a consequential loss of 1,669 jobs. This decision, following the earlier suspension of the Jetstream 41 and 61 programmes at Prestwick, marked the end of BAE SYSTEMS construction of complete aircraft for the civil market.

The Wider Industry

Outside BAe/BAE SYSTEMS, Shorts produced the SD330 and 360 developments of their 'ugly-duckling' Skyvan, and went on to supply the RAF with an extensively developed version of the Embraer Tucano for basic training. The last SD360 was built in 1991, and the last Tucano in 1992. Purchased by Bombardier in 1989, the company has become increasingly centred upon aerospace component manufacture and assembly. It is unlikely that the company will ever build another complete aircraft.

The boom that Westland experienced in the late 1970s could not last. Partly as a result of its ill-starred WG30 civil helicopter venture, Westland found itself in financial difficulties in 1986. A huge political row erupted over whether WHL should accept a possible European rescue package, or one offered by Sikorsky. After much acrimony, including the resignation of Michael Heseltine from the cabinet, the Sikorsky option was taken.

Westland, like BAe, has taken an increasingly international route to secure its future. This has centred on the EH101 helicopter developed with Italy. WHL was purchased by GKN in 1994. During 1998, GKN announced its intention to combine its helicopter operations with

The commercial aerospace market has proven troublesome for BAE SYSTEMS plc. The two RJX prototypes are seen here flying together, shortly before the programme was cancelled in the aftermath of the terrorist attack on New York on 11 September 2001. (BAE SYSTEMS plc)

those of the Italian company Agusta SpA. This merger has resulted in the formation of a new company, AgustaWestland, which has a mix of civil and military products, and involvement in both the EH101 and NH90 programmes. In the UK, the company has the EH101 and the WAH-64 Apache in production. The Lynx also remains in production, having gained export success in the form of the Super Lynx 300. The helicopter marketplace world-wide still features over-capacity, and AgustaWestland will continue to need good penetration in export markets to secure its long-term future.

In the general aviation sector, the almost immortal Islander continues in limited production. Private aircraft have, for the most part, remained a bleak area for the British industry. Success has, however, been achieved by three products – the Slingsby T67 Firefly, the CFM Shadow and the Europa.

- Slingsby redesigned the wooden Fournier RF6 (T67A), adopting an all-composite structure and installing increased power to produce a highly successful fully aerobatic trainer, which has found favour at entry level with a number of air forces around the world.
- The CFM (Cook Flying Machines) Shadow was designed by David Cook of Leiston, Suffolk. More than 400 of these aircraft have been built in a number of variants, including the high-performance Streak Shadow which flies at up to 105 knots on its 64hp. The Shadow and Streak Shadow have been sold in more than thirty-six countries, and have completed many notable flights, including from England to Australia. As with so many British aircraft manufacturers, there have been trading difficulties along the way. CFM Metal Fax Ltd went into liquidation in November 1996 and was taken over by CFM Aircraft Ltd in 1997. CFM Aircraft was, itself, in receivership in Autumn 2002 before being taken over by CFM Airborne Inc. of Texas, who announced in November 2002 the setting up of a UK facility: CFM Airborne (UK) Ltd.
- Ivan Shaw's all-composite Europa, designed for the home-built and kit construction market, first flew in September 1992. Within ten years, more than 900 kits had been sold in thirty-four countries, and more than 300 aircraft were flying.

Future Prospects

Where does the future of the British industry lie? Shrinking defence markets have forced rationalisation in the USA. To some extent, this was also the engine for the creation of Hawker Siddeley and BAC, and subsequently the formation of British Aerospace and BAE SYSTEMS.

Developed using the Lynx dynamic system, the WG30 was a brave but unsuccessful attempt by Westland to diversify into the civil market.
(J.S. Smith)

The all-composite Europa has been an outstanding success, with more than 900 kits sold in thirty-four countries. (Europa Aircraft Co.)

With an increasing trend toward collaborative projects, and the large scale of investment required to launch new projects, aerospace is rapidly moving towards being a global business.

Lockheed, Martin Marietta, General Dynamics (Fort Worth Division), IBM, Loral, and Vought have already coalesced into a single corporation. Northrop and Grumman have merged to become Northrop Grumman, and McDonnell and Douglas being absorbed into the Boeing Company. Faced with these giant businesses, European re-structuring has become inevitable. British Aerospace took a 35% share in Saab of Sweden and spent a period in ultimately unsuccessful restructuring discussions with DaimlerChrysler Aerospace of Germany (DASA).

On 19 January 1999, BAe and GEC announced that they had reached agreement on the merger of BAe with Marconi Electronic Systems (the defence interests of GEC). This merger, effective from the end of November 1999, created BAE SYSTEMS, then Europe's largest defence company, ranking at third largest in the world with a workforce of nearly 100,000 employees.

In response to the creation of BAE SYSTEMS, DaimlerChrysler announced in June 1999 that they were acquiring the Spanish company CASA, thereby strengthening their position for future restructuring discussions. An agreement with Aérospatiale Matra followed, leading to the formation of EADS (European Aeronautic Defence & Space Co.) on 10 July 2000. EADS is the world's third largest defence organisation behind Boeing and Lockheed Martin, displacing BAE SYSTEMS from this position.

With transatlantic projects such as JSF looking to secure global export markets, overtures from the major players in the USA may not be long delayed. A future global aerospace business may yet be created by one of the major US defence conglomerates acting in partnership with BAE SYSTEMS and/or EADS. In ten years time, it is hard to believe that the current structure of the industry will not have seen further upheaval – we will have to wait and see. By that time, indeed, it may seem almost quaint to refer to the British Aircraft Industry.

8
The Genealogy of
British Aerospace/BAE SYSTEMS
and GKN Westland Helicopters

The preceding narrative has charted the evolution of the British aircraft industry. Much of the manufacturing capacity of the industry is now in the hands of only two companies: BAE SYSTEMS, previously British Aerospace plc, manufacturing military and commercial fixed-wing aircraft; and AgustaWestland (previously GKN Westland Helicopters Ltd) manufacturing military helicopters.

Although the narrative has shown how political and commercial imperatives led to progressive re-structuring of the industry into these companies, the impact of these changes is best appreciated when presented graphically in the form of a family tree. BAE SYSTEMS came into being with the merger between British Aerospace and the defence interests of GEC, Marconi Electronic Systems (MES). As MES did not include any UK aircraft manufacturers in its heritage, the following family trees represent only the British Aerospace heritage that passed into BAE SYSTEMS.

Four diagrams are presented:

1. British Aerospace: The Big Picture
2. BAe: Hawker Siddeley Companies
3. BAe: British Aircraft Corporation and Scottish Aviation
4. British Rotorcraft Industry

Whilst in many respects these diagrams speak for themselves, a few observations are worth making:

- British Aerospace was formed in 1977 by the merging of three companies: Hawker Siddeley Aviation Ltd, the British Aircraft Corporation (BAC) and Scottish Aviation Ltd. Short Brothers & Harland were the only major fixed-wing aircraft manufacturer that remained independent of this group.
- Because Scottish Aviation Ltd had acquired the rump of the Beagle Aircraft Ltd and Handley Page Ltd activities, they effectively brought with them into the BAe family tree the heritage of these firms. This encompasses (via Handley Page Ltd) Martinsyde Ltd and Phillips & Powis/Miles Aircraft Ltd, and (via Beagle) Auster Aircaft Ltd and Taylorcraft Aeroplanes (England) Ltd.
- Hawker Siddeley Aviation Ltd (HSAL) added Blackburn & General Aircraft Ltd, the de Havilland Aeroplane Co. Ltd and Folland Aircraft Ltd to the group of Hawker Siddeley companies which had already been merged in 1935, although continuing to trade under their original identities (A.V. Roe & Co. Ltd, Hawker Aircraft Ltd, Gloster Aircraft Co. Ltd, and Sir W.G. Armstrong Whitworth Aircraft Ltd).
- The less familiar antecedents of HSAL include H.H. Martyn & Co. (via Gloster), William Denny & Bros Ltd, General Aircraft Ltd and CWA Ltd (via Blackburn) and Airspeed Ltd, May, Harden & May and Wycombe Aircraft Constructors (via AIRCO/de Havilland).

- Only four companies were grouped into BAC, these being English Electric Aviation Ltd, Bristol Aircraft Ltd (previously the Bristol Aeroplane Co. Ltd), Vickers-Armstrongs (Aircraft) Ltd and Hunting Aircraft Ltd (previously Percival Aircraft Ltd). The Vickers-Armstrongs heritage includes The Supermarine Aviation Works Ltd and Pemberton-Billing Ltd. The aircraft interests of The English Electric Co. Ltd were originally formed by merging the aircraft activities of Coventry Ordnance Works, Phoenix Dynamo Co. Ltd and Dick, Kerr & Co. in December 1918.
- Between 1919 and 1921 many company names were changed, and a number of new companies were founded following the closure of closely linked predecessors. This reflects the impact of taxation imposed after the First World War on companies which were considered to have made excess profits.
- On the helicopter side, only one major cycle of contraction is apparent with the Saunders-Roe Ltd, the Bristol Aircraft Ltd (Helicopter Division) and the Fairey Aviation Co. Ltd helicopter interests merging into Westland Aircraft Ltd in 1959-1960. Saunders-Roe had acquired the helicopter interests of The Cierva Autogiro Co. Ltd in 1951. Both The Fairey Aviation Co. Ltd and Saunders-Roe Ltd were, of course, notable manufacturers of fixed-wing aircraft, in addition to their helicopter interests.

BAe – The Big Picture

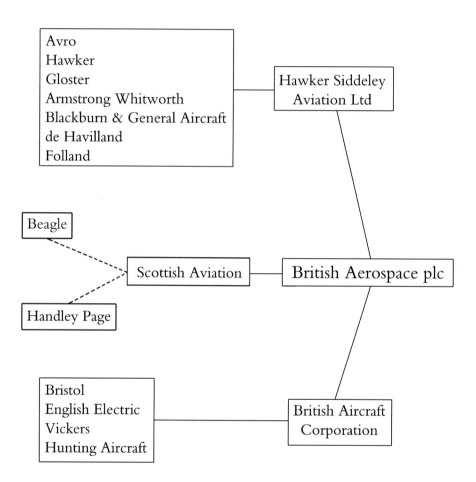

British Aerospace – Hawker Siddeley Companies

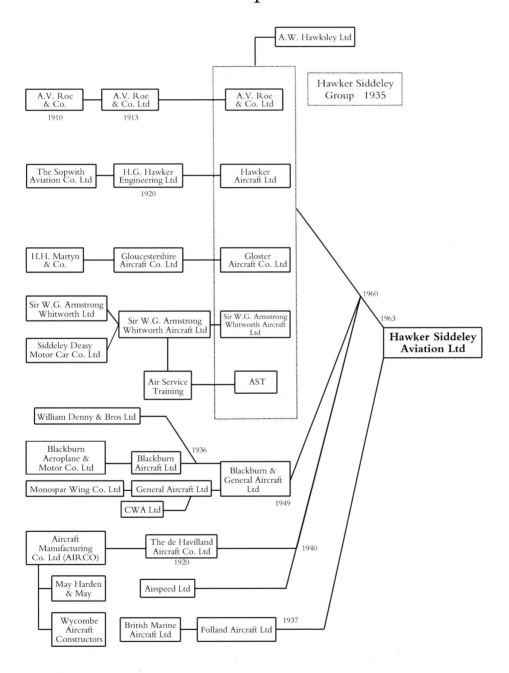

BAe: British Aircraft Corporation & Scottish Aviation

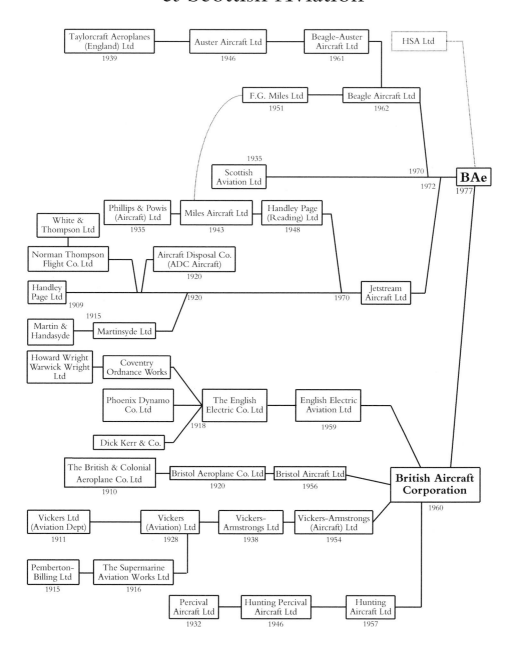

Taylorcraft Aeroplanes (England) Ltd — 1939

Auster Aircraft Ltd — 1946

Beagle-Auster Aircraft Ltd — 1961

HSA Ltd

F.G. Miles Ltd — 1951

Beagle Aircraft Ltd — 1962

Scottish Aviation Ltd — 1935

BAe — 1977

1970

1972

Phillips & Powis (Aircraft) Ltd — 1935

Miles Aircraft Ltd — 1943

Handley Page (Reading) Ltd — 1948

White & Thompson Ltd

Norman Thompson Flight Co. Ltd

Aircraft Disposal Co. (ADC Aircraft) — 1920

Handley Page Ltd — 1909

1920

Jetstream Aircraft Ltd — 1970

Martin & Handasyde — 1915

Martinsyde Ltd

Howard Wright Warwick Wright Ltd

Coventry Ordnance Works

Phoenix Dynamo Co. Ltd

The English Electric Co. Ltd — 1918

English Electric Aviation Ltd — 1959

Dick Kerr & Co.

The British & Colonial Aeroplane Co. Ltd — 1910

Bristol Aeroplane Co. Ltd — 1920

Bristol Aircraft Ltd — 1956

British Aircraft Corporation — 1960

Vickers Ltd (Aviation Dept) — 1911

Vickers (Aviation) Ltd — 1928

Vickers-Armstrongs Ltd — 1938

Vickers-Armstrongs (Aircraft) Ltd — 1954

Pemberton-Billing Ltd — 1915

The Supermarine Aviation Works Ltd — 1916

Percival Aircraft Ltd — 1932

Hunting Percival Aircraft Ltd — 1946

Hunting Aircraft Ltd — 1957

British Rotorcraft Industry

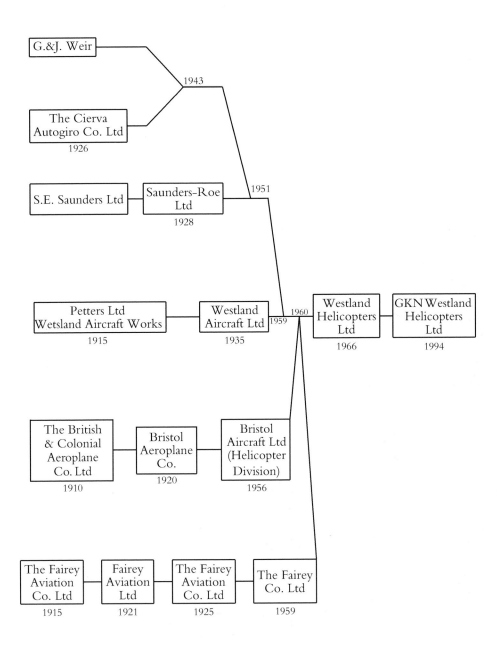

The Aircraft Manufacturers of South West and Central Southern England

As indicated in the introduction, for the purpose of this work, South West and Central Southern England is deemed to comprise the following: the Channel Islands, Cornwall, Devon, Dorset, Gloucestershire, Hampshire, the Isle of Wight, Somerset and Wiltshire.

Channel Islands

Guernsey

The **Nöel (Parmentier)** Wee Mite G-ACRL was flown (unregistered) in April 1933 from Vazon Bay sands. The ABC Scorpion-powered Wee Mite was designed by Cecil Nöel and built by Harold le Parmentier and other helpers. The aircraft was a parasol monoplane seating two in tandem, with a deep, not to say bath-like, appearance to the fuselage. The aircraft was re-engined with a Salmson radial after a forced landing, and withdrawn from use in 1936. This short life suggests that the type was not particularly successful, although the machine did complete a successful aerial circumnavigation of Guernsey in September 1933.

Cornwall

Bodmin

Trago Mills Ltd (Aircraft Division): The SAH1, a low-wing two-seat side-by-side training monoplane, was designed by Sydney Holloway and built by Trago Mills Ltd at Bodmin. The prototype G-SAHI was first flown at Bodmin on 23 August 1983 and showed excellent handling and great promise.

The Holloway/ Trago Mills SAH1 prototype has failed to live up to its early promise, with a number of companies taking up its development with only limited success. (Trago Mills via Ken Ellis)

Orca Aircraft Ltd: The Trago Mills aircraft activities were renamed as Orca Aircraft Ltd in August 1988. Although Orca entered administration a year later, the SAH1 rights were sold to **FLS Lovaux** at Hurn, who continued development of the design as the FLS Sprint (see Hurn, Dorset, for further details).

The ill-fated **Leisure Sport** Supermarine S.5 replica G–BDFF was based here after being rebuilt in 1986, flying again in October of that year. The aircraft crashed fatally following structural failure on 23 May 1987 (see also Thruxton and Calshot, Hampshire).

The **Whittaker** MW2B Excalibur G–BDDX, a low-wing monoplane with a pusher-ducted fan propulsor, flew only once on 1 July 1986 at Bodmin (see also Wootton-under-Edge, Gloucestershire).

Lands End

Western Airways, run by the late V.H. 'Viv' Bellamy and his son Rod, is noted for a series of highly authentic flying replica aircraft. The types constructed have mainly been from the First World War or the inter-war period. The origin of these replicas is generally indicated by their serial numbers (WA/1, WA/2, etc.) for Western Aircraft. The following were flown between 1976 and 1985:

- Fokker Dr1 G–BEFR (WA/1) first flown St Just in December 1976.
- Sopwith Camel G–BFCZ/B7270 first flown at St Just in 1977 and subsequently displayed in the Brooklands Museum.
- The Fairey Flycatcher replica G–BEYB 'S1287' (WA/3) was completed by John Hall and Maurice Gilbank on John Fairey's estate at King's Somborne, Hants, flying for the first time in July 1979.
- The DH2 replica G–BFVH (WA/4) was built for Thorpe Water Park and first flew in mid-1978. It proved to be slow and underpowered, with heavy controls and ineffective ailerons.
- Sopwith 1½ Strutter G–BIDW (WA/5) first flew in November 1980 and was displayed in the RAF Museum as '9382', it now being exhibited as A8226.
- Hawker Fury G–BKBB/K1930 (WA/6) was built over a period of four years for the late Hon. Patrick Lindsay, first flying on 11 December 1985.

The first of the Western Airways replicas was Fokker Dr1 G-BEFR. (Author)

Viv Bellamy was also responsible for managing the restoration work on the Fleet Air Arm Museum Fairey Albacore N4389 (also quoted as N4172), which was assembled from the remains of no less than four aircraft. Mr Bellamy was associated with the Hampshire Aero Club at Eastleigh, where he constructed the Pfalz replica G-ATIJ (flown in August 1965) for the film *The Blue Max*. He also built a Le Rhône-powered Avro 504K replica which was built and flown at Blackbushe, Hants, over a period of only twelve weeks in 1966. A trial installation of a Rover V8 engine was made in Auster J/1 G-AHAP, carrying out ground running in mid-1981, also at Blackbushe.

St Columb

Wombat Gyrocopters, of Higher Fraddon, Indian Queens, St Columb, designed and built a recreational autogyro, the first example being registered G-WBAT.

This AIRCO DH2 replica was built at Lands End for Thorpe Park, and is here seen at the 2000 SBAC Show. (Author)

One of Britain's varied selection of sporting autogyros, G-WBAT was built by Wombat Gyrocopters in Cornwall. (Author)

N500/G-BWRA is a modification of John Penny's home-built Sopwith Triplane replica G-PENY. The aircraft is seen here on a farm strip in East Devon. (Author)

Devon

Barnstaple

Lundy & Atlantic Coast Air Services, which originally operated air services between Barnstaple, Lundy and Torbay, worked within the Tiger Moth Civilian Repair Organisation during the Second World War.

Dunkeswell

Roger Hardy has designed a single-seat light biplane, the Hardy RH7B Tigerlight. Mostly completed by Mr Hardy, the prototype G-MZGT has been taken over by John McNab of Shebbear, and was reported (in *Popular Flying* of November/December 2001) as having been taken to Dunkeswell in preparation for its first flight.

David Silsbury: G-PENY was a Sopwith Triplane replica built by **John Penny** of Eckington (South Yorkshire) and flown during the late summer of 1988. The aircraft was only loosely based on the Sopwith design, the fuselage being widened to accommodate two occupants and power being supplied by a Lycoming 0-320. Following a landing accident, David Silsbury rebuilt the aircraft in Devon. In its modified form, the fuselage was rebuilt to the original width and the engine replaced with a Warner Scarab radial for an altogether more original appearance. Re-registered as G-BWRA and marked as N500, the aircraft was at Dunkeswell for testing during late 1996 and early 1997. The first flight in its rebuilt configuration was made on 31 August 1996.

Exeter

Air Service Training Ltd: During the Second World War, part of the Spitfire Civilian Repair Organisation repair work of AST Ltd was dispersed to Exeter. A hangar was built at the airport for assembly and additional premises (including a bus depot and various garages) were requisitioned in Exeter.

Chrislea Super Ace G-AKUW in 'as new' condition when celebrating Shoreham's sixty years as a municipal airport. (Author)

Chrislea Aircraft Co. Ltd moved to Exeter from Heston in April 1947 and (reportedly) took over the hangar previously occupied by AST. The Super Ace II G-AKFD was flown here in February 1948, with a Gipsy Major engine replacing the Lycoming of the original Ace, G-AHLG. The prototype initially retained the unconventional controls of the Ace, but eventually it, and all production aircraft, was modified to fit conventional rudder controls.

The difficulties encountered when flying the aircraft in its initial configuration can be surmised from some comments in a flight test conducted by R.G. Worcester for *The Aeroplane* magazine. After summarising the flying controls – conventional ailerons, side-to-side movement of the control wheel to apply rudder, vertical translation of the control wheel to apply elevator, and foot pedal throttle – he commented with fine understatement: 'It must be admitted that these actions are not altogether instinctive.'

He went on to say that 'Pilots who are used to conventional take-off controls should restrain a wild impulse to pull the control column out of its socket. To leave the ground the stick must be lowered a ½ inch with a finger-tip movement. A slight swing may tend to develop to starboard, and coarse application of the rudder (i.e. swinging the wheel sideways to the left) is necessary to keep the aircraft straight. In the air, the machine is very sensitive, and the controls are beautifully light and well harmonised.' His final, perhaps tongue-in-cheek, remark was that 'aerobatics would, however, demand a certain confidence in the controls, which was not acquired in my short series of flights.' In May 1948, Chrislea announced a free familiarisation course to any 'A' Licence holder who bought a Super Ace aircraft. By mid-October 1948, the flight controls of the Super Ace had been modified. Yaw control was provided conventionally by rudder pedals, and only the elevator remained unconventional, retaining vertical translation of the control wheel for its control input.

Thirty-three aircraft were built, comprising the original Ace, twenty-seven Super Ace aircraft, and five Skyjeep utility aircraft with tailwheel undercarriage and conventional stick and rudder controls. The first Skyjeep, G-AKVS, flew at Exeter on 21 November 1949.

Chrislea's assets were acquired by **C.E. Harper Aircraft** in 1952. As it is known that a number of the aircraft constructed by Chrislea were not flown, it seems likely that these were the main assets passed to C.E. Harper Aircraft.

Folland Aircraft Ltd are reported to have had dispersed capacity at Exeter during the Second World War.

Gould & Co., of London Inn Square, Exeter, built a copy of the Blériot monoplane in 1910. *British Aircraft before the Great War* indicates that this machine was designed by Mr George Weeks.

Parkhouse Monoplane: This unregistered home-built aircraft was photographed in October 1919, inverted after an accident. The machine was a parasol monoplane powered by a radial engine, with a wing of low aspect ratio and wire spoke wheels. Ord-Hume indicates that this accident occurred next to the Exeter to Cullompton road, to the north of Exeter. The precise identity of the machine is not clear however, with a report in *Aeroplane Monthly*, illustrated by the same photograph, describing it as a parasol monoplane designed and built by T.S. Baldwin. This machine was said to have been flown unregistered 'in the South Devon area', and to have been powered by an Anzani radial engine.

Plymouth/Torquay

During the Second World War, **W. Mumford** operated a repair centre at Plymouth within the Civilian Repair Organisation, specialising in Tiger Moth repairs. W. Mumford is also reported in *British Aircraft before the Great War* to have constructed a monoplane at Devonport 'of Blériot type' in 1910, which is also said to have been the first monoplane constructed 'in the West Country'.

Shapley Aircraft Ltd was registered on 6 November 1937 to build the Shapley Kittiwake. Named after its designer, E.S. Shapley, the Kittiwake was indeed shapely (if not a little rotund), with a monocoque wooden fuselage and gull wings. Single-seat (Mk I) and two-seat (Mk II) examples were constructed pre-war, these flying at Plymouth (Roborough) during 1937 (Mk I, G-AEZN) and 1938 (Mk II, G-AFRP).

Test-flying showed that the type had great promise in terms of both performance and handling qualities. G-AFRP survived the Second World War and development work was continued after the end of hostilities. Unfortunately, this was halted when the Pobjoy Niagara III-powered Mk II crashed while conducting spinning trials on 10 May 1946. The aircraft was constructed in a store room at Starkey's Iron Foundry, Swan Street, Torquay.

Dorset

Bournemouth (see also Hurn)

The Bournemouth Aviation Co., Talbot Village Aerodrome, Bournemouth. This company set up a flying school (from late 1915) with London & Provincial Caudron trainers, several of which they themselves constructed. In December 1915, London & Provincial had two aircraft under construction for Bournemouth Aviation, who had just set up a new flying ground of 200-250 acres of level, well-drained ground at Talbot Village, north west of Bournemouth. In November 1916, the company was advertising: 'School Biplanes supplied' and 'School Machines (Caudron Type) built to order. Immediate delivery.'

One of the Caudron-related designs, powered by an 80hp Anzani, is reported to have flown to 7,500ft, with a passenger, in May 1917. By the end of August 1917 the company was reported to be creating a new flying field extending to some 100 acres about a mile away from Talbot Village. In August 1918, the school had twelve solo and dual aeroplanes in use and more than twenty other aeroplanes and engines in stock.

Hampshire Woodcrafts Ltd acquired the business of manufacturers of aeroplanes and spare parts known as **The Bournemouth Aviation Co. Ltd**, and had offices at Wharf Road, Bournemouth, in November 1918.

'Historic Talbot Village' is sited to the north of the A3049 and is an enclave of private roads and playing fields to the north of Bournemouth town centre. The 1924 Ordnance Survey map shows Bournemouth Aerodrome just to the north of Talbot Village in the vicinity of the modern-day Kingleigh School, between East Howe and Ensbury Park.

Motor Mac's Ltd of 35 Holdenhurst Road, Bournemouth, was run by William Edward McArdle, Bournemouth's first pilot. The garage advertised itself as 'The Finest Garage in England' and was on a site subsequently occupied by Hartwells Ltd. Other advertising included: 'Aeroplane Manufacturers' (May 1917); 'On War Office List. Aeroplane manufacturers and makers of component parts'; 'Sheet metal, welding, die stamping work' (January 1917); 'Fittings as used on Sopwith wings, centre section, ailerons, RE8 rudders, Scarff gun mounts, Scarff Dibowsky interrupter gear, bracing struts and wiring plates for BE2E, DH6 wiring plates, DH9 wings and tail units' and 'Aeroplane, Motor & General Engineers. Contractors to Admiralty, War Office and Ministry of Munitions' (August 1918).

Having learned to fly in 1909-1910 at the Blériot school at Chalons and Issy-les-Moulineaux, McArdle flew a Blériot monoplane, initially from two fields near Vine Farm, Wallisdown. Vine Farm lay immediately to the south of Talbot Village, and the street names of Vine Farm Close and Vine Farm Road are contained within the modern housing estate on Talbot Heath, opposite Bournemouth College of Art. During the Second World War, this site was used for a short period (around the time of the D-Day landings) by US Army liaison aircraft.

McCardle joined forces with the American J.A. Drexel to set up a training school with seven Blériots on the Dorset side of Redhill Common at Ensbury Park a mile or so east of Talbot Village. A number of the Blériot aircraft used were constructed at McArdle's Garage, and *British Aircraft before the Great War* indicates that there were also reports of three biplanes being under construction during 1910. The Dorset side of Redhill Common remains flat open ground, presently in use as playing fields.

McArdle & Drexel were, in 1910, regarded as 'the foremost Blériot exponents resident in England at the time'. The school moved again to East Boldre, near Beaulieu, becoming the New Forest Aviation School. A number of Blériot monoplanes used by the school were sold to the Eastbourne Aviation Co. when the school ceased trading in late 1911.

Poole Aviation Co., of 24 West Quay Road, Poole, advertised as 'Contractors to HM Government', and used the telegraphic address 'Aviation, Poole.' Despite this company's title, it is very likely that it only manufactured parts and sub-assemblies.

Worms Aircraft Construction Co. Ltd – Business address: Rutland Works, Rutland Road, Bournemouth. This company is linked to the **Worms Aircraft Construction Co.** (Max Worms) of Sackville Street, Piccadilly, which had works at Twickenham and Chelsea. The London company advertised its capability to supply 'complete metal and wood components for all types of aircraft.' The formation of a limited company with works in Bournemouth took place in April 1918. Nothing else is known.

Christchurch Airfield

Christchurch was used for aircraft manufacture by Airspeed Ltd, later the Christchurch division of The de Havilland Aircraft Co. Ltd, from 1941 until 1962.

Airspeed (1934) Ltd used Christchurch to provide additional manufacturing capacity to that available at Portsmouth; for a summary of the company history, refer to the entry for Portsmouth, Hants. The types constructed at Christchurch were the Airspeed Oxford (550 out of a total production run in excess of 8,500), Airspeed Horsa glider (695 at Christchurch), de Havilland Mosquito (422) and, as the Airspeed Division of de Havilland, the Ambassador airliner.

The first Christchurch-built Oxford was X6250, which flew in March 1941. One of Airspeed's main contributions to the war effort was the Horsa glider built at Christchurch, which was prominent in the D–Day landings. The aircraft was designed for dispersed production, with modules coming together at RAF maintenance units for final assembly. All told, nearly 3,800 were built, with extensive sub-contracting to furniture manufacturers. Airspeed built some 700, the **Harris Lebus** 'group' adding around 2,700 others and **Austin Motors Ltd** a further 365. The first Christchurch-built example, DG604, flew on 22 February 1942, towed by a Whitley. Airspeed Ltd also built a total of 122 de Havilland Mosquito B.35s and 300 FB. VIs.

The Airspeed Horsa assault glider was one of the company's most important products during the Second World War. (BAE SYSTEMS plc)

The first Airspeed Ambassador, G-AGUA, flew at Christchurch on 10 July 1947. An elegant design, the Ambassador had its origins as the Brabazon Committee's Type IIA. The Ambassador was designed by Arthur Hagg at Fairmile Manor, Cobham, Surrey from 1943 onwards. The programme was held back by delays in validation of the wing design and fuselage pressurisation testing, which was carried out by submerging a test fuselage in Portsmouth Docks.

Ambassador production was limited to twenty-three aircraft. The type entered service as the BEA Elizabethan Class on 13 March 1952 and was progressively replaced in BEA service by the Viscount from 1957. The last BEA Ambassador service was flown on 30 July 1958. Subsequently the type saw service with a number of smaller airlines such as Autair International, BKS and Dan Air.

The Ambassador was used as a test bed for a number of engine types. The second prototype, G-AKRD, tested the Proteus 705 for the Britannia, the Tyne for the Vanguard (as G-37-3), and the Dart, as the Ambassador P. Special. A second Tyne Ambassador, G-ALZR, was used with G-AKRD for route-proving operations of the Tyne, prior to the introduction of the Vanguard. G-ALFR was used by Napier at Luton for flight testing the Napier Eland.

At the 1948 SBAC Show, the Ambassador gave a spectacular (and possibly never equalled) exhibition by taxiing out with the port engine stopped and its propeller feathered. The aircraft then took off and completed its entire demonstration on one engine.

The Airspeed Ambassador second proto-type G-AKRD was extensively used as a test bed. Here it is seen on propeller development trials, subsequently being used for Proteus, Dart and Tyne testing. (BAE SYSTEMS plc)

Airspeed/ de Havilland activities at Christchurch included Ambassador production and responsibility for the Vampire Trainer, here represented by a Swedish example, 28413. (BAE SYSTEMS plc)

The de Havilland Aircraft Co. Ltd purchased the Swan Hunter & Wigham Richardson shares in Airspeed (1934) Ltd in May 1940. From 1 January 1944, the company was re-named **Airspeed Ltd**, operating as the Airspeed Division of de Havilland. In 1951, the company was re-organised, integrated into the de Havilland company organisation and thereafter traded under its parent's name as the de Havilland Christchurch Division. The following types were built at Christchurch: Consul, Sea Venom, Vampire Trainer, night fighter versions of the Vampire and Venom, and the Sea Vixen.

The Sea Vixen was developed from the DH110, two of which were built at Hatfield. Sea Vixen production comprised the Sea Vixen Mk 20X pre-production aircraft, XF828, which flew on 20 June 1955, and 114 FAW1, the first (XJ474) flying on 20 March 1957. Production then switched to the Sea Vixen FAW2, the total for this variant comprising two prototypes, twenty-nine new-build aircraft and sixty-seven conversions from FAW1. Sea Vixen FAW2 production was centred at Chester. The first FAW2 (conversion of FAW1 XN684) was flown on 1 June 1962. A proportion of the Vampire Trainer (T.11) and Sea Vampire (T.22) were also built by the de Havilland Christchurch Division, production being shared with Hatfield and Chester. Vampire trainers were also built for export (T.55) for countries including New Zealand, South Africa, Norway, Venezuala, Portugal, Iraq, Sweden and the Lebanon, totalling some forty-three aircraft.

A Sea Vixen FAW2 XJ580 was, for a number of years, proudly displayed on the corner of the old airfield site, but was subsequently moved to Tangmere in West Sussex. A sign beneath the aircraft recorded the use of the site for aircraft manufacture and listed the types constructed at Christchurch, as follows:

> *This aircraft was built near this site, a corner of what used to be Christchurch Airfield, where once the Airspeed-de Havilland factory stood. Between 1942-62 the following aircraft were built here:*
> *Horsa Assault Glider, Oxford, Seafire II, Mosquito P.R.34 & B.35, Consul, Ambassador Airliner, Vampire Jet Trainer, Vampire & Venom Night Fighters, Sea Venom & Sea Vixen.*

The factory buildings remain, but the airfield itself has disappeared beneath an industrial estate and housing development. Local street names reflect Britain's aviation heritage and include: Airspeed Road, Airfield Way, The Runway, De Havilland Way, the Beaver and Sea Vixen Industrial Estates, and streets commemorating the Hunter, Valiant, Halifax, Blenheim, Comet, Stirling, Viscount, Brabazon, Swordfish, Auster, Britannia, Vulcan, Sunderland, Beaufighter, Wellesley, Andover, Lysander, Wessex, Lancaster, Wellington, Ambassador and Grebe – an extraordinary collection!

Portsmouth Aviation Ltd had a hangar at the end of Warren Avenue on the south side of Christchurch airfield, which was used to overhaul and refurbish RAF Oxford aircraft during the Second World War. This hangar remained in use by 622 Gliding School/171 Squadron ATC until July 1963.

The **Scintillex** premises in Bridge Street were used during the Second World War for the manufacture of Airspeed Horsa assemblies.

Hurn

Prior to the establishment of Heathrow, Hurn was the main post-war operational base of BOAC, although services were also operated from Northolt and Poole.

Airwork Ltd is remembered by the author for its running, at Hurn, of the Fleet Requirements Unit, operating Supermarine Scimitar fighters and Meteor TT20 target tugs.

The Fleet Requirements Unit was established at Hurn in 1952 and used an incredible variety of aircraft types, which included (in approximate chronological sequence) the following: Sea Mosquito, Sea Hornet, Sea Fury, Attacker, Sea Hawk, Firefly, Meteor, Scimitar, Hunter and Canberra. Three Dragonfly helicopters were also employed. The Fleet Requirements Unit moved to Yeovilton in late 1972.

The company operated from a number of locations and ferried several British-built aircraft to export customers from Hurn. Examples include twelve Indonesian Fairey Gannets delivered from Hurn to Surabaya, three Hunting Provost trainers to Khartoum, Sudan, and a further six to Kuala Lumpur, Malaysia. A number of BAC 167 Strikemaster aircraft were also delivered to the Middle East from Hurn.

After the formation of the **British Aircraft Corporation**, production and flight test of the BAC One-Eleven was carried out at Hurn. The design of the BAC One-Eleven was evolved by BAC from the Hunting H.107 project. The BAC One-Eleven Srs 200 prototype G-ASHG first flew at Hurn on 20 August 1963, to be followed by the Srs 400 on 13 July 1965, Srs 500 G-ASYD on 30 June 1967, and the Srs 475 (also G-ASYD) on 27 August 1970. UK production was completed in 1984, with a sales total of 232 aircraft.

The de Havilland Aircraft Co. Ltd: Hurn was used by BOAC as the base for its Comet Unit as the type was first introduced into service. The association of Hurn with de Havilland products continued with the use of Hurn for the flight testing of a number of Christchurch-built types, including the Sea Vixen, until the early 1960s. To support this activity, de Havilland Christchurch operated a production, development and experimental hangar at Hurn which was particularly active in support of Vampire Trainer production.

Flight Refuelling Ltd/FR Aviation/Cobham plc: Flight Refuelling Ltd has taken over the civilian Fleet Requirements Unit operations (providing calibration targets, electronic warfare and target-towing aircraft for the Royal Navy) previously provided by Airwork Ltd. A fleet of modified Falcon 20 aircraft, which are based at Hurn, currently meets these requirements.

The company has carried out a range of aircraft modification programmes at Hurn, including a programme to convert Sea Vixen aircraft to pilotless D3 drone configuration; a similar (but unsuccessful) programme based around F-100 Super Sabre conversions; and the modification of eight RAF VC-10 aircraft to flight refuelling tanker configuration under contract from British Aerospace.

Cobham plc was awarded the contract for major airframe refurbishment in support of the Nimrod MRA.4 programme. Unfortunately, this contract was subsequently cancelled, with the work being brought back in-house by BAE SYSTEMS.

FLS Aerospace (Lovaux Ltd): FLS acquired the Brooklands Aerospace Group in July 1990 and moved Optica production from Old Sarum to Hurn. A total of twenty-two Optica had been built by various concerns up to mid-1995. In 1996 it was reported that a Memorandum of Understanding had been signed with Gegasi Industries of Malaysia which would lead to production in that country.

FLS acquired the SAH1 design from Orca Aircraft in October 1991 and re-named it the FLS Sprint. The first production Sprint 160, G-FLSI, flew on 16 December 1993. Further Sprint aircraft have been registered, including G-BVNU, G-BXWU, G-BXWV and G-SCLX. G-BVNU is a Sprint Club, powered by a 118hp O-235 engine. During 1998, the FLS Sprint rights were purchased by Mike Woodley of North Weald. FLS Aerospace operates maintenance facilities for wide-bodied commercial aircraft at both Stansted and Manchester.

The BAC One-Eleven did not achieve the success of the DC9, but has proven to be rugged and reliable in service. This photograph shows two BUA aircraft at Gatwick Airport including, in the foreground, G-ASJA, the first aircraft to be delivered. (Via Author)

Both Hurn (seen here) and Tarrant Rushton were used for the production test-flying of de Havilland Vampire Trainers built at Christchurch. (BAE SYSTEMS plc)

The Holloway/ Trago Mills/ Orca SAH1 is seen here at the SBAC Show in its then guise as the FLS1 Sprint. (Author)

Above: *Of the 163 Varsity aircraft built, the majority were assembled at Vickers-Armstrongs' Hurn factory.* (J.S. Smith)

Left: *An advertisement for the Vickers-Armstrongs Ltd Varsity.* (Copyright: BAE SYSTEMS plc)

Below: *Vickers' successful Viscount is represented here by the Hurn-built YI-ACL of Iraqi Airways.* (Marshalls Aerospace Ltd)

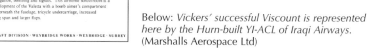

Vickers–Armstrongs Ltd used Hurn as a production and test facility to supplement their capacity at Weybridge and Wisley, making use of the hangars previously occupied by BOAC. The Viscount and the Varsity were manufactured at Hurn, which was also used briefly in 1951 for early flight testing of the Valiant prototype, whilst a hard runway was laid at Wisley. 146 Varsity aircraft, from the total production run of 163, were built at Hurn, the remainder being built at Weybridge. The last Varsity to leave the production line was flown on 28 February 1954.

279 Viscount were built at Hurn from a production total of 445, the type seeing service with more than sixty operators. The two Viscount-erecting shops at Hurn were extended in length from 342ft to 796ft (more than doubled) in late 1954 and early 1955. This enabled production work to continue on twenty-four aircraft simultaneously. In the late 1990s, fifty years after the type's first flight, sixteen aircraft remained in service, mainly in the cargo role.

Kimmeridge Hill

Kimmeridge Hill near Purbeck was used by the Westland test pilot **Harald Penrose** in 1935 to fly his home–designed and built glider, the 34ft-span Pegasus.

Tarrant Rushton

The de Havilland Aircraft Co. Ltd: Tarrant Rushton was used for the production flight testing of Christchurch-built de Havilland Vampire T.11 aircraft.

Flight Refuelling Ltd: In June 1948, the operations division of Flight Refuelling Ltd moved from Ford Aerodrome to Tarrant Rushton. During the Berlin Air Lift, Flight Refuelling used Avro Lancaster and Lancastrian aircraft converted into flying tankers to deliver nearly seven million pounds of fuel to Berlin.

Flight Refuelling is perhaps best known for its development of the probe and drogue technique of in–flight refuelling. The development aircraft used from April 1949 included Lancaster aircraft G-33-1, G-33-2 (ex-PB972) and Meteor III EE397. The first air-to-air refuelling of the Meteor took place on 6 April 1949. A twelve-hour non-stop flight was made by the Meteor on 7 August 1949. The company later made use of Lincoln RA657 and Meteor IV VZ389.

Flight Refuelling Ltd carried out Meteor overhaul and modification activity at Tarrant Rushton, and was responsible for the conversion of Meteor aircraft to drone configura-

Two hangars are the only survivors as the runways, dispersals and perimeter track of Tarrant Rushton fade into the agricultural landscape. (Author)

tion. This extensive programme included some 200 aircraft, with ninety-two Meteor F.4 converted to U.15 and more than 100 F.8 converted to either U.16 or U.21. The first pilotless take-off by a Meteor U.15 took place on 11 March 1955, the aircraft concerned being RA421. In 1953, the company was promoting itself thus: 'Flight Refuelling Ltd. Specialists in retrospective modifications from design through to flight test.' Another aircraft modification programme was the conversion of a number of Bristol Brigand aircraft to the Brigand T.4 trainer configuration. The company also conducted overhaul and modification work for the Belgian Air Force, types handled including the T-33 and F-84. Conversions to RF-84 were carried out for both the Belgian Air Force and the USAF.

During February 1955 the Meteor programme was underway, with the company advertising for airframe fitters for Meteor overhaul at Tarrant Rushton, this being supported by a 'special bus service from Salisbury, Ringwood, Bournemouth, Christchurch and Poole.' In addition to drone conversions, a significant number of ex-RAF aircraft were prepared at Tarrant Rushton for export to mainly Middle Eastern customers in a programme that ran from mid-1954 until mid-1956. Customers included Ecuador (twelve FR.9), Egypt (eight F.8, three T.7), Syria (seven F.8, two FR.9), Israel (seven FR.9, two T.7), Sweden (two T.7) and a single T.7 to France.

A Sea Vixen made the final flight from Tarrant Rushton on 30 September 1980.

General Aircraft Ltd: In Spring 1944, General Aircraft Ltd had a works team providing maintenance and repair support to Hamilcar gliders at Tarrant Rushton.

Gloucestershire

Almondsbury

The **Lynn Williams** Z-1 Flitzer is a single-seat home-built biplane with the purported style of a 1920s German design. It was first flown from a farm strip at Brickhouse Farm, one mile to the east of the M4/M5 interchange at Almondsbury. This miniature biplane (G-BVAW) is Volkswagen-powered and carries the marks D692 in imitation of a period colour scheme and is also marked with the fictitious name **Staaken Flugzeugbau**, Berlin. The aircraft first flew in the spring of 1995 and has since had its initial 1600cc Volkswagen engine replaced by the more powerful 1834cc version. A second aircraft, G-FLIZ, has since flown.

The Lynn Williams Z-1 Flitzer was first flown from the farm strip at Brickhouse Farm near Bristol, where this photograph was taken.
(J.S. Smith)

Only the buildings give a hint of the aeronautical heritage of the Gloster experimental site at Bentham, as seen in September 2000. (Ken Ellis Collection)

Bentham

Gloster Aircraft Co. Ltd set up experimental works at Bentham close to Brockworth. Bentham was used for design and prototype manufacture, with the prototypes subsequently being disassembled for road transport, being typically flown from Moreton Valence or Boscombe Down. The Gloster E.1/44 prototype SM809 was built here, but damaged during its road move to Boscombe Down, being replaced by TX145. After its first flight at Boscombe Down, TX145 was subsequently tested at Moreton Valence and RAE Farnborough.

Bristol Area

Aircraft construction in the Bristol area is presented below in the following sequence: aircraft construction in Bristol itself, including Brislington, Eastville, Fishponds and Park Row; the long-lived operations of The British & Colonial Aeroplane Co. Ltd and its successors at Filton which continues to the present day; and activity at the pre-war airfield of Whitchurch (Hengrove Park).

Bristol Area – City of Bristol

The **British & Colonial Aeroplane Co. Ltd** had sawmills and a woodworking workshop in the Tramway Co.'s works at Brislington. These were used for the construction of six Boxkite and twenty-four TB8s for the RNAS. A second F.2B production line was established here, building 1,045 aircraft, the first Brislington built F.2B being delivered in April 1917. For further details see Filton.

Parnall & Sons Ltd (shopfitters) built a substantial number of aircraft during the First World War, orders including eighty Avro 504B, thirty Avro 504G, 600 Avro 504J/K, 115 Fairey Hamble Baby (130 ordered, but not all are known to have been delivered), twenty Short 827 and six Short Bombers. A number of the Hamble Baby aircraft were delivered in landplane form, these being known as Hamble Baby Converts.

The original aircraft works were at Broadmead, Bristol, supplemented by a new factory at Mivart Street, Eastville, which previously belonged to a clothing manufacturer (although it is also stated to have been used for cabinet making). The erecting shop was a conversion of the Coliseum skating rink in Park Row, and there was a further factory that was taken over at Brislington for experimental work and propeller manufacture. There were two additional

Above: *Among the types constructed by Parnall & Sons during the First World War was the Short 827, seen here in the company's Coliseum Works.* (Ken Wixey)

factories at Baptist Mills and Fairfax Street, which were used for wing manufacture and doping. During this period Parnall–built aircraft were test flown at Filton.

In 1920, following the sale of Parnall & Sons to W. & T. Avery, George Parnall set up a new company, **George Parnall & Co. Ltd**, initially still at Park Row, but later at Yate. In 1921 the company was advertising: 'George Parnall & Co. Designers and manufacturers of all types of modern aircraft. Coliseum Works, Park Row, Bristol. Works also at Feeder Road, Bristol.' In September 1929 the company was advertising as: 'Aircraft Designers and Constructors, Specialists in light aircraft.' Telegraphic address: 'Warplanes, Bristol.'

The **Parnall & Sons Ltd** concern, under W. & T. Avery, accepted contracts from 1939 for the manufacture of aircraft components as a result of the Second World War expansion of aircraft production. This work was performed at Lodge Causeway, Fishponds, in a factory previously occupied by the engine manufacturer, Cosmos Engineering. Production at Fishponds included major structural components for the de Havilland Tiger Moth, Airspeed Oxford (wings), Airspeed Horsa (fuselages), and smaller components for the Fairey Barracuda, Handley Page Halifax, de Havilland Mosquito, Bristol Beaufighter and Short Stirling. This activity at Fishponds continued post-war, notably with components for de Havilland/Hawker Siddeley (Comet, Dove, Heron, Vampire, HS125), and for the Bristol Freighter and Britannia.

Pride Monoplane. *British Aircraft before the Great War* reports that Mr Christopher Pride of Fishponds, Bristol, built a monoplane of unconventional configuration ('a tandem monoplane ... with propellers front and rear') which made one flight on 18 July 1909. This flight extended to a very creditable 976yds, but was abruptly terminated when the aircraft hit a tree.

The **Redcliffe Aircraft Co. Ltd** of Harford Street, Cathay, Bristol, was registered in July 1918 with £1,000 capital as manufacturers of wings and parts for aeroplanes, nothing else known.

Bristol Area - Filton

Filton is the site in Britain which has the longest record of continuous aircraft manufacture. The presentation below gives a chronological record of the Bristol Aeroplane Co. Ltd from its founding as the British & Colonial Aeroplane Co. Ltd to its present-day successors BAE SYSTEMS. There follows a summary of flight test activity associated with the development of Bristol engines, and of the activities of Parnall at Filton.

Pioneering period (1908-1914)

The British & Colonial Aeroplane Co. Ltd: Telegrams, 'Aviation, Bristol.' The company was founded (and funded) by Sir George White, Bt., the Bristol-based pioneer of the electric tram, in February 1910. Sir George was not a pioneering pilot. Rather, he saw the aeroplane as a commercial opportunity from the outset, and this enterprise proved to be extremely successful. The initial works at Filton were originally two Bristol Tramways sheds, on the corner of Homestead Road and Fairlawn Avenue, emblazoned with the new company name. The general offices were set up in Filton House, which was purchased in 1912, and still exists within the BAE SYSTEMS site.

The airfield at Filton has been in continuous use for aircraft manufacture since the formation of The British & Colonial Aeroplane Co. Ltd in February 1910. (Author)

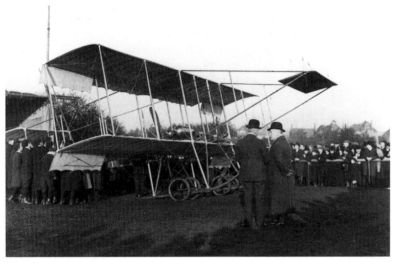

The Bristol Standard Biplane, or Boxkite, was one of the most important aircraft to fly in Britain before the First World War. Seventy-eight of these aircraft were built. Sir George White, the founder of The British & Colonial Aeroplane Co. Ltd, is seen here (to the right) in conversation with another gentleman. (Rolls-Royce via Ken Ellis)

The Bristol F2B Fighter was a long-serving workhorse. With Handley Page slots and a much enlarged rudder, this is the final version, the Fighter Mk IV. This aircraft shows an array of additional paraphernalia, including a message collection hook between the undercarriage legs. (Ken Ellis Collection)

Below: A selection of Bristol & Colonial advertisements. (Copyright: BAE SYSTEMS plc)

British & Colonial built many successful early designs that were used for school flying, notably at Larkhill and Brooklands. These ranged from Farman-type biplanes typified by the Boxkite (seventy-eight built) and sleek monoplanes such as the Bristol Prier series, thirty-four of which were built. Other early products included the Gordon England biplanes (five), Coanda Monoplane (thirty-four), and subsequent biplane developments including fifty-three Bristol TB8 aircraft, a number of which were conversions from Coanda Monoplanes. Eric Gordon England joined the company in August 1911 and carried out both design work and flight testing before leaving in November 1912 to work with James Radley on his Waterplane project. F.S. Barnwell joined the company as Experimental Designer (later becoming Chief Designer) in December 1911. Some idea of the early success of the British & Colonial Aeroplane Co. can be gained by their construction of more than 100 aeroplanes in 1911. To reinforce the point, the company was advertising at this time that 'no fewer than three machines can be turned out weekly.'

In January 1913 the company was advertising: 'The Bristol Monoplane. Contractors to HM War Office and Admiralty and all the important European Governments. The most successful machine of the day.' Note that although the company name was British & Colonial, it referred to its products as Bristol types from the outset. Thus, another advertisement from later in 1913 refers to 'The celebrated "Bristol" Aeroplanes'.

First World War Production

During the First World War, The British & Colonial Aeroplane Co. Ltd built a range of fighter aircraft, the most successful and famous being the Bristol F.2B Fighter. During this period, the company's normal advertising style was: 'The British & Colonial Aeroplane Company Ltd. Filton, Bristol. The "Bristol" Aeroplanes. Contractors to HM Admiralty & War Office.'

An early military design that achieved production and service success was the Bristol Scout. This machine had its origins in the Scout A, which was first flown at Larkhill on 23 February 1914. The prototype was followed by two Scout Bs, before the main production variants – the Scout C and D – appeared. Production comprised 161 Scout C and 160 Scout D, the type serving with both the RNAS and the RFC.

As indicated above, the company's most important product during the First World War was the Bristol Fighter. The first of two prototypes of the F.2A, A3303, was flown on 9 September 1916. The F.2B version was undoubtedly among the best aircraft developed during the war. Following on from the production of fifty F.2A, the Bristol F.2B Fighter remained in virtually continuous production from 1917 to 1927; 4,747 were built up to 1919, and the type remained in RAF service until 1932. 1,583 Bristol Fighters were in service with the RAF at the time of the Armistice.

The type was built by several sub-contractors including Sir W.G. Armstrong, Whitworth & Co. Ltd, Angus Sanderson & Co., The Austin Motor Co. (1914) Ltd, The Gloucestershire Aircraft Co. Ltd, Harris & Sheldon Ltd, Marshall & Sons, The Standard Motor Co. Ltd and the National Aircraft Factory No.3 at Aintree. Production (post-war) of army co-operation machines included 215 new-build aircraft and 200 conversions from the existing fleet. Eighty-four aircraft were built up from spare parts in 1925, and a further 144 reconditioned in 1926. A new variant, the Fighter Mk III contributed a further eighty aircraft, production ending in June 1927. It is perhaps not surprising that total numbers are clouded with some uncertainty, but *Bristol Aircraft Since 1910* gives a grand total of 5,252 (some other sources differ; British Aerospace's own publication *Proud Heritage*, for example, gives a total of 5,308, with Putnam's *The British Fighter Since 1912* giving 5,329).

Another product of note was the M1 monoplane, 130 of which were built, mostly for overseas service. The M1A first flew at Filton on 14 July 1916. Contract production by British & Colonial during the First World War included a small number of RE8 and BE8, and some 1,174 BE2 of all variants, for which type British & Colonial were one of the most important manufacturers.

During the First World War, Filton was used as the **South West Aircraft Acceptance Park.**

Collapse and Re-birth Between the Wars

In March 1920 the company transferred its assets to **The Bristol Aeroplane Co. Ltd** (founded on 9 February 1920) and then went into liquidation. As with many of the established aircraft companies, the catalyst for this apparently extreme action was the demand for payment of Excess Profits Duty, which threatened the survival of the industry. It transpired that voluntary liquidation, and the transfer of assets to a new company, allowed the effects of the Duty largely to be avoided.

The early post-war years were as lean for Bristol as they were for many other companies across the industry. The company received only a few prototype orders, which are not detailed here. One type worthy of mention, not least for its advanced features such as a retractable undercarriage and fully-faired engine installation, was the Bristol Type 72 Racer. Of strikingly corpulent appearance, the single example built (G-EBDR) was flown in July 1922, but made only six further flights before being abandoned.

Small numbers of assorted civilian designs were also built, including such types as the Bristol Tourer, Taxiplane/Type 83 School Machine and the Type 89 Jupiter Trainer. Continued Bristol Fighter production and modification, together with sub-contract work, were essential to the survival of the aircraft business.

The prototype Bristol Brownie G-EBJK was first flown at Filton on 6 August 1924, ahead of the 1924 Lympne Light Aeroplane Trials, for which it was an entrant. Unsuccessful designs included the Bristol Braemar, Pullman and Tramp four-engine triplanes, the Type 75 Ten Seater (G-EAWY) and Type 75A (G-EBEV).

The fortunes of the company improved with the selection of the Bristol Bulldog single-seat fighter for RAF service, leading to a large production run for the RAF and for export customers. 441 were built at Filton, the first being flown on 17 May 1927. The Bulldog II production prototype, J9480, was flown on 21 January 1928. The main production variants were the Bulldog II and IIA. The Bulldog was exported to Australia, Denmark, Estonia, Finland, Latvia, Siam, Sweden and USA.

The Bulldog was heavily promoted by Bristol for its use of steel construction. In May 1930, Bristol were advertising: 'Pilots speak with enthusiasm of the Bristol Bulldog all-steel fighter because it combines the splendid combination of a high performance aeroplane capable of every "stunt" and manoeuvre, yet is easily flown by any pilot. The all-steel structure also gives strength with lightness, reduced maintenance cares and makes repair a matter of simplicity and ease. The finest example of steel construction the aeronautical world can show today.' A more general advertising slogan was: 'Bristol – Designers and Manufacturers of High Performance Aircraft for Civil and Military Purposes, and Radial Air-cooled Aero Engines.'

The Bristol 120 R-6, which was flown in January 1932, was a private venture prototype competing for General Purpose specification G.4/31. This demanding requirement resulted in prototype offerings from Armstrong Witworth, Blackburn, Bristol, Fairey (two designs), Handley Page, Hawker (two designs), Parnall, Vickers and Westland. With its gun turret and stretcher accommodation in the rear fuselage, the Bristol 120 was already a pretty daunting prospect; the type was abandoned after the specification was modified to add a requirement for a torpedo carriage. This requirement was subsequently deleted; dive bombing being added to the list of roles to be fulfilled. No production contracts were placed for any of the participants in this sorry tale.

A most significant prototype was flown on 12 April 1935. This was the Bristol Type 142 *Britain First*, a high speed transport to the order of Lord Rothermere. A modern twin-engine

The unmistakeable, but equally unsuccessful, Bristol Type 72 Racer G-EBDR, which was first flown in 1922. (Rolls-Royce via Ken Ellis)

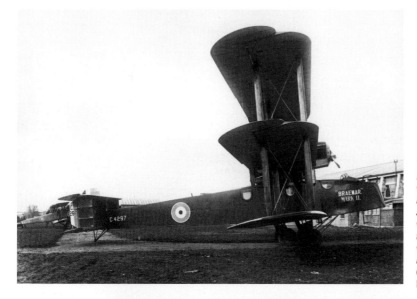

The towering Bristol Braemar was followed by the Pullman and Tramp; all were four-engine triplanes, which met with little success. (Rolls-Royce via Ken Ellis)

Bulldogs under construction for the Royal Australian Air Force. (Military Aircraft Photographs)

Above and opposite above: A selection of Bristol Aeroplane Co. Ltd advertisments. (Copyright: BAE SYSTEMS plc)

Opposite below: The General-Purpose specification G.4/31 spawned the Bristol 120 and a number of competitors. Unfortunately the demands of the requirement resulted in a 'Jack-of-all-trades, but master of none', and none of the contenders entered production. (Ken Ellis Collection)

machine with retractable undercarriage, the *Britain First* was 50mph faster than the Gloster Gauntlet. The prototype, R–12/K7557, was subsequently developed into a military variant, the Blenheim. The type was advertised in February 1936 as: 'Britain First – Bristol built. All Metal Aircraft. Designed and Manufactured by The Bristol Aeroplane Co. Ltd.'

A final Bristol product of this period was the Bombay. The prototype of this twin-engine, high-wing transport, K3583, was flown on 22 June 1935. Fifty production aircraft were built by Short & Harland Ltd at Belfast.

Although Bristol built mainly aircraft of their own design, sub-contract production included 150 Parnall Panther, eighty-five Armstrong Whitworth Siskin IIIA and 141 Hawker Audax. One outstanding achievement during this period was the flight of the Bristol 138A high-altitude monoplane to a new altitude record of 53,937ft on 30 June 1937.

Second World War Mass Production

The main Bristol designs that were developed for use in the Second World War are summarised in the following table:

Type	Serial/Registration	Comments
Blenheim I	K7033	First flown at Filton 25 June 1935. Advertised in September 1936 as 'Probably the World's Fastest Bomber'. Production consisted of 1,501 aircraft (including 1,390 for the RAF) built by: The Bristol Aeroplane Co. Ltd at Filton (718); A.V. Roe & Co. Ltd, Chadderton (250); and Rootes Securities Ltd, Speke (422). Fifty for export to Finland, Yugoslavia and Turkey, with sixty-one further aircraft built in Finland and Yugoslavia.
Blenheim IV (Bolingbroke)	K7072	Prototype, converted from Blenheim I, flown 24 September 1937. Production: The Bristol Aeroplane Co. Ltd, Filton (312); A.V. Roe & Co. Ltd, Chadderton (750); Rootes Securities Ltd, Speke and Blythe Bridge (2,060). 676 additional aircraft in Canada.
Blenheim V (Bisley)	AD657	First flown 24 February 1941. 942 built, all by Rootes Securities Ltd at Blythe Bridge.
Beaufort	L4441	Torpedo bomber/mine layer/reconnaissance. First flown 15 October 1938. Produced in various marks in Britain and Australia. Production totals: The Bristol Aeroplane Co. Ltd 1,429, plus 700 in Australia.
Beaufighter	R2052	Heavily-armed strike aircraft and night fighter. First flown 17 July 1939. UK production comprised 1,469 at Filton, 3,336 at Weston-super-Mare shadow factory, 500 by Fairey Aviation Ltd at Stockport, and 260 by Rootes Securities Ltd at Blythe Bridge.
Buckingham	DX249	Medium bomber and high-speed transport. First flown 4 February 1943. Four prototypes and 119 production aircraft built, many delivered to store and then scrapped.
Buckmaster	TJ714	Trainer, first flown 27 October 1944, 112 built.
Brigand	MX988	Torpedo bomber and strike aircraft. Flown 4 December 1944; four prototypes and 143 production aircraft.

During the Second World War, Bristol also built the Hawker Tempest II at Filton and Banwell. The famous Bristol designer F.S. Barnwell was assisted by L.G. Frise (the inventor of the Frise aileron), who took over design responsibility after Barnwell's death (see Whitchurch). Frise contributed to, or oversaw, the design of the Bulldog, *Britain First* and Bombay, together with the wartime mainstays of the company, the Blenheim, Beaufort, and Beaufighter, together with the other aircraft tabulated above. In the immediate post-war period, Frise was responsible for the Bristol 170 and Brabazon, before leaving Bristol to join Percival Aircraft Ltd in 1948.

Post War (1945-1960)

During the immediate post-war period, The Bristol Aeroplane Co. Ltd embraced the civil transport market and set up a helicopter division, which produced its own designs for civil and military use. The company's products are described in the table below.

Above: *Blenheim prototype K7033 is, with its polished metal finish, reminiscent of the Type 142* Britain First. (Ken Ellis Collection)

Right: (Copyright: BAE SYSTEMS plc)

Below: *Bristol's aggressive Beaufighter is seen here toward the end of its service life, when in use as a target tug at Exeter. This aircraft, RD862, was built at the Old Mixon shadow factory at Weston-super-Mare.* (H.E. North)

Type	Serial/Registration	Comments
Type 170 Freighter	G-AGPV	Freight and car transport. Flown on 2 December 1945; 214 built. Most familiar for its cross-channel operations with Silver City Airways, Bristol advertised the Freighter as 'The carry anything aircraft'. The Mk 32, with its lengthened nose which increased capacity to three 14ft cars and twenty passengers, was first flown on 16 January 1953. See additional comments below.
Type 167 Brabazon 1	G-AGPW	First flown on 4 September 1949, see additional comments below.
Type 175 Britannia	G-ALBO	First flown on 16 August 1952, the elegant Britannia was advertised by Bristol as 'The Whispering Giant'. Eighty-five were built, including those sub-contracted to Short Bros & Harland Ltd at Belfast. Later stretched variants were the Series 300, first flown (G-ANCA) on 31 July 1956, and the Series 310, first flown (G-AOVA) on 31 December 1956.
Bristol 171 Sycamore	VL958	Designed to Specification E.20/45 and first flown at Filton on 27 July 1947; production at Filton and Weston-super-Mare of a total of 180 military and civil machines. The military machines were used for general-purpose transport, ambulance, and search and rescue duties. Export customers included Australia and West Germany (fifty examples).
Bristol 173	G-ALBN	Piston-engined tandem rotor helicopter first flown on 3 January 1952, and (after a long struggle) productionised as the turbine-powered Belvedere. Five Bristol 173 were followed by twenty-six production Type 192 Belvedere built for the RAF. The first was XG447, flown on 5 July 1958 at Weston-super-Mare, to which helicopter operations were transferred from 1955.

This fine photograph shows the prototype Britannia G-ALBO, together with the first three production aircraft, at Filton during the aircraft's flight test programme. (BAE SYSTEMS plc via Ken Ellis)

Right: *Bristol 171 Sycamore HC.11 WT933 outside the Brabazon hangar at Filton.* (BAE SYSTEMS plc via Ken Ellis)

Below: *The piston engine-powered Bristol 173 is seen at Filton in April 1953 in its initial configuration with three-bladed rotor and butterfly tail. Extensive development eventually led to the Bristol 192 Belvedere.* (BAE SYSTEMS plc via Ken Ellis)

After the Second World War, some fifty Beaufighter aircraft were converted to the TT10 target-towing variant at Filton, the first TT10 (NT913) being flown in June 1948.

The Bristol Freighter was originally designed for military use in the Far East campaign of the Second World War. With the end of hostilities, the type was marketed as a rugged and capacious transport for both civil and military use. The type gained success as a car ferry and had a very hard-working life in Silver City operation in the days before the cross-channel ferry industry blossomed, the inaugural cross-channel flight being made on 13 July 1948. In 1954 the Silver City Freighter fleet averaged 2,970 landings and take-offs per aircraft in the fleet – just over eight sectors per day, every day of the year. 20,870 flights were completed, carrying 126,000 passengers and 42,500 vehicles. In October 1954, Air Charter Ltd were advertising the following prices for the use of their 'Channel Air Bridge': Motor cars up to 12ft 6in long £7 5s, adult passenger return fare £5 1s. A total of 214 Bristol Freighter aircraft were built.

It is difficult at this distance of time to appreciate the sheer size of the Bristol Brabazon – a tailplane span of 75ft perhaps speaks volumes, as much as the 230ft wingspan (19ft greater than a Boeing 747-400). The undercarriage track was 55ft, undercarriage development requiring the assistance of an Avro Lincoln test aircraft, RE282. One lasting legacy is the 7½ acre Brabazon assembly hall, still in use at Filton and 1,052ft long, 410ft maximum width and 117ft high! Three Lancaster aircraft were used at Filton to support development of the Brabazon flight control system.

One of the last Britannia aircraft to remain in service was this Aer Turas example, which is being used to fly racehorses into Cambridge to compete at Newmarket. (Author)

Work on extending the runway to a length of 2,750yds to meet the needs of the mighty Brabazon began in March 1946. One regrettable effect of this was the total destruction of the village of Charlton, which lay to the west of Filton, directly in line with the runway.

The four-engine Britannia airliner was grandly advertised in 1953 thus: 'The Bristol Britannia – Britain is building commercial aircraft for the world's airlines. The Britannia combines great payload capacity with great range and offers a wider profit margin in operation than any other aircraft.'

The aircraft construction activities were re-formed as **Bristol Aircraft Ltd** from January 1956 prior to the next cycle of industry reorganisation.

Rationalisation (1960-1977)

Two experimental types first flown at Filton during this period were the stainless steel Bristol 188 XF923, which flew on 14 April 1962 at RAE Bedford, and the exotic Fairey Delta 2 derivative, the BAC 221 WG774, which was first flown on 1 May 1964. The BAC 221 was a modification of the first Fairey Delta 2, fitted with a wing of ogival planform, to allow it to carry out high-speed testing in support of the Concorde programme. The BAC 221 first flew at Filton on 1 May 1964.

The Bristol 188 high-speed research aircraft was the last aircraft design of the Bristol Aeroplane Co. Two aircraft (XF923, XF926) were built, but the type's first flight was delayed by persistent engine problems. These problems continued throughout the flight test programme and, in combination with the very limited flight endurance available, prevented the aircraft from achieving its potential.

British Aircraft Corporation Commercial Aircraft Division (BAC Filton Division from February 1960, Commercial Aircraft Division from June 1971): BAC at Filton was responsible, with Aérospatiale, for the design and manufacture of Concorde. Still turning heads and without equal thirty years after its first flight, Concorde was first flown (F-WTSS) at Toulouse on 2 March 1969, the first British prototype (G-BSST) flying on 9 April 1969. The first British production aircraft, G-BBDG, flew at Filton on 13 February 1974. Sixteen production aircraft were built, of which fourteen were sold, the type beginning supersonic passenger service on 21 January 1976. The accident to an Air France Concorde on 25 July 2000, following damage caused by debris on the runway, led to the suspension of the type's Airworthiness Certificate. Following fuel tank and other modifications, the type returned to passenger service on 7 November 2001.

Above: *Concorde: a pinnacle of technical (if not commercial) achievement.* (Author)

Below: *First flight of XF926, the second Bristol 188, during April 1963. The chase aircraft is Hawker Hunter XF509.* (BAE SYSTEMS plc via Ken Ellis)

Modern times

British Aerospace/BAE SYSTEMS: For corporate history see Farnborough, Hants.

British Aerospace Airbus Ltd/BAE SYSTEMS Airbus Ltd. The origins of Airbus Industrie began to crystallise with the signature of a Memorandum of Understanding between the French, German and British governments for the design of the A300, on 26 September 1967. Airbus Industrie was formed on 18 December 1970, with a Hawker Siddeley holding of 20%. Airbus has succeeded in becoming the world's second largest producer of commercial aircraft, and now claims to outperform Boeing in a number of market sectors.

The first A300B F-WUAB flew on 28 October 1972 at Toulouse-Blagnac, the type entering service with Air France on 23 May 1974. Advertising for the A300 (in competition

BAE SYSTEMS Airbus Ltd, the UK component of Airbus has its headquarters at Filton. (Author)

with DC10 and TriStar) emphasised its twin-engine configuration: 'Two's economy, three's a drag.' The first flight dates of subsequent Airbus products were as follows:

A310	3 April 1982
A300-600	8 July 1983
A320	22 February 1987
A340-300	25 October 1991
A330	2 November 1992
A321	11 March 1993
A300-600ST	13 September 1994
	(Built by SATIC for the transport of Airbus airframe assemblies)
A319	25 August 1995
A340-600	23 March 2001
A318	15 January 2002
A340-500	11 February 2002

Significant production statistics for the Airbus range are given below:

11 November 1988	Firm orders for the A300/310 series pass 500
28 February 1989	Total orders exceed 1,000
9 June 1989	Firm orders for A320 exceed 500 and first A321 orders announced
10 June 1989	Delivery of 500th Airbus aircraft
End 1990	Firm orders reach 1,690
March 1993	Delivery of 1,000th Airbus aircraft (Air France's first A340-300)
January 1995	Delivery of 500th A320
1 April 1996	Firm orders pass 2,000
19 February 1997	Delivery of 1,500th Airbus aircraft
9 September 1998	Airbus sales pass 3,000 aircraft
15 April 1999	1,000th aircraft of A320 family (A319/A320/A321) delivered
18 May 1999	Delivery of 2,000th Airbus aircraft (an A340 to Lufthansa)
30 June 2002	Sales total 4,503 aircraft made up of 843 twin-engine A300 and A310, 2,838 single-aisle aircraft (A318, A319, A320, A321), 737 long-range, twin-aisle, A330 (twin-engine) and A340 (four-engine) family, and eighty-five ultra-high capacity A380. Total deliveries stood at 2,984 aircraft. 2,872 aircraft were in operation with 187 operators.

Production rates are high, reaching eighteen single-aisle aircraft and six long-range/twin-aisle aircraft per month in June 1998. Although only portions of these aircraft are designed and manufactured in Britain, the British Aerospace/BAE SYSTEMS content within these advanced technology transport aircraft is of considerable economic and industrial value.

In 1998, BAe Airbus Ltd had some 5,000 employees engaged in the design of wings and fuel systems, and the manufacture of the primary wing structure, for all Airbus products. Additional projects include the Future Large Aircraft project (FLA) – now styled A400M – and the very large A380 project.

The strong pressure to unite Airbus as a 'single corporate entity' finally bore fruit with the announcement of the formation of the Airbus Integrated Co. (AIC) on 23 June 2000, BAE SYSTEMS taking a 20% share. The Airbus Integrated Co. is now fully operational, with **Airbus** being incorporated under French law as an SAS (Société par Action Simplifiée) on 11 July 2001.

British Aerospace Aviation Services (later BAE SYSTEMS Aviation Services) specialised in conversions of Airbus A300B4 aircraft to freight configuration. The first aircraft was delivered in April 1997 to C-S Aviation Services, an American leasing company who are owners of the world's largest fleet of A300B4. British Aerospace Aviation Services delivered twelve A300B4 freighter conversions during 1998, and in September 1998 stated that they held forty-two firm orders and thirteen options for the type. BAE SYSTEMS Aviation Services also conducted major maintenance and modification work on both the A300 and the A310 series.

In late May 2002, BAE SYSTEMS announced that it could not afford to keep the business (Aviation Services) going in the absence of a sustainable forward order book. It was reported in the press that the Airbus A300B4 freighter conversion activity was to close, and that it was not clear whether this also implied that plans that had been mooted for an equivalent A320 freighter conversion programme had also been abandoned. The number of A300B4 conversions completed by January 2002 was thirty-nine aircraft.

Bristol/Bristol Siddeley/Rolls-Royce Ltd engine test activities: Bristol engines were developed and produced at the Patchway site, adjoining Filton airfield. From 1936 to the end of the Second World War, Bristol, together with the shadow factories and dispersed production units, built more than 101,000 piston engines including 57,400 Hercules, 2,500 Centaurus, 20,700 Mercury and 14,400 Pegasus. A summary of engine test bed aircraft

Left and right:
(Copyright: BAE
SYSTEMS plc)

operated in support of Bristol (and Bristol Siddeley/Rolls-Royce) engine development is given below (not all these aircraft necessarily operated from Filton, however).

- Lucifer – modified Bristol M1 Monoplane (M1D) G-EAVP.
- Mercury, Aquila – widespread use of Bristol Bulldog.
- Hydra, Orion – Hawker Harrier J8325 used from 1929.
- Jupiter – Bristol Badger II J6492.
- Jupiter, Pegasus – Hawker Hart G-ABTN.
- Jupiter VIF, Mercury, Aquila – Bristol Type 107 Bullpup J9051.
- Jupiter VII – Bristol Bloodhound G-EBGG. The Bloodhound, which was first flown on 6 June 1925, was used to conduct engine endurance tests of the Jupiter VII. The main trial began on 4 January 1926 and ended on 8 April, the sealed engine having flown over 25,074 miles in 225hr 54min. No replacements were made during the trial, and only two valve components needed to be replaced before the aircraft made a return trip from Croydon to Cairo, starting on 30 June 1926. Three Jupiter VII engines were also subject to a 250hr endurance test, fitted to a Handley Page Hampstead.
- Pegasus, Mercury, Perseus, Taurus – Hawker Hart K3020.
- Pegasus III, Pegasus X, Perseus, Taurus – Hawker PV4 K6926, which first flew at Brooklands on 6 December 1934, and was delivered to Filton for engine trials in October 1935.
- Taurus – The second prototype of the unsuccessful Bristol 148, K6552, was used as a test bed for the Taurus engine. The Bristol 148 was a low-wing, single-engine monoplane intended for army co-operation use, only two examples being built.
- Centaurus – Extensive use was made of the Vickers Warwick GRII as an engine test bed for the development of various marks of the Centaurus engine. Examples included HG341 (Centaurus 130 for the Ambassador); HG342 (Centaurus XII); HG343 (Centaurus VII and Centaurus 57 for the Shetland); HG141 (Centaurus VII); and HG345 (Centaurus 12SM). Hawker Tempest II engine test aircraft included MW374, MW378, MW735 and MW737 on Centaurus XV trials. Hawker Sea Fury FB. Mk 11 VX612 was also used for engine trials.
- Theseus – Avro Lincoln RA716/G, first flown on 17 February 1947 from Filton with Theseus 11 outboard (this aircraft was later flown with Avon engines outboard), plus RE339 and RE418, with Theseus 21 engines outboard. The Handley Page Hermes 5 G-ALEU, G-ALEV also flew with the Theseus on 23 August 1949 and 27 August 1950, respectively.
- Proteus – Avro Lincoln SX972, December 1950; Avro Lincoln RF368; Airspeed Ambassador G-AKRD, early 1954.
- Phoebus – Avro Lincoln RA643 – installation work by D. Napier & Son at Luton in 1947, test-flying from Filton.
- Olympus – English Electric Canberra WD952, first flown on 5 August 1952. On 29 August 1955 this aircraft gained a world altitude record of 65,890ft. Avro Vulcan XA894. Avro Ashton Mk 3, WB493, flown in 1955 with an Olympus outboard of each nacelle. Subsequently (in 1957-1958) the port Olympus was replaced with a Bristol Orpheus.
- Viper – Lancaster SW342 flew in November 1952 with an ASV3 in the tail, this being replaced by an ASV5 in 1954. English Electric Canberra WK163 from 1956 to 1959; English Electric Canberra WK141 – Viper 8 and 11.
- Pegasus – bomb bay installation on the first production Vickers Valiant, WP199, from January 1961.
- Olympus 593 (Concorde development) – Avro Vulcan B2 XA903 from September 1966 to August 1971. (This aircraft was subsequently further modified by Marshall of

Cambridge to flight test the RB199 in support of the Panavia Tornado programme from April 1973 to February 1979.)

• Pegasus 11–61 – Harrier GR5 ZD402 was used in 1989 (during engine flight testing from Filton) to set a number of time to height records. Heintz Frick achieved 0 to 12,000m in 126.63 seconds and 0 to 6,000m in 53.88 seconds. Rolls–Royce test pilot Andy Sephton achieved 0 to 3,000m in 36.88 seconds and 0 to 9,000m in 81.00 seconds.

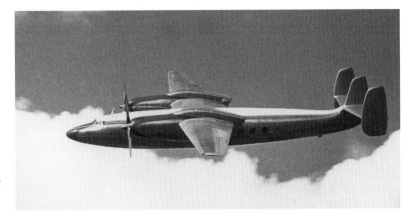

Airspeed Ambassador G-AKRD shows off its fine lines in its Proteus test bed guise. (Via Author)

The record-breaking Olympus Canberra WD952 climbs away over Filton. (BAE SYSTEMS plc via Ken Ellis)

Avro Vulcan B. Mk 2 XA903 was used as a flying test bed for the Olympus 593 engine for Concorde, before being modified by Marshall of Cambridge to test the RB199 engine for the Tornado programme. (Marshall Aerospace Ltd)

Parnall & Sons and George Parnall & Co. used Filton for test flying until the company moved to Yate. The Plover was designed as a single-seat fighter for naval use, competing unsuccessfully with the Fairey Flycatcher. (Ken Ellis Collection)

Aircraft built by **Parnall & Sons** and **George Parnall & Co.** were tested at Filton prior to Parnall's move to Yate. The Parnall Plover was test-flown at Filton in December 1922 and was designed as a single-seat fighter for naval use. It competed unsuccessfully with the Fairey Flycatcher. The Parnall Pixie I/II light aircraft first flew here (Pixie I) on 13 September 1923, and (in Pixie II configuration) on 4 October 1923. The Parnall Possum J6862 was also first flown at Filton on 19 July 1923.

Bristol Area – Whitchurch

HRH Prince George officially opened Bristol Municipal Airport at Whitchurch, now known as Hengrove Park, on 31 May 1930. The airfield was used for the dispersal of the fleets of Imperial Airways and British Airways at the outbreak of the Second World War and was also a major Air Transport Auxiliary base.

Aero Engines Ltd, of Hanham Road, Kingswood, Bristol, were the manufacturers of the Douglas Sprite engine, and built nine Tipsy S2 at Kingswood. These aircraft were flown at Whitchurch during 1936 and 1937, the first example being G-AEOD. Not all the registrations allocated to these aircraft were taken up, and only three machines were formally issued with Authorisations to Fly.

The **Barnwell** BSW 1 G-AFID was designed by Frank Barnwell, the Chief Designer of the Bristol Aeroplane Co. Ltd, and built at Whitchurch by Airwork Ltd. The aircraft was a single-seat low-wing monoplane, powered by a 28hp Scott Squirrel engine. G-AFID flew for the first time on 17 July 1938 but tragically crashed on its second flight, on 2 August 1938, killing its designer. Barnwell was an early pioneer pilot and designer (working with his brother in Scotland), and designed the Bristol Scout, M1 Monoplane, F.2B Fighter, Bulldog and Blenheim.

Bristol Aeroplane Co. Ltd: Beaufighter II aircraft were taken here by road for engines to be installed and other work completed during a period when Merlin engines were in short supply in 1941.

Brockworth

The No.2 Shadow Factory was constructed on the opposite side of the airfield from the **Gloster Aircraft Co. Ltd** factory at Hucclecote (see below). This shadow factory was

Above: *Pre-fabricated housing offered a lifeline to many aircraft manufacturers in the years immediately after the Second World War. This scene shows a kitchen being fitted out as a house moves down the production line.* (BAE SYSTEMS plc)

Right: (Copyright: BAE SYSTEMS plc)

generally known as Brockworth, lying on the other side of the parish boundary from Hucclecote. The factory was built from August 1938 and completed in November 1940, together with a new concrete runway. Short Stirling components were manufactured here during the period when Stirling production was dispersed away from Rochester at the end of 1940. It is not entirely clear whether or not any aircraft were completed here, prior to production being established at South Marston, Wiltshire. The factory was used subsequently for the assembly of the Albemarle, from a dispersed production organisation which manufactured components and major assemblies.

A.W. Hawksley Ltd: This company was set up within the Hawker Siddeley Group with responsibility for the production and assembly of the Albemarle. Six hundred Albemarle were built at Hucclecote, the two prototypes having been built at Hamble. The company name was 'concocted' from **A.W.** (Armstrong Whitworth) and **Hawk**er **S**idde**ley**.

The Albemarle was the first British military aircraft to be specified from the outset to have a tricycle undercarriage, and its construction emphasised the use of 'non-strategic' materials. Early production difficulties were encountered with a workforce that was largely inexperienced in aircraft manufacture. The production of components was, in fact, dispersed to nearly 1,000 companies, very few of which had previous experience of aircraft work. Major sub-contractors included furniture manufacturers Harris Lebus Ltd (tailplanes), The Rover Co. Ltd (centre sections), and The MG Car Co. Ltd (front fuselage).

Albemarle production was split between Special Transport (ST), and General Transport (GT) variants, the type being used primarily for paratroop transport and glider towing. Production quantities by variant are tabulated below:

Mark	Production quantity
Mk I Series 1	32
ST Mk I Series 1	8
GT Mk I Series 2	46
ST Mk I Series 2	14
GT Mk I Series 3	23
ST Mk I Series 3	77
GT Mk II	1
ST Mk II	99
Mk IV	1
ST Mk V	49
ST Mk VI Series 1	133
GT Mk VI Series 2	117

After the war, A.W. Hawksley built no less than 18,000 pre-fabricated houses in this factory. (In June 1948, the Hawker Siddeley Aircraft Co. Ltd's twelfth Annual Report stated: 'A.W. Hawksley Ltd has helped considerably in widening our interests and up to date has made over 12,000 factory-built pre-fabricated houses.')

Cheltenham

In September 1916, three Ruffy-Baumann aircraft were being used by a flying school in Cheltenham, the aerodrome extending to 150 acres. Mr Ruffy was then a director of the **Cheltenham & West of England Aviation Co. Ltd.**

H.H. Martyn & Co., of Sunningend Works, Cheltenham, manufactured the Farman Longhorn and Shorthorn under licence from the Aircraft Manufacturing Co. (AIRCO). The first contract, placed in 1914, was for propellers for Short seaplanes, followed by sub-contracted fuselages and other parts from AIRCO. H.H. Martyn & Co. produced architectural sculpture and ornamental plasterwork and joinery. The company was noted for the reproduction of Grinling Gibbons' carvings.

The Gloucestershire Aircraft Co. Ltd (GAC) was formed on 5 June 1917 with authorised capital of £1,000, being jointly owned by H.H. Martyn & Co. and AIRCO, initially renting the Sunningend works, and '...acquiring the business carried on by A.W. Martyn at Cheltenham as the Gloucestershire Aircraft Co. Ltd. Chairman Mr G. Holt Thomas, Managing Director A.W. Martyn.' Mr A.W. Martyn, whose father founded H.H. Martyn & Co., died on 18 January 1947.

GAC built 150 DH6 (the first being C9336), 435 Bristol F.2B Fighter, the Nieuport Nighthawk and other types at Cheltenham, sub-contracting work to **Savages Ltd, Daniels & Co.** and **Gloucester Carriage & Wagon Co.**

THE
GLOUCESTERSHIRE AIRCRAFT C⁰ L^TD
CHELTENHAM
CONTRACTORS TO HIS MAJESTY'S
GOVERNMENT

DESIGNERS & MANUFACTURERS
OF ALL TYPES OF HEAVIER
THAN AIR MACHINES.

TELEGRAPHIC ADDRESS,
"SUNNINGEND"
TELE PHONE
1181 (2 Lines) CHELTENHAM

HEAD OFFICES & WORKS

SUNNINGEND
WORKS, CHELTENHAM

"We congratulate the Gloucestershire Aviation Co. on their rapid production of such a fine machine."—FLIGHT, July 21st.

The Gloucestershire Aircraft Co., Ltd., winners of the Aerial Derby, 1921, with Mars I. fitted with Napier Lion Engine, possess special facilities for designing and constructing Aircraft of highest possible efficiency.

Enquiries solicited for any type of machine.

THE GLOUCESTERSHIRE AIRCRAFT CO., LTD.,
SUNNINGEND WORKS, CHELTENHAM.

Chief Engineer and Designer: H. P. FOLLAND, F.R.Ae.S.
Contractors to The British Air Ministry and Foreign Governments.

Above and right: (Copyright: BAE SYSTEMS plc)

After the end of the First World War, GAC began to construct aircraft of its own design. The company had been building the Nieuport Nighthawk under contract and took over a number of airframes following the collapse of **Nieuport & General Aircraft Ltd**. The aircraft designer H.P. Folland also moved from Nieuport to GAC, and the company embarked on the production of a series of aircraft based upon the Nighthawk under the family name Gloucestershire Mars. With a keen eye to publicity, the Mars 1, or Bamel, was designed for racing and was highly successful. Later products in this series included the Mars II, III and IV Sparrowhawk (see below), the Mars VI Nighthawk and the Mars X Nightjar.

Survival also depended on other contracts, including building up thirty-five DH9A from stored components (serial numbers from J7073 and J7249) and refurbishing a further ten (from J7347). One attempt at non-aviation diversification was the development in 1920 of a motor scooter under the name Unibus.

In addition to the Sunningend Works, aircraft were also constructed in the Winter Gardens Pavilion, Imperial Square, Cheltenham. Nieuport Nighthawk aircraft were stored in the Winter Gardens Pavilion in 1921, a significant number being modified with the Bentley BR2 rotary before being sold on to Japan as the 'Sparrowhawk'. The total Japanese order was for fifty aircraft (thirty single-seat Sparrowhawk I, ten two-seat Sparrowhawk II and ten Sparrowhawk III with modifications for shipboard use), with a further forty to be assembled by the Yokosuka Naval Air Arsenal. The modifications to the Sparrowhawk III included the fitting of hydroplanes on the undercarriage to increase the chance of survival should the aircraft be ditched.

From 1921, GAC made increasing use of the First World War Acceptance Park at Hucclecote and from 1926 changed its name to **Gloster Aircraft Co. Ltd**. The progressive transfer of all Gloster Aircraft Co. operations to Hucclecote was not completed until 1929. For further details of aircraft manufactured by The Gloucestershire Aircraft Co. Ltd and the Gloster Aircraft Co. Ltd, see Hucclecote.

In 1923, GAC purchased **The Steel Wing Co.** and gained a production contract to design and manufacture all-steel wings and struts for the Wapiti. Steel Wing Co. wings were used on all Wapiti II and most subsequent aircraft. Toward the end of Wapiti production, Westland themselves manufactured the wings and interplane struts to the designs of The Steel Wing Co.

The Gloster E.28/39 experimental jet aircraft was completed at **Regent Motors, Cheltenham** to avoid the risk of bombing at the main factory. A second dispersal facility, **Crabtree's Garage**, was used to install a longer stroke nose-wheel leg prior to first flight. (See also Hucclecote.)

Folland Aircraft Ltd ran an experimental department, and carried out dispersed production of Wellington and Spitfire components, in the **Black and White Coach** garage at Cheltenham from late 1940. Other facilities used include **Steel's Garage**, Bath Road, and **Foyle's Furniture Shop**, also Bath Road. (See also Staverton, Glos.)

Fairford

RAF Fairford was used during the Second World War by glider and airborne forces operating with such types as the Short Stirling, particularly in support of the D-Day landings and the Arnhem operation. The airfield was subsequently used by the **British Aircraft Corporation** as the BAC/Aérospatiale Concorde flight test centre. Fairford was chosen for Concorde flight testing because of its long flat runway, which allowed for the panoramic operation of cameras used for the measurement of the aircraft's take-off and landing performance. Its rural location also limited the noise nuisance associated with these trials. Having visited the test centre during the early trials of the British prototype G-BSST, the author can attest to just how noisy (and smoky) this aircraft was compared with the final production standard.

Hucclecote

Hucclecote was associated with the assembly and flight testing of the products of **The Gloucestershire Aircraft Co. Ltd** and its successor, **Gloster Aircraft Co. Ltd**, virtually throughout the existence of the company. A related company, **A.W. Hawksley Ltd**, built the Albemarle in the adjoining Brockworth shadow factory (see separate entry for Brockworth, above). This section also contains a short entry relating to the **General Aircraft** ST3.

First World War Production

An Aircraft Acceptance Park was established at Hucclecote during the First World War, with aircraft built by **The Gloucestershire Aircraft Co. Ltd** (GAC) being delivered by road from Cheltenham. At the end of the First World War there were twenty-six hangars and storage sheds covering some twenty acres.

The main types produced by H.H. Martyn and The Gloucestershire Aircraft Co. Ltd during the First World War were:

- Farman components under sub-contract to AIRCO (H.H. Martyn & Co.).
- 150 DH6, the first being C9336.
- 550 Bristol F.2B Fighter, not all of which are thought to have been delivered – three batches as follows: 150 C9836 onward, 150 Arab-powered E9507 onward and an order for 250 with serials from H834 onward. At least 135 and possibly as many as 161 aircraft from this last batch were delivered.

During the First World War, the company advertised as: 'Contractors to His Majesty's Government, Designers of all types of heavier than air machines.'

Production between the Wars

GAC rented the No.2 hangar of the Aircraft Acceptance Park at Hucclecote from 1921. The company progressively occupied the site from 1926 and **Gloster Aircraft Co. Ltd** purchased the site in 1928 (the change of company name took effect from 11 December 1926). The move from Cheltenham to the Hucclecote factory, on the west side of the site was completed by 1929.

The main types produced between the wars by The Gloucestershire Aircraft Co. Ltd and Gloster Aircraft Co. Ltd were:

- Nieuport Nighthawk: contract production of the Nighthawk fighter designed by H.P. Folland for Nieuport & General Aircraft Ltd at Cricklewood. Around thirty were completed.

- Mars I 'Bamel' racer (see additional comments below).
- Sparrowhawk – Mars II, III and IV – a Nighthawk derivative for Japan (for further details see Cheltenham).
- Nighthawk (Mars VI): Twenty-nine Nighthawk were rebuilt as Mars VI Nighthawk with either the Jupiter or Jaguar radial, with an additional twenty-five aircraft exported to Greece. Prototype H8534 was flown in late 1920. (One source indicates that thirty-one aircraft were flown for the RAF and some ninety stored unflown, providing the source for the aircraft manufactured for Greece.)
- GAC were responsible for a total of forty-five DH9A in three batches, these being a mix of aircraft built up from stored components and reconditioned airframes.
- Mars X Nightjar: The Nightjar was a Nighthawk with Bentley BR2 and under-carriage modifications making it similar to the Japanese Sparrowhawk III. The prototype conversion was H8535, and twenty-two aircraft were completed.
- Grouse: a private venture two-seat trainer based on the Sparrowhawk, which was developed with an Armstrong Siddeley Lynx. Subsequently modified with a Jaguar radial engine and single-seat configuration as the progenitor to the Grebe.
- Grebe: The Grebe I was the single-seat Jaguar-powered Grouse. The first aircraft, J6969, flew in May 1923 and was followed by two additional prototypes for the Air Ministry, plus a civil demonstrator, G-EBHA, and 108 production Grebe II, renowned for their excellent handling. The lower wing of the Grebe was built by Hawker and the upper wing by A.V. Roe & Co. Ltd. The Grebe IIIDC was a dual control variant, twenty-one being built, the grand total Grebe construction therefore being 133 aircraft.
- The company built the Gannet for the Lympne Light Aeroplane Trials, but did not pursue the private aircraft market, preferring to concentrate their efforts on fighter aircraft. The Gannet G-EBHU had a span of only 18ft and a length of 16ft 8in.
- GAC (in its Gloucestershire and Gloster incarnations) built racing seaplanes for the Schneider Trophy competitions (Gloster II to VI) – see additional comments below.
- Gamecock fighter – basically the Grebe fitted with a Jupiter IV engine. The first prototype Gamecock I, J7497, flew from Hucclecote in February 1925. Including prototypes, ninety-six were built, of which ninety production aircraft were delivered to the RAF, and two to Finland as pattern aircraft for fifteen additional Finnish-built examples. The type was the RAF's last wooden fighter. Like the Grebe, the Gamecock exhibited excellent handling and could perform a 360 degree roll in a vertical climb and then push over and fly away from the top of the manoeuvre.

J6969, seen here prior to competing in the King's Cup Air Race, was the first prototype Grebe. It was developed via the Grouse from the Sparrowhawk, which was itself a derivative of the Nieuport Nighthawk. (Ken Ellis Collection)

- A number of other prototypes were constructed by Gloucestershire and Gloster including the Gnatsnapper, Goldfinch, Gorcock, Goral, Goring, Goshawk and Guan. The Goral was a huge bomber transport with two pairs of Rolls-Royce Kestrel engines mounted in push-pull units between its biplane wings (which were of 95ft span – only 4ft less than a Vulcan B.Mk 1).

After his move to the Gloucestershire Aircraft Co. Ltd from Nieuport & General Aircraft Ltd, the designer H.P. Folland chose to continue the development of a series of racing aircraft, in part to publicise the company.

One of the most notable of these aircraft was the first design, the Mars I Bamel G-EAXZ, which was particularly successful in raising the company's profile and reputation. G-EAXZ first flew at Hucclecote on 20 June 1921 and succeeded in winning a hat-trick of Aerial Derby races in 1921, 1922 and 1923. G-EAXZ was powered by the superlative Napier Lion of 450hp, a huge amount of power for a biplane of only 22ft wing span (the same as a Currie Wot).

On 3 October 1922, the Bamel was timed under FAI supervision at 212mph; it was also capable of the startling climb rate of 3,500ft/min and was timed to 19,500ft in eleven minutes thirty-four seconds. In its final form, as the Gloster I of 1923, its span was reduced to 20ft and the power increased to 530hp – an awesome combination. The aircraft was subsequently trans-ferred to the RAF as J7234 and used as a training aircraft for the RAF Schneider Trophy team.

The subsequent series of Gloster seaplanes are surely among the most elegant biplanes ever flown. Briefly, they consist of Gloster II (J7504 and J7505), Gloster III (N194 and N195) and the beautiful Gloster IV, three of which (N222-N224) were built for the 1927 Schneider Trophy contest. Last of all was the Gloster VI monoplane, two of which were built for the 1929 contest.

By this point, the company had been renamed as the **Gloster Aircraft Co. Ltd**, this change taking effect from 11 December 1926. One relatively little known success was the last Gloster wooden aircraft, the Gambet. Although only one aircraft was built in Britain, flying on 12 December 1927, production of 150 aircraft followed in Japan as the A1N1 and A1N2, replacing the earlier Sparrowhawk aircraft.

Contract production included seventy-four Armstrong Whitworth Siskin III (in 1927-1929), modification and repair of the Siskin and production of metal wings for 525 Wapiti IIA (in 1929-1932), together with the completion of the DH72 Canberra three-engine night bomber J9184, which flew on 28 July 1931.

The Gloster Goring J8764 was constructed against Specification 23/25 with a view to replacing the Hawker Horsley. After initial landplane trials, floats were fitted and trials were then conducted at Calshot. (Ken Ellis Collection)

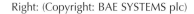

Above: *An impressive line-up of fifteen Gladiators awaiting delivery at Hucclecote.* (BAE SYSTEMS plc via Ken Ellis)

Right: (Copyright: BAE SYSTEMS plc)

In the late 1920s, the industry was making a transition to metal aircraft construction, Gloster benefiting from its involvement in **The Steel Wing Co**. In May 1929, Gloster was advertising: 'The Pioneers of Steel Aircraft. 14 years experience in the use of corrugated metal strip for aircraft construction. 25 types of metal wings designed and constructed for service and civil aircraft of all classes. Due to the unrivalled experience and facilities for the design and construction in metal, we have been entrusted with the execution of large orders for several other firms' Service Aircraft.' Metal wing production included a monospar wing for a Fokker F.VII/3m built to the order of the Air Ministry.

By 1930 the company was advertising the all-metal Gloster AS31 Survey, stating: 'The Gloster Aircraft Co. Ltd are specialising in civil aircraft – Survey, Passenger Carrying, Freight Carrying and Postal Machines.' The pioneering claims were also extended to 'The pioneers of Steel Aircraft and Variable Pitch Propellers'. The AS31 was a large twin-engine biplane with relatively high power to secure good performance in tropical conditions. As a result it could maintain flight on one engine at maximum weight at 9,000ft altitude.

During this period, the most significant of Gloster's own designs were their famous biplane fighters; the Gauntlet and the Gladiator. The Gauntlet had its origins in the Mercury IIA-powered SS.18, J9125, which was designed against specification F.20/27 and flew in January 1929. Progressive modification via the SS.18A (Jupiter VII), SS.18B (Panther III), SS.19 (Jupiter VIIF), SS.19A and SS.19B (Mercury IVS2) resulted in the production Gauntlet (Mercury VIS). The first of twenty-four production Gauntlet I, K4081, flew on 17 December 1934. 204 Gauntlet II followed with structural revisions, together with a further seventeen in Denmark.

The Gladiator was first flown on 12 September 1934 as the SS.37 K5200, designed to meet specification F.7/30. The type was to be the last biplane fighter to serve with the RAF; a total of 747 were built (including ninety-eight Sea Gladiators). Export deliveries were made to Latvia, Lithuania, Norway, Sweden (thirty aircraft subsequently transferred to Finland), Belgium, China, Eire, Greece, Iraq, Egypt and Portugal.

As with many other firms in the industry, diversification was essential to survival, and Gloster found themselves renting out hangar space for use as a bus garage, for mushroom growing, pig farming and for indoor sports facilities. The company also produced a number of non-aviation items, including the almost inevitable car bodies together with milk churns, bomb handlers and a number of light industrial products including fish fryers.

Gloster Aircraft Co. Ltd was purchased by **Hawker Aircraft Ltd** on 20 February 1934, joining the **Hawker Siddeley Group**. Gloster had only built twenty-six aircraft between 1930 and 1934. Although operating as a more or less autonomous unit, Gloster then received a series of production contracts of Hawker types, as indicated below.

Under Hawker sub-contracts, Gloster built:

- Twenty-five Audax
- Seventy-two Hart – forty Hart Special and thirty-two Hart Trainer, originally ordered as Audax
- Two Hartbees
- Forty-seven Hardy, the first Gloster production example being K4050

Second World War Mass Production

During the pre-Second World War expansion period, the No.2 Shadow Factory was built at Brockworth (on the east side of the airfield). This also resulted in the construction of a hard runway, which came into use in 1938. Contract work from Hawker Aircraft Ltd continued, notably with the Hurricane and Typhoon, until the Gloster Meteor became the main focus as the Second World War drew to a close. The aircraft built under contract from Hawker included the Henley (all 200 production examples, the first being L3243). The Hawker Henley served as a target tug, but suffered from frequent engine failures in service due to the sustained high power demands of this role. The Henley was followed by 2,750 Hurricane – the first Gloster-built aircraft, P2535, flying on 20 October 1939 (some sources state 27 October).

Hurricane production by Gloster proceeded at a high rate – 1,211 aircraft were built in 1940 and 1,359 in 1941. At peak production six aircraft were produced in a working day, with the additional delivery of twenty to twenty-five wing sets per week to Hawker. The

Gloster produced large numbers of Hawker aircraft during the Second World War including 3,300 Typhoon, 2,750 Hurricane and all 200 production examples of the Henley. This photograph shows Henley and Hurricane production in full swing. (Ken Ellis Collection)

peak production rate was 130 per month (160 per month is quoted in a *Flight* article). Forty-three local firms were involved in this effort, the last Gloster-built aircraft being delivered on 21 March 1942.

Gloster manufactured 3,300 Hawker Typhoon. This was all but seventeen of the type, the remainder consisting of two prototypes and the first fifteen production aircraft built by Hawker. The first Gloster-built example, R7576, flew on 27 May 1941.

Gloster built two prototypes of the F.5/34 Mercury IX-powered low-wing monoplane fighter, the first prototype, K5064, being flown in December 1937. Equally unsuccessful was the F.9/37, two of which were built; this was a stub-nosed twin-engined fighter, which resembled a twin-finned version of the Beaufighter. The Taurus-powered prototype, L7999, was flown from Hucclecote on 3 April 1939. The second Peregrine-powered aircraft, L8002, flew during July 1940.

Gloster is, of course, famously associated with British jet aircraft development. Britain's first jet aircraft, the E.28/39, W4041/G, completed taxiing trials at Hucclecote, including some initial hops, on 7/8 April 1941, before going to Cranwell for flight test. In modern procurement parlance, the E.28/39 proved to be a perfect Technology Demonstration Programme and provided a flight envelope that extended to a maximum speed of 466mph and a maximum altitude of 42,170ft.

Gloster's most successful design was the twin-engined Meteor jet fighter, whose production spanned from the latter years of the Second World War into the mid-1950s. Eight development aircraft (known as the F.9/40) were used for a wide range of engine proving trials as summarised below:

Serial	Powerplant/Comments
DG202/G	Rover W.2B. Ground running 29 June 1942. Taxiing trials and short hops at Newmarket Heath 10 July 1942. Later Rolls-Royce B.23 Welland.
DG203/G	Power Jets W.2/500 and W.2/700 and pressure cabin
DG204/G	Metropolitan-Vickers F.2, F.3/1. Axial engines slung below the wing due to their smaller diameter.
DG205/G	Rover W.2B, later Rolls-Royce B.23 Welland
DG206/G	De Havilland Halford H.1 (later Goblin). First true flight 5 March 1943 at Cranwell.
DG207/G	De Havilland Halford H.1B and pressure cabin. Sole Meteor II prototype, used by de Havilland for engine development flying.
DG208/G	Rolls-Royce WR1
DG209/G	Rolls-Royce B.23 (later W.2B/37 Derwent)

Twenty pre-series Meteor F Mk I were built powered by the Welland, with the first, EE210/G, flying on 12 January 1944. Although nominally production aircraft, these were used for a wide ranging series of engine and airframe development trials, this usage continuing with the F Mk III and F Mk IV.

Serial	Test Configuration
EE210/G	F Mk I prototype flown on 12 January 1944
EE211/G	Long chord nacelles
EE212/G	Revised fin and rudder, also flown at Boscombe Down as a two seater
EE214/G	Under fuselage fuel tank
EE215/G	Welland reheat trials
EE219/G	Auxiliary fins on tailplane
EE221/G	W.2/700 engines
EE227/G	No fin or rudder above tailplane. Later modified to Trent Meteor, first turboprop to fly on 20 September 1945. Subsequently converted to Derwent II.
EE230	F Mk III prototype, first flown September 1944

Serial	Test Configuration
EE246	F Mk III, ejector seat trials
EE337	Derwent 5, short nacelles, arrester hook. Flown from *HMS Implacable*.
EE338	Ejector seat trials
EE360/G	Modified as F Mk IV prototype, first flown 15 May 1945 with Derwent 5
EE387	Deck landing trials
EE397	Flight refuelling probe
EE416	Ejector seat trials
EE445	Griffith boundary layer control wing built by Armstrong Whitworth.
EE454 and EE455	F Mk IV, specially cleaned up for world speed record 7 November 1945, 606.38mph achieved by EE454
EE519	Pylon and fuel system development for the F.8
EE531	Folding wing tests
EE548 to EE550	Further world speed record flying. Gp Capt. Donaldson flew EE549 to 615.78mph on 7 September 1946.

Post-war (1945-1960)

After the Second World War, Gloster, like a number of other manufacturers, produced aluminium bungalows to maintain production employment. Those built by Gloster were sold as Hawker Siddeley bungalows. Post-war component production on behalf of Hawker included the forward fuselage of the prototype Hunter WB188.

The extensive use of the Meteor in trials configurations continued with the later marks: prototypes and a selection of the diverse trials configurations are tabulated below:

Serial	Test Configuration
G-AKPK	T.7 prototype built as a private venture, first flown 19 March 1948
RA382	F Mk IV with lengthened nose, 30in fuselage extension behind cockpit and ninety-five gallon increase in fuel capacity
RA435	Derwent Meteor reheat trials with Rolls-Royce
RA490	F Mk IV with Metropolitan-Vickers Beryl, later used for jet deflection Nene trials, flying in this form on 15 May 1954. See Merryfield, Somerset.
RA491	F Mk IV with Rolls-Royce Avon and (later) SNECMA Atar engines, fitted by AST Ltd
VS968	Meteor PR.10 prototype, first flown on 29 March 1950
VT150	F.8 prototype (from F Mk IV), Derwent 8 engines, lengthened fuselage and revised tail surfaces, flown 12 October 1948
VT196	Derwent reheat trials
VT347	F Mk IV converted to sole PR.5, crashed on first flight 15 June 1949
VW360	FR.9 prototype, first flown on 23 March 1950
VW364	FR.9 used for Martin-Baker ejector seat trials
VW411	Hybrid trials aircraft with FR.9 nose, T.7 fuselage and F.8 tail surfaces
VW413	T.7 modified as aerodynamic test aircraft for the Meteor NF.11
VZ389	Armstrong Whitworth-built F Mk IV. Flight refuelling probe and trials
VZ517	F.8 with Armstrong Siddeley Screamer rocket under fuselage
VZ608	FR.9 with RB108 lift jet engine mounted in centre fuselage by F.G. Miles Ltd
WA546	Meteor NF.11 prototype, first flown on 31 May 1950
WA820	Sapphire Meteor (F.8) modified by AST Ltd. Set a number of time to climb records on 31 August 1951, as follows: 9,843ft in 76 seconds, 19,685ft in 110 seconds, 29,500ft in 149 seconds, 39,370ft in 187 seconds.
WA982	F.8 with wing-tip mounted Rolls-Royce Soar turbojets
WD604	NF.11 flown with tip tanks in early 1952
WH320	F.8 used for brake parachute trials

Serial	Test Configuration
G-AMCJ and G-7-1	Private venture ground attack demonstrator based on F.8 with twenty-four rocket projectiles and two wing-tip fuel tanks, flown on 4 September 1950
G-ANSO	Meteor 7/8 hybrid, the private venture Meteor G-AMCJ fitted with a T.7 cockpit and nose, first flown on 9 August 1951
WK935	Prone-pilot F.8 Meteor, first flown 10 February 1954
WL375	F.8/FR.9 hybrid
WM261	Meteor NF.14 prototype, first flown on 23 October 1953
WM308	Meteor NF.13 prototype, first flown on 21 December 1952
WS950	Meteor NF.12 prototype, first flown on 21 April 1953

Above: (Copyright: BAE SYSTEMS plc)

Right: *The Meteor has been a popular platform for experimental and research flying, this example having served with the CEV in France.* (Author)

Above: *The Meteor F.8 was the most numerous of the single-seat versions. More than 1,000 were built, with licence production undertaken in Belgium and the Netherlands.* (BAE SYSTEMS plc via Ken Ellis)

Left: *TX145, the first of the E.1/44 prototypes to fly, photographed at Moreton Valence.* (BAE SYSTEMS plc via Ken Ellis)

Gloster Meteor production figures are not quoted consistently in the various references consulted during the preparation of this volume. Based upon the data tabulated below, it would appear that Gloster built some 2,500 Meteor aircraft, the main production marks being the F. Mk IV, T.7 and F.8. Sir W.G. Armstrong Whitworth Aircraft Ltd built some 1,050 Meteor aircraft at Coventry, and took responsibility for the development and production of night fighter variants. 330 F.8 aircraft were built under licence in the Netherlands and Belgium. Meteor production exceeded 3,850 aircraft, more than any other British jet aircraft. Because of the large number of aircraft ordered, extensive use was made of sub-contracted production for both components and assemblies, with the factory at Hucclecote being effectively a final assembly organisation. The aircraft was ultimately a great success despite (to quote Constance Babbington-Smith) being 'a cross breed between the old breed of airframe and the new breed of engine'.

Gloster Meteor Production Data

Mark	Gloster Aircraft Co. Ltd	Sir W.G. Armstrong Whitworth Aircraft Ltd	Licence	Total
F9/40	8	–	–	8
F. Mk I	20	–	–	20
F. Mk II	(1, within F. Mk I, above)	–	–	–
F. Mk III	210	–	–	210
F. Mk IV	613 ★	45 (figures up to 48 also quoted)	–	658
FR.5	1	–	–	1
T.7	712 (most widely quoted figure)	–	–	712
F.8	753 ★★	430 widely quoted	330	1513
FR.9	126	–	–	126
PR.10	59	–	–	59
NF.11	–	335 (334 and 338 also quoted)	–	335
NF.12	–	100	–	100
NF.13	–	40	–	40
NF.14	–	100	–	100
Totals	**2502**	**1050**	**330**	**3882**

★   If AWA total of 45 and widely quoted production total of 658 are correct.

★★ If AWA total of 430 and overall UK total of 1,183 are correct, but UK total figures of 1,079 and 1,181 are also quoted.

One unsuccessful product was the E.1/44, a mid-wing monoplane powered by a single 5,000lb-thrust Nene 2. The prototype SM809 was damaged whilst en route to Boscombe Down by road for its first flight. Two additional aircraft were built, the first, TX145, being flown at Boscombe Down on 9 March 1948. The type is chiefly notable for the fact that the second prototype, TX148, featured revised angular tail surfaces with a mid-set tailplane, which were subsequently adopted for the Meteor (F.8 and subsequent marks).

The last design of the Gloster Aircraft Co. Ltd was the Javelin all-weather fighter, with its unique tailed delta configuration. The first prototype Gloster GA.5, WD804, was taken by road from Hucclecote to Moreton Valence for its first flight, which took place on 26 November 1951. The first production Javelin FAW.1, XA544, was flown on 22 July 1954.

Air Service Training at Hamble was responsible for the design of the forward fuselage modifications for the Gloster Javelin T. Mk 3. The T. Mk 3 prototype, WT841, was assembled at Hamble before being disassembled and moved by road to Gloucester for its first flight. This took place on 20 August 1956, and a further twenty-two production Javelin T. Mk 3 were subsequently built by Gloster. Including the GA.5 prototypes, Gloster built 302 Javelin aircraft, and Sir W.G. Armstrong Whitworth Aircraft Ltd built a further 133 at Coventry, giving a total of 435 aircraft. The most important marks were the FAW.4 (fifty aircraft, first flown 19 September 1955), FAW.5 (sixty-four) and the FAW.7 (142). Seventy-six of the FAW.7 aircraft were subsequently modified to become Javelin FAW. 9. Some Javelin aircraft were flown off the short runway at Hucclecote for the short flight to the Moreton Valence flight test centre.

Modern Times

On completion of Javelin production, the Hucclecote site was sold to Gloster Trading Estates in 1964. The Gloster factory site has been demolished, although two very fine Belfast hangars remained untouched during site re-development (underway in mid-1997). The developers were, at that time, enforcing a rule of 'no photography is allowed on site'. This rule was, regrettably, extended to the E.28/39 memorial, which is situated just inside the site entrance, preventing the author from photographing it. The memorial not only records that the E.28/39, the first British jet aircraft, was designed and constructed on this site, but also stands in tribute to all Gloster Aircraft Co. Ltd personnel who contributed so much to the 1939-1945 war effort. 'The Flying Machine' public house lies close by for those seeking solace at the sad condition of this once important manufacturing site.

The **General Aircraft** ST3 G-AARP (also known as the Gloster–Monospar SS1) was built by Gloster for **The Monospar Wing Co. Ltd**, and first flew on 27 November 1930 at Hucclecote. **General Aircraft Ltd** continued with development of the type into the Monospar series at Croydon and Hanworth.

RAF Kemble (near Cirencester)

Kemble was a major RAF Maintenance Unit (MU) throughout the Second World War and into the 1980s. Although not directly associated with aircraft manufacture, units such as this were involved in aircraft modification, preparation for service of both British and foreign types of aircraft, aircraft storage and the assembly of Horsa and Hotspur gliders delivered in parts from dispersed production facilities.

Whilst this book does not, in general, list Maintenance Units as manufacturers, the work at Kemble was so varied that it is included here to represent other RAF MU modification and preparation centres. No.5 MU was formed here in 1938, no less than 500 aircraft being in store by December 1939. Many aircraft were passed from the MU to an Overseas Air Delivery Flight, later No.1 Overseas Air Preparation Unit, based on the airfield.

Types handled included Hind, Whitley, Blenheim, Wellington, Spitfire, Hurricane (converted to fighter bombers), glider assembly, Typhoon, Beaufort, Albemarle and Lancaster. More than 500 Wellington were prepared for Middle East service at Kemble. Lancaster aircraft were re-engined here with Merlin 24 engines in 1944. Many impressed civilian aircraft were stored here, and a veritable treasure trove of more than fifty such aircraft were sold from storage in December 1945.

Kemble was also home to No.2 Transport Aircraft Modification Section. (No.1, para-doxically the *second* to be established, was at Tempsford.) The main activity of this group was Dakota conversions for passenger transport, trooping, freighter, glider tug, paratroop or ambulance use. In addition to the Dakota, the unit also carried out Lancastrian, Stirling, Halifax and Oxford conversions.

After the Second World War, No.5 MU continued its activities with modifications to Vampire aircraft in 1948; acceptance and painting of 559 Canadair CL-13 Sabre for the RAF from 1952; and Hunter modification activities. Alongside these major programmes, many other types operated by the RAF passed through including Canberra, Shackleton, Varsity, Jet Provost, Andover and Chipmunk. The entire RAF fleet of Belfast transport aircraft spent some time lined up on the airfield at Kemble whilst awaiting disposal.

RAF Little Rissington (south of Stow-on-the-Wold)

The RAF Maintenance Unit on this airfield handled a huge variety of aircraft, and was responsible for the erection of both Hotspur and Horsa gliders.

Moreton Valence

The **Gloster Aircraft Co. Ltd** used Moreton Valence (originally known as Haresfield aerodrome) for flight test activities from October 1943, and the airfield is particularly associated with Gloster Meteor and Javelin production flight test and other experimental flying. The prototype Meteor F. Mk 8 VT150 was first flown from Moreton Valence on 12 October 1948. The prototype Javelin (GA.5) WD804 first flew from Moreton Valence on 26 November 1951.

The **Rotol** Flight Test Department operated at Moreton Valence from June 1947 until 1954, flying Spitfire, Sea Fury, Wyvern and other types. Rotol was a joint company founded in 1937 by **Ro**lls-Royce Ltd and the Bris**tol** Aeroplane Co. Ltd for propeller development and production. (See also Staverton.)

The airfield is now bisected by the M5 and has been returned to agricultural use. Part of the factory site is in use as a garden centre, and a number of buildings are used as warehouses by the Bilton Cargo Centre. Further buildings are also due to be constructed for warehouse use on the site.

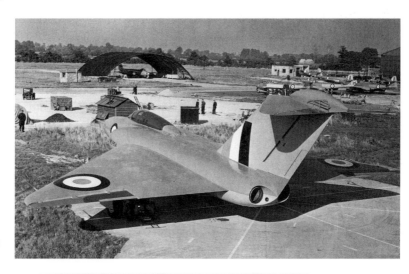

The prototype Gloster GA.5 WD804 photographed at Moreton Valence, where it made its first flight on 26 November 1951. (BAE SYSTEMS plc via Ken Ellis)

XA699 is a Javelin FAW.5, this type being closely associated with Moreton Valence. This particular example was built by Sir W.G. Armstrong Whitworth Aircraft Ltd. (J.S. Smith)

Newent

The **Gloster Aircraft Co. Ltd** used a factory at Newent, some ten miles north west of Gloucester, which was built in 1939 and had an area of some 50,000sq.ft. In early 1946, this factory was taken over by **Charlesworth Bodies (1931) Ltd**, of Coventry and Gloucester. During the Second World War, Charlesworth Bodies worked on a number of aircraft types including the Whitley, Lancaster, Lincoln, Beaufighter, Defiant, Barracuda, Whirlwind, Mosquito and Horsa, manufacturing some 50,000 components for these aircraft.

On the takeover of this ex-Gloster factory, the company held a dance in celebration. Charlesworth Bodies had, prior to the Second World War, been engaged in building coachwork for 'high class automobiles'. Components had been built for more than 3,000 Lancaster aircraft during the war, but by 1946 the company was engaged in the production of aircraft galley equipment for such types as the Viking.

Staverton (Gloucester Airport)

Staverton was used by **Dowty** for undercarriage development trials, for example on the Halifax. The company were later to produce composite propellers for a number of types of turboprop aircraft.

Folland Aircraft Ltd: Ten of the twelve Folland F43/37 specialist engine test aircraft (P1774 to P1785) were assembled at Staverton, and all twelve were based here at some point during their test careers (although British Aerospace data indicates that only eight aircraft were flown). From Staverton, these aircraft were then sent either to Napier at Luton, Bristol at Filton (Hercules and Centaurus development), or de Havilland Engines at Hatfield. At least four were supplied for the use of Napier. Engines tested by this fleet included Sabre I, II, III, V, VII, E.113, Hercules VIII, XI, Centaurus in various versions, and (fitted but probably not flown) the Deerhound, Vulture, Exe and Merlin. A partial allocation of these engine types to individual airframes is given in the table below:

Serial Number	Engine Types Fitted
P1774	Sabre I, Sabre II, Centaurus
P1775	Hercules VIII, Centaurus IV
P1776	Sabre I, Centaurus
P1777	Sabre I, Centaurus I
P1778	Sabre I, Centaurus, Griffon
P1779	Hercules XI, Sabre I
P1780	Hercules XI, Sabre I, Sabre V, Sabre VII
P1781	Centaurus IV
P1782	Hercules XI
P1783	Hercules XI
P1784	Hercules XI
P1785	Hercules XI

Flight Refuelling Ltd was based at Staverton from 1941 to 1946 and converted four Lancasters (G-AHJT to G-AHJW) to tanker/receiver aircraft, these aircraft later moving on to operate from Ford and then Tarrant Rushton. During the Second World War, Flight Refuelling activity included towed Hurricane and Spitfire experiments (behind Wellington tug aircraft). The design activity and offices to support this work was located in the requisitioned Morgan motor works at Malvern Link, Worcestershire.

Glos-Air Ltd: The Victa Airtourer two-seat light aircraft was initially directly imported into the UK from Australia, but was later assembled by **Glos-Air Ltd** at Staverton. Aircraft assembled by Glos-Air were known as the Glos-Airtourer. These aircraft were shipped from New Zealand in a 'partly knocked-down' condition (production having transferred in October 1967 from Victa Ltd in Australia to AESL in Hamilton, NZ) and re-assembled, painted and test flown by Glos-Air. Twenty-three aircraft were imported between 1967 and 1972, in addition to eleven aircraft imported directly from Victa Ltd.

At times of peak production activity, Staverton was used for the flight testing of Hawker Typhoon aircraft built by **Gloster Aircraft Co. Ltd**.

Rotol Ltd Flight Test Department operated a fleet of trials aircraft at Staverton, including such types as Whitley, Wellington VI DR475, Spitfire and Tempest. Rotol produced some 100,000 propellers during the Second World War, these being used on more than sixty types of aircraft.

The sole Hawker Tornado built by A.V. Roe & Co. Ltd (R7936, which flew at Woodford on 29 August 1941) was used by Rotol Ltd at Staverton for contra-rotating propeller trials before moving on to similar duties with de Havilland Propellers at Hatfield. Rotol also used Hawker Typhoon R7638, Tempest V JN874, Tempest VI NX188 and Sea Fury FB. Mk 11 VR923, VW664 and VX613 for propeller development. (See also Moreton Valence.) The Martin-Baker MB5 was also flown at Staverton on Rotol trials.

Smiths Industries Ltd (Aviation Division) based their Dove (G-AOSE), Varsity (G-APAZ, G-ARFP) and Hawker Siddeley HS748 (G-ASJT) test aircraft at Staverton in the 1960s, and was responsible for management of the airport from 1956 until 1962. The Smiths Flying Unit was set up in 1947 and was based at Luton and then Moreton Valence before moving to Staverton. Other types operated included Avro XIX G-AHKX, Proctor G-AHFK, and DC-3 G-AMZE.

The early fleet of Smith's Aircraft Instruments Ltd lined up outside their hangar at Staverton. The Proctor, Anson and DC-3 were to be replaced by a de Havilland Dove, two Vickers Varsity and an HS748. (BAE SYSTEMS plc)

Stoke Orchard

The **Gloster Aircraft Co. Ltd** set up a factory at Stoke Orchard airfield (next to the present day M5, to the north of Cheltenham) which was used to provide additional Typhoon production capacity, and for modification and repair activity.

Stroud

The Dudbridge Iron Works Ltd: Head office 87 Victoria Street, SW1, and works at Stroud. This company acted as sole UK agents for (and manufacturer of) Salmson engines. The Dudbridge Iron Works Ltd was a founder member of the SBAC.

Wootton-under-Edge

Mr Mike Whittaker has built a long and successful series of microlights, which fall outside the scope of this book. One of his first designs, the MW2 Excalibur, was a conventional aircraft with a low-wing pusher layout and twin tailbooms. Powered by a VW engine driving a ducted fan, it flew only once at Bodmin, on 1 July 1976, and was not successfully developed.

Yate

No.3 (Western) Aircraft Repair Depot remanufactured a large number of aircraft at Yate during the First World War, including BE2, RE8, 1½ Strutter, F.2B, Camel, SE5A and Avro 504. At least 260 aircraft were built up from spares and salvage. Four Blackburn Kangaroo were built at Yate.

George Parnall & Co. Ltd of Park Row, Bristol, began to use Yate from 1925, it subsequently becoming the company's main operating base. During the First World War, the company (then **Parnall & Sons**) had built more than 750 aircraft at their Park Row factory; see the Bristol entry for details.

During the 1920s, the company built and re-furbished about thirty DH9A. Other aircraft produced under contract in the 1930s included the single Miles Satyr and the initial batch of

The diminutive Miles Satyr G-ABVG was built at Yate by George Parnall & Co. Ltd to the design of Mr F.G. Miles. Contemporary descriptions emphasise the type's high performance and good handling. (Via Ken Ellis)

G-ACFY is a Percival Gull 4, one of twenty-four built at Yate by George Parnall & Co. Ltd. (Andrew Rae)

Percival Gull aircraft. The company was reformed as **Parnall Aircraft Ltd** (incorporating Nash & Thompson and Hendy Aircraft) in May 1935.

The **Miles** M.1 Satyr, G-ABVG, was designed by F.G. Miles and his wife in 1931 in a rented room over a shop in Sevenoaks and constructed by Parnall. F.G. Miles first flew the Satyr on 31 July 1932. With its light weight (900lb) and 75hp Pobjoy, the Satyr was noted for its sprightly performance, matched by delightful handling. G-ABVG was a tiny (21ft span) I-strutted biplane, and was capable of a top speed of 120mph and a rate of climb of 1,400ft/min.

Parnall also built the **Hendy** 302, a two-seat monoplane which, but for its deep fuselage and tandem seats, in many ways anticipated the later Percival Gull. Although the Hendy 302 was designed for Capt. E.W. Percival, the aircraft were quite independent of each other. Capt. Percival wanted a machine to race in the 1930 King's Cup, and joined with Basil Henderson and Mr H.A. Miles in developing the specification for the Hendy 302. G-AAVT was powered by a Cirrus Hermes engine, with the design, construction and flight testing being completed in four months. In racing trim, the Hendy 302 proved itself capable of high speeds, averaging 128.5mph in winning a race of over 108 miles on 9 July 1930 – an extremely good performance on its 105hp.

The first twenty-four production **Percival** Gull aircraft were built by Parnall at Yate, the aircraft being marketed directly by E.W. Percival from 81 St George's Square, and 20 Grosvenor Place, London. Basil Henderson and Edgar Percival were later to dispute the extent to which the Gull was dependent upon Henderson's designs. The particular point at issue seemed to be whether the Gull not only used the Henderson spar design (over which Parnall held the rights), but also the Henderson-designed aerofoil section, which had been used on the Hendy 302. Strongly held views were expressed by the two principals in this matter.

The **Hendy** 3308 Heck was built to the order of Whitney Straight (see Yeovil). The Hendy 3308 led to the Parnall Heck II, with reconfigured cockpit and fixed undercarriage, six of which were built at Yate, the first example being G-AEGH. A related aircraft, the Parnall 382 Heck III G-AFKF, was built in 1938 against training specification T.1/37. This design featured tandem open cockpits and a Gipsy Six engine and was reported to have very pleasant handling when tested, marked as J1, at Martlesham Heath. Unfortunately, like many other promising aircraft of its time, it failed to receive a production order and was later impressed as R9138.

A selection of Parnall's own designs are listed below:

Type	Comments
Panther	Prototype N91 and five others built by Parnall. 150 Panther built by British & Colonial Aeroplane Co. at Filton.
Plover	Prototype N160 flown in late 1922 or early 1923. Competitor to the Fairey Flycatcher. Three prototypes and ten or eleven production aircraft.
Possum	An ungainly triplane with a single Lion engine in the fuselage driving two wing-mounted propellers. Prototype J6862 was first flown at Filton on 19 July 1923. Two built.
Pixie	Entrants for the 1923/1924 Lympne Light Aircraft competitions, see additional comments below.
Peto	A folding biplane of great ingenuity built, for carriage by the ill-fated submarine M2, in a hangar only 8ft wide. Serials N181 and N182 (N181 rebuilt as N225).
Pipit	An elegant biplane fighter to Naval Specification N.21/26. Powered by a Rolls-Royce F.XIIS, the type was reminiscent of the Hawker Fury, but for its taller tail and squarer wing tips. Two prototypes only were built, the first, N232, flying in mid-1928. Both aircraft unfortunately suffered from structural failures in flight.
C.10, C.11	Unsuccessful autogiros of 1927, see comments below.
Imp	An innovative biplane with stressed skin wings, a swept upper wing and single inter-plane struts. Prototype G-EBTE flown in February 1927. See additional comments below.
Elf	Warren-braced biplane, prototype G-AAFH first flown in mid-1929. Three built, one of which, G-AAIN, is preserved at the Shuttleworth Trust. G-AAIN has been restored to flying condition, taking to the air for the first time since its rebuild on 25 June 1980.

The Pixie could be flown in two different low-wing monoplane configurations. Alternative engines (500cc or 700cc Douglas) and propellers could be fitted, and two sizes of monoplane wing were manufactured (span 28ft 6in or 17ft 10in), allowing the aircraft's performance to be tailored to each different aspect of the trials included in the Light Aircraft Competition. First flight of the Pixie I (large wings, small engine) was on 13 September 1923, followed on 4 October by the same aircraft in Pixie II configuration (small wings, large engine). These flights were made at Filton.

In the 1924 competitions a modified two-seat configuration, known as the Pixie III, was used. The Pixie III could also optimise its performance to the competition requirements by a change in configuration, this time with a removable biplane wing. Two Pixie III were built, G-EBJG and G-EBKK, the first flying from Yate on 5 September 1924. Pixie II, G-EBKM, was still flying in 1939.

The Parnall-built Cierva C.10 and C.11 had almost identically disastrous histories. C.10 J9038 rolled over on its first attempted take-off at Yate on 26 April 1928, and repeated this performance on its second attempt at Andover on 5 November of the same year. The second aircraft, the 120hp Airdisco V8-powered C.11 G-EBQG, followed the example of the C.10 and also overturned on take-off at Yate.

The Parnall Imp featured the unusual arrangement of an unswept lower wing and a markedly swept upper wing; this had the advantage of allowing clear access to the front cockpit without requiring a tall (and drag-inducing) cabane strut arrangement. Initially powered by a Genet II, the Imp was re-engined in 1929 and served as a test bed for the new Pobjoy radial engine. Other less successful Parnall types included the Puffin, Perch, Pike, Prawn, Parasol (two aircraft used for variable incidence wing tests, built in 1929) and the Parnall G.4/31 prototype K2772. Parnall advertised the Parasol as being: 'designed to fulfil the function of securing true full scale data, and of measuring the aerodynamic forces acting on the wings of an aircraft.'

The two-seat Parnall Pixie III was designed for the 1924 Lympne Light Aircraft Competition. The type, whose upper wing was removable, was first flown at Yate on 5 September 1924. (Parnall via Ken Ellis)

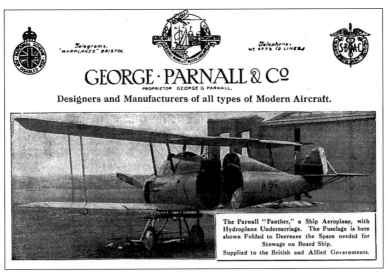

Telegrams.
"WARPLANES" BRISTOL

Telephone.
Nº 4773 (2 LINES)

GEORGE · PARNALL & Cº
PROPRIETOR GEORGE G PARNALL.
Designers and Manufacturers of all types of Modern Aircraft.

The Parnall "Panther," a Ship Aeroplane, with Hydroplane Undercarriage. The Fuselage is here shown Folded to Decrease the Space needed for Stowage on Board Ship.
Supplied to the British and Allied Governments.

The extraordinary Parnall Prawn demonstrates its articulated engine mounting, which kept the propeller tips clear of the surface when operating from water. (Via Ken Ellis)

Parnall's factory lies behind the railway station at Yate and is now used for the manufacture of domestic, rather than military, products. (Author)

Work during the Second World War concentrated on Fraser-Nash gun turrets and radar development, although some Spitfire airframe manufacture was also undertaken, together with component manufacture for other types, including parts for the Gloster Meteor. The factory at Yate was badly damaged in a series of German attacks in 1941. The company set up satellite works at Temple Cloud, which were used for the manufacture of Lancaster components, including fins, rudders and rear fuselage assemblies.

Parnall's factory lies next to the railway station at Yate and is readily distinguished by having two characteristic arch-roofed hangars in the centre of a long run of traditional saw-tooth ridged factory buildings. The site is now used for the manufacture of Hotpoint and Creda domestic appliances, a field into which Parnall moved at the end of the Second World War. The airfield has been developed for housing.

Hampshire

Andover

George Parnall & Co. Ltd: The Parnall-built Cierva C.10 J9058 was tested unsuccessfully at Andover on 5 November 1928.

Westland Aircraft Works (Branch of Petters Ltd): The airfield at RAF Andover was sometimes used by Westland for prototype testing, particularly when there was concern over the length of the runway available at Yeovil. Aircraft tested at Andover included the Westland Westbury J7765 (1926), Witch J8596 (January 1928), Westland F.7/30 K2981, Pterodactyl 1A J9251 (June 1928) and Pterodactyl V K2770 (May 1934).

Beaulieu

Beaulieu was used for early flying experiments, including some flying by E. Rowland Moon, and testing of Patrick Hamilton's Deperdussin two-seater following structural strengthening and duplication of its flying wires (this work having been completed by Mr Moon).

British Aircraft before the Great War reports that **Messrs. Perry & Beadle** flew a single-seat tractor biplane, with wings of unequal span, at Beaulieu in 1913. The collaborators who built this machine were later to form the **Perry, Beadle & Co.**, at Gould Road, Twickenham, London. The T.2, a modified version of the machine flown at Bealieu, was flying from Brooklands in 1914.

During the Second World War, Beaulieu became the site of the Airborne Forces Experimental Establishment.

Blackbushe Airfield

The airfield at Hartford Bridge Flats was constructed by Sir Robert McAlpine Ltd and (among other uses) was used by the Royal Aircraft Establishment for glider trials prior to the establishment of the Airborne Forces Experimental Establishment at Beaulieu. The RAE glider activity took place in late 1942 and 1943, involving the investigation of multiple tow techniques and 'snatch' towing to pick a glider off the ground using an already airborne tug. The types involved included the Horsa, Hamilcar and Hadrian.

The airfield was named Blackbushe on 2 December 1944 and became a Ministry of Civil Aviation airfield from February 1947. Blackbushe was a very active passenger transport airfield after the Second World War. Resident airlines in 1948 included Westminster Airways, Silver City Airways and Airwork Ltd. The airfield originally extended on both sides of the A30, with the Westminster Airways and Silver City Airways hangars being to the south of the main road. Blackbushe was much used by heavy charter aircraft, and for diversions from Northolt and London due to its fog dispersal equipment (FIDO).

The Hawker Hurricane Mk XII BE417/G-HURR, rebuilt by **Autokraft Ltd** at Brooklands, was first flown after its rebuild at Blackbushe on 14 January 1996.

Whilst not strictly being a manufacturing activity, there was an interesting example of early contracting from the MoD when **Eagle Aviation Ltd** at Blackbushe provided maintenance for NX739, a Lancaster used by the MoD as a photo-chase aircraft for experimental flying at Farnborough. This was clearly a successful enterprise, as the arrangement continued with the Lancaster's replacement, Lincoln RF322.

The Westland Westbury J7765 was one of a number of Westland designs to make its first flight at Andover. Two aircraft were built to Specification 4/24. (Westland)

Fairtravel Linnet G-ASMT was one of those completed at Blackbushe. G-ASMT is seen here at Brienne le Chateau.
(Author)

The Mitchell Kittiwake II was a two-seat derivative of the Mitchell Procter Kittiwake I. It is seen here at Blackbushe during testing in 1972, fitted with temporary spin recovery strakes ahead of the tailplane.
(Author)

Fairtravel Ltd built the Fairtravel Linnet II at Blackbushe. The aircraft was an anglicised Piel Emeraude derived from the Garland-Bianchi Linnet I, the first of which, G-APNS, had been built at White Waltham and flown at Fairoaks on 1 September 1958. Three aircraft were built by Fairtravel Ltd, the first, G-ASFW, flying on 20 March 1963.

Hampshire Aeroplane Co.: V.H. Bellamy modified Auster J/1 Autocrat G-AGVI at Blackbushe to be powered by a Rover TP90 turboprop engine in 1965. An Avro 504K replica, G-ATXL, also constructed by V.H. Bellamy, flew here on 17 August 1966. This aircraft was built and flown in the space of twelve weeks. See also Eastleigh, Hants, and Lands End, Cornwall.

The **Mitchell** Kittiwake II, G-AWGM, a two-seat development of the Mitchell Procter Kittiwake I, was developed by Dr C.G.B. Mitchell of 17 Tavistock Road, Fleet. G-AWGM was flown at Blackbushe on 19 March 1972, having been built by **Robinson Aircraft** at Blackbushe. See also the entry for Lasham.

Robinson Aircraft began the construction of John Fairey's Flycatcher replica, and built Luton Major G-AVXG, which was flown in 1968. Further information concerning the Flycatcher replica can be found under Lands End, Cornwall, and King's Somborne, Hants.

Vickers–Armstrongs Ltd: Limited Supermarine flight test activity was conducted at Blackbushe (Hartford Bridge Flats) in the spring of 1943.

Warbirds of GB Ltd: This organisation, which was set up by Doug Arnold, operated at Blackbushe from around 1976 until 1985. The company imported an array of Second World War aircraft (many from India), carried out restoration work and returned a number of aircraft to airworthy condition. The company also operated at Bitteswell and Biggin Hill. A partial list of the aircraft that passed through Blackbushe is given below:

Type	Individual Aircraft/Comments
CASA 2.111E	G-BDYA (ex-Spanish Air Force, 1976 to 1977, exported to USA)
CASA 352	G-BECL, G-BFHD, G-BFHE, G-BFHF, G-BFHE (ex-Spanish Air Force)
De Havilland Mosquito	RS709/G-ASKA/G-MOSI (present 1981 to 1983)
Gloster Meteor TT. Mk 20	WM167/G-LOSM
Hawker Tempest II	MW376, MW401, MW404, MW758, MW763, MW810, PR538 (all ex-Indian Air Force)
Hawker Sea Fury T.20	D-CAMI/G-BCKH, D-CACE/G-BCOV, D-CAFO/G-BCKV
Hawker Hunter T. Mk 54	ET-271 (Royal Danish Air Force)
Republic P-47D Thunderbolt	G-BLZW (1985, exported to USA)
Supermarine Spitfire	• MV262/IAF '42' • MV293/IAF '48'/G-SPIT, FR. Mk XIV • NH238/G-Mk IX, LF. Mk IXc flown at Blackbushe after rebuild 6 May 1984 • NH799 (ex-IAF), FR. Mk XIV • RW386/G-BXVI, LF. Mk XVIe • SM832/G-WWII, F. Mk XIV (ex-IAF) • SM969/HS877 (IAF)/G-BRAF, FR. Mk XVIIIe flown at Blackbushe after rebuild 12 October 1985 • TE392, LF. Mk XVIe
Westland Lysander	G-BCWL

An anonymous ex-Indian Air Force Spitfire fuselage awaits restoration in the Warbirds of GB Ltd workshop at Blackbushe. (Nick Blackman)

Calshot Castle

Calshot is chiefly notable for its use as an operating base for the British Schneider Trophy teams. A number of the competing aircraft were flown for the first time at Calshot, examples being tabulated below.

Type	Serial Numbers	Date and Comments
Supermarine S.5	N219–N221	August 1927. N220 won the event, flown by Fl. Lt Webster at 281.656mph. Fl. Lt D'Arcy Greig, DFC, AFC subsequently used N220 to set a new British speed record of 319.57mph at Calshot on 4 November 1928.
Gloster IV	N222–N224	August 1927. N223 set a biplane speed record of 277mph.
Gloster VI	N249, N250	Entrants for the 1929 contest. N249 first flew on 25 August 1929. 'Gloster VI – Certified World's Speed Record 336.3mph 10 September 1929. Pioneers of Steel Aircraft and Variable Pitch Propellers. GLOSTER.' This record did not last long before being overtaken by that of the Supermarine S6 (see next entry).
Supermarine S.6	N247, N248	N247 first flew on 10 August 1929 and won the 1929 contest, flown by Fl. Lt Waghorn at 328.63mph. Sqdn Ldr A.H. Orlebar, AFC, flew the S.6 N247 to set a world speed record of 357.7mph (575.7kph) on 12 September 1929.
Supermarine S.6B	S1595, S1596	S1595 first flew on 29 July 1931. The Schneider Trophy was gained permanently for Britain when Fl. Lt Boothman flew S1595 to victory at 340.08mph. Fl. Lt Stainforth subsequently set a world speed record of 407.5mph flying S.6B S1595 on 29 September 1931.

The **Leisure Sport** Supermarine S.5 replica G-BDFF was first flown from Calshot on 28 August 1975, some forty-eight years after the original S.5 first flew from the same site. (For additional references relating to G-BDFF, see Thruxton, Hants and Bodmin, Cornwall.)

The three **Saunders–Roe** Princess flying boat airframes were cocooned at Calshot until they were finally scrapped in 1967.

Supermarine S.5 replica G-BDFF was constructed at Thruxton and first flown at Calshot on 28 August 1975. This photograph was taken at Bodmin after its 1986 re-build. (Author)

Folland Midge prototype G-39-1 photographed in May 1955. (Bristol Siddeley Engines via Ken Ellis)

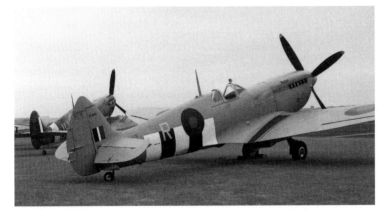

PL965 is a Vickers-Armstrongs-built Spitfire PR Mk XI from a batch whose construction was split between Chattis Hill and Aldermaston. (Author)

Chattis Hill

Vickers-Armstrongs Ltd: Chattis Hill was established as an airfield in 1917 and was used from 1940 for Supermarine Spitfire assembly and flight test. The hangars and aircraft were concealed among the surrounding trees and every effort was made to disguise the significance of the site, which had been in use as racehorse gallops. The 1917 airfield was situated immediately to the east of that used by Vickers-Armstrongs from 1940, to the north and east of Chattis Hill House. The airfield closed on 31 May 1948.

Chilbolton Airfield

Folland Aircraft Ltd began occupation of Chilbolton in 1953, the airfield being used for Folland Midge and Gnat testing from 11 August 1954 when the Midge G-39-1 first flew at Boscombe Down. On the day of its first flight, the Midge completed a total of four flights, ending with a flight from Boscombe Down to Chilbolton. The Folland Gnat was the production variant of the Midge, the first Gnat F.1, G-39-2, flying at Boscombe Down on 18 July 1955. Folland also used Chilbolton for development flying associated with their lightweight ejector seat, this activity being supported by the use of two Gloster Meteor T.7 aircraft, WA690 and WF877.

In 1961, following expiry of their lease, Folland (now part of Hawker Siddeley) progressively transferred Gnat T.1 flight test activity to Dunsfold from 20 February 1961 onward.

THE SUPERMARINE 510, developed from the "Attacker," has swept-back wings and tail unit to delay the onset of compressibility effects. The superb finish on all surfaces ensures a high aerodynamic efficiency which makes full use of the thrust of the Rolls-Royce Nene Engine.

VICKERS-ARMSTRONGS LIMITED · AIRCRAFT DIVISION · WEYBRIDGE AND SUPERMARINE WORKS

Above: *Swift F. Mk 1 WK196 in a busy flight test hangar at Chilbolton.* (Philip Jarrett)

Left: (Copyright: BAE SYSTEMS plc)

Vickers-Armstrongs Ltd (Supermarine Division): Chilbolton was used by Supermarine for flight test from 1947 to 1957, although activity was progressively moved to Wisley from 1956. Testing in this period included a rapid sequence of jet prototypes, covering the development of the Attacker, Swift and Scimitar. Supermarine flew the Types 392, 398, Attacker, 508, 510, 517, 525, 528, 529, Swift, 535, 541, 544 and Scimitar between July 1946 and January 1957 – a very heavy workload for all concerned!

Tracing the hectic development paths of Supermarine aircraft is complicated by the company policy of issuing a new type number for every significant modification. Rather than making an attempt to unravel the maze for every individual model, its complexity can be illustrated by looking at the development history of the Type 510.

The Supermarine 510 VV106 was, in effect, a swept-wing Attacker, flown at Boscombe Down on 29 December 1948. The second aircraft, VV119, had a modified engine air intake and cockpit canopy, resulting in the designation Type 528, and flew on 27 March 1950. After some six weeks flying, the aircraft was modified to a nosewheel configuration as the Type 535, flying again on 23 August 1950. In parallel with this activity, VV106 (the Type 510) acquired a variable incidence tailplane, to become the Type 517. Relatively minor modifications to the Type 535 led to two Swift prototypes (strictly Supermarine Type 541 WJ960 and WJ965), which finally allowed transition to an initial production configuration, the Swift F. Mk 1.

For further details of Supermarine jet aircraft production, see South Marston, Wiltshire.

Farnborough

With its Army Balloon Factory heritage, Farnborough is probably the site of the earliest organised flying and testing activity in Britain. The discussion below traces the development of the Government establishments on this site from the Balloon Factory to the Defence Experimental Research Agency (DERA), now split into DSTL (retained within the Ministry of Defence) and QinetiQ. This is followed by a review of British Aerospace/BAE SYSTEMS activities, including a summary of the company's corporate organisation, history and current projects. The entry is concluded with an alphabetical listing of other activities at this busy airfield.

The **Army Balloon Factory** moved from Aldershot to Farnborough in 1906; the later telegraphic address of the Royal Aircraft Factory and the RAE, 'Ballooning, Farnborough', reveals this ancestry. It was re-named **His Majesty's Balloon Factory** in April 1908, becoming the **Army Aircraft Factory** on 26 April 1911, and the **Royal Aircraft Factory** on 11 April 1912. The Factory cunningly produced completely new aircraft types under the guise of repairing existing machines.

During the First World War, the Royal Aircraft Factory and its designers were subjected to a sustained campaign of vitriolic abuse in the columns of *The Aeroplane* by its editor, Mr C.G. Grey, which would almost certainly be actionable were it to be published today. Its authors justified the campaign, partly on the grounds that they considered that the Factory represented a subsidised threat to private industry, but also because of the loss of life being suffered in France by inadequately trained pilots, who were flying machines that were outclassed by those of the enemy.

Reading the editorials today, their tone seems rather extreme. Every opportunity was taken to point out alleged defects of Government aeroplanes 'designed by untrustworthy science', in a manner that can scarcely have increased confidence in the population of a nation at war. In other instances, Grey referred to the 'futility, vacuity, and general ineptitude of the Royal Aircraft Factory', and berated that 'time and shop space is wasted in weird theoretical designs by Government employees.'

Despite the scorn of C.G. Grey, such designs as the BE2, BE12, FE2, RE8 and SE5A made an important contribution to the war in the air. Grey was aided and abetted in his campaign by Mr Noel Pemberton Billing in Parliament. Thus from (March 1917): 'When I asked certain officers why it was called "the Camel", they said it was because it gave the official designers the hump.' A further instance from March 1916 stated: 'officials responsible for deciding types of machine for the RFC failed either through ignorance, intrigue or incompetence to provide the best that this country could produce.' Mr Pemberton Billing is also well known for his claim that RFC pilots were being 'murdered, rather than killed' (a repetition of a statement originally made by Col. Walter Faber MP).

(Note that the above comment concerning the naming of the Camel is a piece of Parliamentary exaggeration. Harald Penrose quotes Sir Henry Tizard as saying it was because one of the pilots of the RFC test squadron at Martlesham Heath said 'just to look at the beast gives me the hump at the thought of flying it'. Most authors attribute the name to the raised forward fuselage fairing which provided access from the cockpit to the twin gun cocking mechanisms to allow the pilot to clear stoppages.)

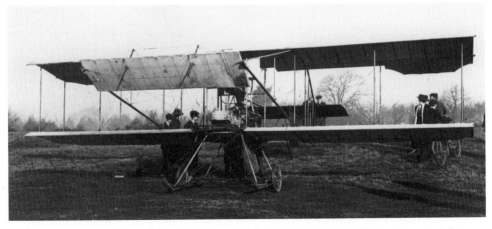

Geoffrey de Havilland's first successful machine was purchased by the Balloon Factory and flown at Farnborough, where this photograph was taken, as the FE1. (BAE SYSTEMS plc)

Despite the heat that they generated, the activities of Mr Grey and Mr Pemberton Billing were viewed less than favourably by the higher echelons of the RFC. Maurice Baring comments upon 'Air agitation going on in England in Parliament, etc.', saying that the net results were that not a single spare part, or extra machine, arrived earlier at the Front, and that the process generated alarm and despondency among serving personnel, a factor which 'never seemed to occur to anyone in England.'

Early **Dunne** biplanes were constructed at the Balloon Factory with official funding, but these were unsuccessful. Development of the Dunne design continued at Blair Atholl in Scotland and Eastchurch on the Isle of Sheppey.

The early pace of development was prodigious, as witnessed by the number of types flown between 1911 and 1914, and included in the following table, which covers the main Royal Aircraft Factory types.

Type	First Flight	Comments
DH No.2 FE1	10 Sept 1910	First flown at Newbury, subsequently purchased by the Balloon Factory and flown as the FE1 at Farnborough in January 1911. Geoffrey de Havilland joined the Balloon Factory as a designer in late 1910.
SE1	June 1911	Nominally created from components of a crashed Blériot and first flown by Geoffrey de Havilland. Crashed fatally on 18 August 1911.
FE2	Sept 1911	Rebuilt FE1 with a Gnome engine flown in September 1911. Tested as a seaplane on Fleet Pond in April 1912.
BE1	1 Jan 1912	Serial 201 (some sources give first flight as 27 December 1911). Nominally a repair of a damaged Voisin pusher.
BE2	Feb 1912	First flown by Geoffrey de Havilland. On 12 August 1912 the aircraft was flown with a passenger to 10,560ft in forty-five minutes.
BE3 to BE8	May 1912 to Aug 1913	BE3 serial 203; BE4 serials 204, 303; BE7 serial 438; and at least nineteen BE8 built by the Factory, with others by The British & Colonial Aeroplane Co. Ltd and Vickers Ltd. Developed into the more successful BE8A built by Vickers Ltd and Coventry Ordnance Works Ltd.
SE2	Oct 1913	Rebuilt BS1 (Blériot Scout) first flown by Geoffrey de Havilland as the BS1 in March 1913. The SE2 was later modified to become the SE2A, serial 609.
RE1	About May 1913	Built as an improved BE design. Two aircraft, nos 607 and 608.
RE2	1 July 1913	Tested unsuccessfully on floats at Fleet Pond in 1913.
RE5	Jan 1914	More than twenty built, a figure of twenty-four or twenty-five being usually quoted.
BE2B	Early 1914	Built at the Royal Aircraft Factory and extensively contracted.
BE2C	May 1914	More than 3,400 BE2 of all variants built by contractors
BE2E	Feb 1916	including Sir W.G. Armstrong, Whitworth & Co. Ltd; Barclay, Curle & Co. Ltd; William Beardmore & Co. Ltd; British Caudron Co. Ltd; The British & Colonial Aeroplane Co. Ltd; Coventry Ordnance Works Ltd; The Daimler Co. Ltd; Wm Denny & Bros; The Grahame-White Aviation Co. Ltd; Hewlett & Blondeau Ltd; Martinsyde Ltd; Napier & Miller Ltd; Ruston, Proctor & Co. Ltd; Vickers Ltd; The Vulcan Motor & Engineering Co. (1906) Ltd; G. & J. Weir group and Wolseley Motors Ltd. A number of other contractors built small numbers of the type.

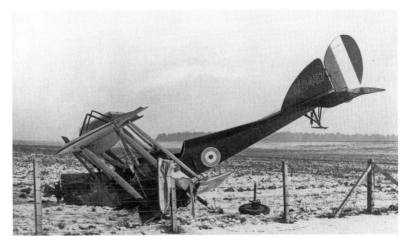

*The Royal
Aircraft Factory
BE2E was one of
the most widely
contracted
designs of the
First World War.
This example
was built by The
British & Colonial
Aeroplane Co.
Ltd. (Via
J.S. Smith)*

*This RE8,
F3556, was
contract-built by
The Daimler Co.
Ltd at Radford,
Coventry.
(Author)*

*The Royal
Aircraft Factory
FE2 was
another widely
contracted
type, this
example being
operated by 100
Squadron, RFC.
(Terry Treadwell
& Alan C. Wood)*

Type	First Flight	Comments
SE4	June 1914	Designed by Henry Folland and noteworthy for its streamlined construction and high performance. Serial 628.
FE2A	26 Jan 1915	Twelve built, prototype 2864.
SE4A	June 1915 (other dates also quoted)	Four built by the Royal Aircraft Factory, serials 5609 to 5612.
BE12	July 1915	Single-seat BE2C derivative with increased power, prototype 1697. Fifty BE12A built by the Coventry Ordnance Works Ltd, with additional aircraft from The Daimler Co. Ltd (BE12/12A/12B) and The Standard Motor Co. Ltd. First BE12B with 200hp Hispano-Suiza engine built by No.1 Southern Aircraft Repair Depot.
FE4	March 1916	Resembling a pusher DH10, prototypes 7993, 7994.
FE2B and FE2D	7 April 1916	Built at the Royal Aircraft Factory and extensively contracted. One source gives an FE2B production total of 1,939 aircraft. Royal Aircraft Factory production consisted of fifty-one FE2B and eighty-five FE2D, plus the FE2D prototype 7995. A total of about 2,300 FE2A/B/D were ordered from contractors including Barclay, Curle & Co. Ltd; Richard Garrett & Sons; G. & J. Weir group; Boulton & Paul Ltd; The Standard Motor Co. Ltd and Ransomes, Sims & Jeffries.
RE8	17 June 1916	At least fifty, and possibly seventy, RE8 were built by the Royal Aircraft Factory, and some 4,000 by contractors. These included orders from The British & Colonial Aeroplane Co. Ltd; Coventry Ordnance Works Ltd; D. Napier & Sons Ltd; The Standard Motor Co. Ltd; The Daimler Co. Ltd; The Austin Motor Co. (1914) Ltd and The Siddeley-Deasy Motor Car Co. Ltd. The prototype was serial number 7996. 1,913 RE8 were on RAF charge at the time of the Armistice.
FE8	15 Oct 1916	Two aircraft built at the Royal Aircraft Factory and production of some 275 aircraft contracted with Vickers Ltd and The Darracq Motor Engineering Co. Ltd. Prototypes 7456, 7457. The FE8 was designed by John Kenworthy.
SE5	22 Nov 1916	Prototype A4561. Some seventy-four production aircraft by the Royal Aircraft Factory, at least fifteen of which were completed as SE5A.
SE5A	12 Jan 1917	The best British fighter of the First World War. The third SE5 prototype was flown with a 200hp Hispano-Suiza engine in January 1917 and was effectively the prototype SE5A. Around 215 were built at the Royal Aircraft Factory and the type was extensively contracted, including Vickers Ltd; Martinsyde Ltd; The Austin Motor Co. (1914) Ltd; Wolseley Motors Ltd; Blériot & Spad/The Air Navigation Co. Ltd. A total of more than 5,000 SE5A were built in Britain and 2,696 SE5A were on RAF charge at the time of the Armistice.

The BE8 cannot be regarded as a total success. F. Warren Merriam, in his autobiography *First Through the Clouds*, refers to it as 'that flying death trap'. A further Royal Aircraft Factory type was the RE7, some 250 of which were built by contractors including the Coventry Ordnance Works Ltd (fifty); The Austin Motor Co. (1914) Ltd (at least thirty); D. Napier & Sons Ltd (fifty); and The Siddeley-Deasy Motor Car Co. Ltd (100).

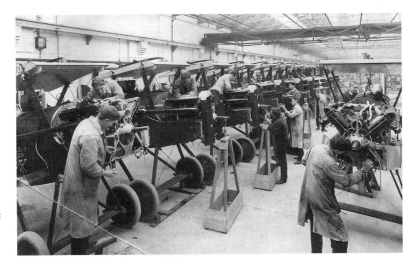

Production of the SE5A in full swing at Wolseley Motors Ltd. (Terry Treadwell & Alan C. Wood)

Designed by Henry Folland, seventy-five SE5 and about 215 SE5A were built at Farnborough out of a total (according to official figures) of 5,205 SE5 and SE5A (serials numbers were issued for 5,793 aircraft, a number of contracts being cancelled at the end of the war). The picture is clouded by the existence of aircraft repaired by depots in France and the UK which were issued with new serial numbers.

Of other designs, the Factory built twenty-four Handley Page O/400, at least six Vimy from a contract for thirty (F2915-F2920) and about ten further Vimy (H651–H660) from an order for twenty aircraft. The Factory tested a substantial number of captured German aircraft at Farnborough. Employment peaked at more than 5,000 in 1916 and some 500 aircraft of about thirty types were built here during the First World War.

The Royal Aircraft Factory became the **Royal Aircraft Establishment** in June 1918. (Reference: *Forever Farnborough – Flying the Limits 1904-96*, P.J. Cooper.) Although only a research establishment with no design or manufacturing role, many interesting activities continued here, highlights being summarised below:

- Acceptance testing of service aircraft.
- Research into flaps and high lift systems; investigation of configuration effects on stability and control and upon spinning characteristics.
- More than ten modified Avro 504K aircraft were used by the RAE for diverse tests including steel spar tests, instrumentation trials, low speed flight control and research into automatic flight control.
- Seven Nieuport Nighthawk were used by the RAE for engine testing. Two of these aircraft, J6928 and J6829, were in fact built by the RAE.
- A de Havilland DH60M Moth, K2235, was built up from spare parts by the RAE.
- Catapult, arrester gear and deck landing trials.
- Early air-to-air refuelling testing.
- Evaluation of captured enemy aircraft during the Second World War.
- Boundary layer control and laminar flow research (supported by Anson, Magister, Monospar and Hurricane test aircraft).
- Flexible deck landing trials.
- Radio control drone development – the first drone Meteor flew from Farnborough in January 1955. Other types included Queen Wasp and Queen Martinet.
- Flying in support of infra-red and other sensor development.
- Meteorological research flights.

Research flying ceased at Farnborough with the move of the last of the DRA/DERA research fleet to Boscombe Down on 18 October 1994.

British Aerospace (BAe) (now **BAE SYSTEMS**) has its Corporate Headquarters at Farnborough. For convenience, the main events in the history of BAe/BAE SYSTEMS are summarised here.

BAe was formally formed on 29 April 1977 under the terms of the Aircraft and Shipbuilding Industries Act (which received its Royal Assent on 17 March 1977). This established BAe as a nationalised corporation, merging **British Aircraft Corporation**, **Hawker Siddeley Aviation Ltd**, **Hawker Siddeley Dynamics Ltd** and **Scottish Aviation Ltd**.

The **British Aerospace Aircraft Group** was formed on 1 January 1978 to control the airframe interests of British Aerospace with (at that time) Operating Divisions as follows: Hatfield/Chester, Kingston/Brough, Manchester, Warton, Scottish and Weybridge/Bristol.

On 1 January 1981, BAe became a public limited company (plc) and 51.75% of the government-held shares were sold to the public in February 1981. The remaining government shares (with the exception of a £1 'golden share') were sold in May 1985. In January 1992, the defence interests of BAe began trading as **British Aerospace Defence Ltd**.

The main military aircraft design and manufacturing activity was carried out, under BAe, by **BAe Military Aircraft & Aerostructures** which, in 1998, had 18,500 employees working on the following products and projects:

- Eurofighter (620 aircraft required by UK, Spain, Germany and Italy)
- Harrier (Sea Harrier FA.2 and T.8; Harrier II GR.7, T.10 and AV-8B; Harrier II Plus)
- Hawk and T-45 Goshawk for the US Navy (first flown 16 April 1988)
- Tornado (GR.4 mid-life improvement programme)
- Nimrod MRA.4
- Joint Strike Fighter

Aerostructures contracts include:

- Boeing 737 flap components
- 747 engine struts
- MD-80 and MD-90 inboard flaps and vanes
- Strakes for the Boeing C-17
- Lockheed P-3 horizontal and vertical stabilisers

The British Aerospace Harrier design team moved to Farnborough after the closure of the factory and design offices at Kingston-upon-Thames. Here the Harrier T.10 prototype, ZH653, is shown climbing away from Dunsfold. (Author)

- Airbus wing components
- TriStar freighter components for Marshall of Cambridge
- RJ series wings, empennage and the rear fuselage
- Doors, elevators, flaps and ventral tanks for the Raytheon Hawker series

Finally, support is provided for out-of-production aircraft, notably the VC-10. These activities are dispersed around the various company sites.

The company's civil aircraft business has been the subject of a number of re-organisations, the highlights of which are summarised below.

In 1988, the company's civil business was conducted by **British Aerospace Civil Aircraft Division**, this being replaced by a subsidiary company, **British Aerospace (Civil Aircraft) Ltd**, on 25 August 1988. On 15 December 1988, this company was renamed **British Aerospace (Commercial Aircraft) Ltd**. From January 1989, this business conducted its operations through three divisions: Corporate Jets Division, Airlines Division and Airbus division. On 28 January 1992 the previous **British Aerospace (Commercial Aircraft) Ltd** was renamed **British Aerospace Regional Aircraft Ltd** (based at Hatfield). On 1 February 1992 **British Aerospace (Airbus) Ltd** was formed as a separate company at Filton. At the same time, **British Aerospace Corporate Jets Ltd** took over from the previous Division. This company was renamed **Corporate Jets Ltd** in May 1992. On 1 June 1993, **Corporate Jets Ltd** was sold to **Raytheon Corporation**.

On 24 September 1992, **Jetstream Holdings Ltd** was formed to be a holding company for BAe's regional turboprop business. In October 1992, assembly of the ATP aircraft was transferred to Prestwick, Scotland (from Woodford). The Prestwick ATP manufacturing activity became **Jetstream Aircraft Ltd** (which had been formed as an operating subsidiary of Jetstrem Holdings Ltd). All activities (for the design, manufacture and non-US support of Jetstream designs) were merged into Jetstream Aircraft Ltd on 24 September 1993. Hatfield was closed as a manufacturing site in 1994 with BAe146 production transferred to Woodford and renamed as **Avro International Aerospace Division**. This division (of British Aerospace Regional Aircraft Ltd) was formed on 1 January 1993.

Regional aircraft production was rationalised with an agreement between BAe, Aérospatiale and Alenia to set up a joint venture activity as **Aero International (Regional) (AI(R))**. AI(R) (with headquarters in Toulouse) began operations on 1 January 1996, and included the Avro International Aerospace regional jet activity at Woodford and the Jetstream activity at Prestwick. By July 1996, the previous Avro International Aerospace, Jetstream Aircraft Ltd and British Aerospace Regional Aircraft Ltd had all ceased to trade.

BAe announced the decision to break up the AI(R) joint venture on 24 April 1998, less than three years after it had been formed. This decision was partially due to the desire of the partners to promote their products separately, but also because of failure to agree on a new seventy-seat regional aircraft project. The break-up was completed by the end of June 1998. In response to the break-up of AI(R), BAe reintroduced **British Aerospace Regional Aircraft** to continue management of the RJ programme.

Under **BAE SYSTEMS**, the ongoing civil activities were renamed as **BAE SYSTEMS, Airbus** and **BAE SYSTEMS, Regional Aircraft**. On 1 January 2001, BAE SYSTEMS Regional Aircraft was merged with BAE SYSTEMS Aviation Services (see Filton) to become **BAE SYSTEMS Aviation Services Group**. BAE SYSTEMS' regional aircraft activity effectively ceased (other than support and training activity) with the announcement on 27 November 2001 of the cancellation of the RJX programme and the cessation of RJ build. On 24 June 2002, the last RJ85 to be built (construction number E2394) departed from Woodford to Filton for storage, whilst awaiting sale.

It was announced in April 1998 that BAe had acquired a 35% holding in Saab, linked to the marketing of the Saab Gripen, which fits well between the BAe Hawk and Eurofighter products. On 11 March 1998, the Government announced that foreign share ownership limits in BAe were being raised to 49.5% (with a maximum of 15% for any one investor), allowing potential equity exchanges with future partners. The foreign share ownership limit has now been lifted, although the government retains its £1 'golden share'.

For an extended period BAe was in negotiation with DASA (now DaimlerChrysler Aerospace) with a view to merging and setting up a European Aerospace and Defence company. Such a move also seemed likely to be associated with a potential BAe shareholding in CASA. These aspirations were essentially brought to a halt as a result of the announcement on 19 January 1999 that BAe and GEC had reached agreement on the takeover, by BAe, of the GEC defence interests (Marconi Electronic Systems).

This merger created, on 30 November 1999, **BAE SYSTEMS**, and acted as a catalyst for the formation, by BAe's putative European partners (DASA, Aérospatiale, CASA) of EADS (European Aeronautic Defence & Space Co.). In January 2001 it was anticipated that Alenia Aerospazio would join in a Joint Venture arrangement with EADS. This teaming arrangement would result in the JV partners holding 62.5% of the Eurofighter programme, 57.5% of Tornado and 71% of Airbus A400M project. Both BAE SYSTEMS and EADS have indicated their interest in transatlantic as well as European partnerships, and it seems that the future will continue to be turbulent.

British Aerospace Harrier flight test activity was temporarily transferred to Farnborough during the summer of 1996, whilst the Dunsfold runway was being re-surfaced. On 24 June 1999, BAe announced that with the completion of the Harrier production programme, it would be closing its Dunsfold site by the end of the year 2000. BAE SYSTEMS has now concentrated its military aircraft production at its sites in northern England (Brough, Samlesbury and Warton).

A.V. Roe & Co. Ltd: The Dart-powered second prototype of the Athena T.1A, VM129, made its first flight at Farnborough on 17 September 1949.

Beagle Aircraft Ltd (British Executive and General Aviation Ltd) had offices at Lynchford Road, Farnborough.

Above: (Copyright: BAE SYSTEMS plc)

The Cody III Circuit of Britain biplane was used to win the Michelin Prizes of 1911. (Terry Treadwell & Alan C. Wood)

The Cody monoplane at Farnborough. This machine, which was intended to compete in the 1912 Military Trials, crashed before it could do so. (Andrew Rae)

The **Brennan** helicopter was flown with official funding, but limited success, from March 1922 (indoor tethered flights) until October 1925. Outdoor flight trials took place from May 1925 and many short (barely controlled) flights were made before accident damage brought the programme to a halt.

The Bristol Aeroplane Co. Ltd: On 28 September 1936, the Bristol 138A high altitude monoplane K4879 set an altitude record with a flight from Farnborough, achieving 49,967ft. This was further extended by the Bristol 138A to 53,937ft on 30 June 1937. The 1936 flight was featured in company advertising thus: 'A Bristol Monoplane fitted with a Bristol Pegasus Engine secures the record for Great Britain: 49,967ft. Another Bristol world record beating the previous record by 1,269 ft.' (See advert on opposite page, extreme left.)

S.F. Cody: Already well known for his work on kites, S.F. Cody began experimenting with gliders at Farnborough in 1905. By 1907, he had begun constructing the British Army Aeroplane No.1 in the Balloon Factory airship shed. Trials began in September 1908 and were quickly successful; on 16 October 1908, Cody flew the British Army Aeroplane No.1 over a distance of 1,390ft (463yds) at heights of 15-30ft. By August 1909, Cody's machine had been extensively modified, with the engine now mounted behind the pilot, and was flying successfully with a passenger. Flights of five to six miles were being achieved, with a flight of more than one hour duration occurring on 8 September 1909.

The types built by Cody were:

- British Army Aeroplane No.1
- Michelin Cup Biplane (flown for four hours and forty-six minutes over a distance of 185.46 miles on the last day of 1910)

- Circuit of Britain Biplane (flown for five hours and fifteen minutes over a distance of 261.5 miles on 29 October 1911)
- Cody monoplane, which crashed before it could compete in the 1912 Military Trials
- Military Trials biplane (which, in addition to winning the Military Trials, was used by Cody to win the Michelin Cup for the third year running in 1912)
- Hydro-biplane built for the 1913 Circuit of Britain. This was the aircraft that Cody was flying, with W.H.B. Evans as passenger, when both were killed on 7 August 1913 due to failure of the structure in flight.

Although appearing antiquated, Cody's machines were reliable performers and good load carriers, as his successes in the Michelin Cup and the 1912 Military Trials demonstrate. Wilfred Parke reported that the later Circuit of Britain biplane was easy to fly despite its unconventional controls, but needed to be watched continuously for lateral balance, 'probably due to the inverted dihedral'.

E.H. Industries, the holders of the contract for the development of the EH101, is based at *Solartron House,* Farnborough.

Farnborough-Aircraft.com is a company set up by Richard Noble (well known for his land speed record, ThrustSSC and ARV endeavours) to develop a single-engine, all composite, turboprop aircraft, the F1, for air taxi use. Developed at Farnborough by a small team with a range of partners, and financed partially through public subscription raised over the internet, the F1 offers an alternative to the executive jet as a source of point-to-point business travel. A key to this is the acceptance of single-engine IFR passenger transport, which has been accepted by many countries for turboprop aircraft such as the Pilatus PC12.

The F1 is currently defined around a single pilot plus five passengers, PT6A-60A engine, good short field performance and high operating performance. A mock-up of the design was shown at the Farnborough International 2000 SBAC Show, and wind tunnel and other development work is underway.

The F1 air taxi concept has yet to be proven, and financing the development and certification of this new type remains a challenge. Satisfactory operating costs and market penetration must also be achieved, and it will be some time before the success or failure of this innovative and entrepreneurial project can be judged. In late 2001, it was announced that funding and manpower constraints were slowing the programme, with first flight now targeted as late 2004.

The **General Aircraft Ltd** GAL 56 tailless glider, TS507, was first flown here on 13 November 1944. The three aircraft built were later tested at Wittering, Lasham and Beaulieu (Airborne Forces Experimental Establishment). The second and third aircraft featured different wing planforms and were flown, respectively, on 27 February 1946 (TS510D) and 30 May 1946 (TS513B).

Gloster Aircraft Co. Ltd: The Gloster E.28/39 carried out trials from Farnborough in late 1942 and early 1943. The third prototype Meteor (DG204/G) first flew at Farnborough in November 1943.

Hawker Aircraft Ltd: Test-flying of the P.1040 and P.1052 jet prototypes was carried out at Farnborough during 1947 and 1948, due to the unsuitability of Langley, with its proximity to Heathrow and lack of a hard runway. The novelty of the swept wing (at least in Britain) in 1950 is reflected in Hawker's advertising: 'Performance improvement – The swept back wing Hawker P.1052 interceptor is being developed to improve still further the high all

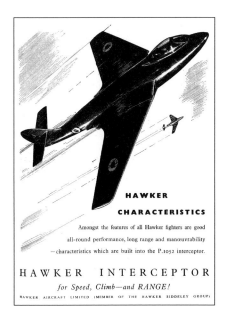

HAWKER

CHARACTERISTICS

Amongst the features of all Hawker fighters are good
all-round performance, long range and manœuvrability
—characteristics which are built into the P.1052 interceptor.

HAWKER   INTERCEPTOR

for Speed, Climb—and RANGE!

HAWKER AIRCRAFT LIMITED (MEMBER OF THE HAWKER SIDDELEY GROUP)

(Copyright: BAE SYSTEMS plc)

round performance of this versatile line of famous fighters. HAWKER INTERCEPTOR for Speed, Climb – and RANGE!'

The Hawker P.1081 was an experimental prototype between the P.1052 and the P.1067 Hunter. The P.1081 had a straight through jet pipe rather than the bifurcated exhaust of the P.1052. VX729 was first flown on 9 June 1950, *The Aeroplane* of 30 June 1950 reporting that this flight took place at Farnborough.

Professor G.T.R. Hill: The Hill Pterodactyl 1 was tested at Farnborough in November 1925, before Professor Hill moved to Westland Aircraft Works.

The **No,1 (Southern) Aircraft Repair Depot** at South Farnborough (Jersey Brow) reconstructed and repaired at least 700 aircraft during First World War. Many types were handled, including BE2C, BE12, RE8, DH4, DH9, Bristol F.2B, Bristol Scout, Nieuport 17, FK8, SE5A, Camel, DH5, FE2B, Sopwith Dolphin, Pup, 1½ Strutter, Spad VII and Martinsyde. The ten sheds used were not dismantled until the 1970s.

RAE Aero Club: This club, founded in October 1922, designed and built entrants for the 1923 *Daily Mail* motor glider competition at Lympne (Hurricane/Zephyr) and the 1926 light aircraft competition (Sirocco). The Zephyr G-EBGW first flew at Farnborough on 6 September 1923 and had the general configuration of a single-seat, half-size Farman Shorthorn. The Zephyr was powered by a 600cc Douglas engine. The Hurricane was a diminutive (23ft span) shoulder wing cantilever monoplane with a fuselage of triangular cross-section, which also first flew in September 1923. Having had its Douglas engine replaced by a 32hp Bristol Cherub, Hurricane G-EBHS achieved notable racing success at Lympne in August 1925, turning in a speed of 81.19mph to win the Grosvenor Challenge Cup, and winning two other races at the same meeting.

The RAE Sirocco had to be abandoned when, after construction, it was found that the centre of gravity was, disastrously, 29in aft of the calculated position. In February 1932 a further design, the Scarab G-ABOH, was flown. The Scarab was a parasol monoplane that made use of the flying surfaces of a DH53, combined with a new fuselage, power being provided by a 32hp Bristol Cherub.

The RAE Aero Club remains active today, ninety years after its foundation.

W.G. Tarrant: The Tarrant Tabor was a six-engine triplane, serial F1765, with a wing span of more than 130ft, wing area of nearly 5,000sq.ft and height of more than 37ft. The high engine thrust line caused the aircraft to nose over on take-off on its attempted first flight on 26 May 1919, killing its two pilots. **W.G. Tarrant**, who constructed the aircraft, were building contractors with works in Byfleet.

Vickers-Armstrongs Ltd: The prototype Vickers Windsor, DW506, was first flown at Farnborough on 23 October 1943. Only three were built. The Vickers 432, DZ217, was first flown here on Christmas Eve 1942.

Gosport

Camper & Nicholsons Ltd, Mumby Road, Gosport: This famous firm of yacht designers and boat builders, which was founded in 1782, built twenty-seven flying boat hulls in 1917-1918 at its Gosport Yard.

Nicholson's connection with racing yachts is perhaps best illustrated by his design of the Americas Cup J-Class racers *Endeavour* and *Endeavour II* for Sir Thomas Sopwith, and the *Shamrock IV* and *Shamrock V* for Sir Thomas Lipton. In 1929, Charles E. Nicholson also constructed the 12m *Flica* and the motor yacht *Evadne* for that other aviator yachtsman, Sir Richard Fairey. Camper & Nicholsons built the 12m yachts *Mouette* and *Tomahawk* for T.O.M. Sopwith, together with the magnificent motor yacht *Philante*, which was later to become the Norwegian Royal Yacht *Norge*. A possible spin-off from aircraft manufacture was the firm's later involvement in hollow spar manufacture for yachts as a result of their shareholding in the McGruer Hollow Spar Co.

The **Gosport Aircraft Co.** was located at the corner of Little Beach Street and Chapel Lane, Gosport, with additional facilities at Northam. The company, also known as GAC, was formed in 1916 by Sir Charles Allom of White, Allom & Co. Ltd, owner of a number of racing yachts, and Mr Charles E. Nicholson of Camper & Nicholsons. 'We rented a waterside timberyard at Southampton for the fitting of the wings to the hulls and were soon getting into quite good production. The finished article was lifted into the Itchen and our test pilot, David Carnegie, did his stuff. We went on to the construction of the larger F.3 type flying boats, and finally F.5s which carried a crew of 5.' (*Great Years in Yachting* by John Nicholson.)

The company's initial order was for sixty FBA Type B flying boats for use at Lee-on-Solent, the first being flown in December 1917. The first aircraft was N2680, and at least thirty were delivered. Sub-contract work was carried out on both wings and flying boat hulls. GAC built sixteen Felixstowe F.3 hulls and six Felixstowe F.2A hulls. Hull manufacture was sub-contracted to the main Camper & Nicholsons Yard at Gosport, with the hulls being towed from Gosport to Northam prior to assembly. Ten Felixstowe F.5 flying boats

were completed (N4630 to N4639) from an order for fifty cancelled following the Armistice. These larger aircraft required more space for assembly, and were erected in leased timber sheds at Northam. The location of these sheds are not known positively, but are believed to have been close to Millstone Point.

An experimental hull, the N4 Atalanta N118, was designed by Charles Nicholson and built by the Gosport Aircraft Co. The hull was then taken by road to the Phoenix Dynamo works at Bradford, united with its superstructure, and then moved from Bradford to the Isle of Grain for testing. This aircraft was completed, but never flown.

Aircraft from the curtailed F.5 order continued to be built for a period after the cessation of hostilities, including G-EAIK, a Felixstowe F.5 completed in 1919. The Gosport Aircraft Co. had close links to J.C. Porte, and held his flying boat patents. J.C. Porte joined the firm in August 1919, sadly dying from tuberculosis in October of the same year. In 1919, the company was advertising under the slogan 'Designers and Builders of Flying Boats for the Air Ministry and for commercial and pleasure use.' GAC was closed in October 1920.

The **United Aircraft Co. Ltd** of 4 Great Marlborough Street, W1; Gosport, Hants; and South Road, Southall, was advertising in August 1918 as 'Contractors to the Air Board'.

Hamble

Hamble, like a number of other areas of sheltered water (such as the Humber Estuary (Brough), the Medway at Rochester, Calshot, Cowes, Felixstowe and Lake Windermere), proved, almost from the first days of British aviation, to be a favoured location for the testing of seaplanes. Contemporary photographs show early seaplanes such as the Short 166 being launched from a rudimentary slipway almost opposite the Crab and Lobster public house at Warsash. In addition to the most recently used airfield site, a number of other locations in the near vicinity of Hamble and Hamble Point have been used for aircraft construction and test-flying purposes, all of which are grouped under this entry.

Aerostructures Hamble Ltd. See the entry for British Aerospace, below.

Air Service Training Ltd (AST): AST was an Armstrong Whitworth company and a member of the Hawker Siddeley Group. The company was formed at Whitley in February 1931 and moved to Hamble in April 1931. New hangars were erected, and use was also made of the A.V. Roe & Co. Ltd factory for the assembly of aircraft for AST's own fleet, which included a large number of Avro Cadet aircraft.

During the Second World War AST was the largest fighter Civilian Repair Organisation (CRO) in the country and repaired 3,400 Spitfires (from 1940 to 1946 the total number repaired was 3,507). The company also performed around 136 Seafire IB conversions from Spitfire VB, and carried out B-17 and Mustang modifications for RAF use. One example of the latter was the installation of special long-range fuel tanks on Mustang FR901. The first Seafire conversion was flown on 23 March 1942. Trial installations were designed and implemented on a number of other American types, including the North American Mitchell.

After the Second World War, a number of aircraft were modified by AST at Hamble for specialist engine test bed usage. Examples include:

- Mamba test bed Avro Lancaster VI ND784/G, first flown on 14 October 1947 at Hamble following modification by AST. This aircraft was originally flown with a bomb bay-mounted ASX in April 1943 (also quoted as June 1945).
- Avro Lancaster SW432, also with nose-mounted Mamba, January 1949.
- Avro Lancaster 80001 of the Swedish Air Force with bomb bay-mounted Dovern and subsequently after-burning Ghost for the Saab J29. First flown on 24 April 1951.

Air Service Training were responsible for the design of the forward fuselage modifications to produce the Javelin T. Mk 3. The prototype, seen here at Moreton Valence, was erected at Hamble before being moved by road to the Gloster Aircraft Co. Ltd prior to its first flight. (BAE SYSTEMS plc via Ken Ellis)

Armstrong Whitworth built the Ensign at Hamble, due to production pressures at Coventry for the Whitley Bomber. The size of the prototype G-ADSR is emphasised by the Armstrong-Siddeley car parked between its undercarriage legs. (British Airways via Ken Ellis)

- Sapphire 1 Avro Lancastrian VM733, first flown on 18 January 1950 from Hamble (also quoted as 19 January).
- Rolls-Royce Derwent afterburner test bed Avro Lincoln SX971, which flew in October 1950.
- Python Lincoln RF403.
- Gloster Meteor 4 RA491 was modified by AST to test the SNECMA Atar 101B-21 engine, following its use as a test bed for the Rolls-Royce Avon. The aircraft was first flown with Atar engines on 31 October 1951.

AST was responsible for the design of the forward fuselage modifications for the Gloster Javelin T. Mk 3. The prototype, WT841, was assembled at Hamble before being disassembled and moved by road to Gloucester for its first flight. This took place on 20 August 1956, and a further twenty-two production Javelin T. Mk 3 were subsequently built by Gloster.

Sir W.G. Armstrong Whitworth Aircraft Ltd: The Armstrong Whitworth Ensign was built in the Air Service Training (ex A.V. Roe & Co. Ltd) hangars due to the company works at Baginton being fully occupied with Whitley production. The first Ensign (G-ADSR) flew from Hamble on 23 January 1938, and was the largest Imperial Airways landplane used before the Second World War. A total of fourteen Ensign were built and, although an elegant and refined design, it proved to be unreliable and difficult to maintain in service.

The two Armstrong Whitworth Albemarle prototypes were also built in the AST hangars at Hamble; the first, P1360, flying on 20 March 1940. By all accounts the space available was barely sufficient for the take-off run required. Subsequent production was the responsibility of **A.W. Hawksley Ltd** at Brockworth.

A.V. Roe & Co. Ltd: The lack of experimental flight test facilities close to the Manchester factories led A.V. Roe to select Hamble on the South Coast for aircraft erection and test-flying. The Hamble facilities also provided additional production capacity, although the main use of Hamble remained the test-flying of prototype aircraft. A.V. Roe & Co. Ltd used Hamble for all new types until Mr A.V. Roe left the company, after which activities were increasingly centred on Manchester. Harry Holmes indicates in *Avro – The History of an Aircraft Company* that the move from Hamble was completed by 14 December 1932, although limited activity continued after that date (testing of float-equipped Tutors and the erection of aircraft for use by AST Ltd). The last known use made of Hamble by A.V. Roe & Co. Ltd was the launching of a float-equipped Chilean Avro 626 from the slipway on 30 May 1935.

A.V. Roe & Co. Ltd initially used a site to the south of the later Hamble airfield, in an area extending to the north west and south of the present Ensign Way, and to the south east of the later British Marine Aircraft/Folland/Hawker Siddeley/British Aerospace works. A.V. Roe & Co. Ltd purchased land for the larger northern airfield in 1924, and this was opened in 1926. The southern airfield was closed in 1933. A.V. Roe & Co. Ltd aircraft were flown at Hamble from Spring 1916, the first type to make its first flight here being the Avro 523 Pike in May 1916. Other A.V. Roe & Co. Ltd designs that were first flown at Hamble are listed below:

Type	Comments
529/529A	An enlarged Pike, prototype RFC serial 3694, flown March 1917; 529A flown 23 October 1917.
530	Two-seat fighter first flown 4 July 1917; an unsuccessful competitor to the Bristol F.2B, only two were built.
531 Spider	A sesquiplane single-seat fighter with complex strut arrangements eliminating the need for rigging wires, first flown April 1918.
533 Manchester	Twin-engine bomber. The prototype F3492, built entirely at Hamble, was first flown in December 1918.
504L	Floatplane version of the Avro 504. Prototype C4329, a modified 504J, was first flown on 4 February 1919.
534 Baby	First flown at Hamble on 30 April 1919 – see additional comments, below.
536	A widened Avro 504 for pleasure flying with four passengers in the rear cockpit. Eight production aircraft built at Hamble, twelve more at Manchester, first flown in April 1919.
539	G-EALG, built as an entrant in the 1919 Schneider Trophy contest and first flown on 29 August 1919.
548	Generic description of the Avro 504 when powered by other than a rotary or radial engine (also Avro 545 and 548A). The prototype G-EAPQ (with three individual cockpits) was first flown in late 1919, before testing at Farnborough on 13 January 1920, powered by an 80hp Renault. Other engines used included Curtiss OX-5 (Type 545) and 120hp Airdisco (548A).
547 Triplane	A triplane with an enclosed passenger cabin and a slab-sided fuselage. One of Avro's least attractive designs, the prototype G-EAQX was first flown on 6 February 1920.
549 Aldershot	J6852, the first of two prototypes, was flown in September 1921. Later re-engined with the unprecedentedly powerful 1,000hp Napier Cub, flying with this engine on 15 December 1922. The fifteen Manchester-built production aircraft were built powered by the Rolls-Royce Condor.

Above and left: (Copyright: BAE SYSTEMS plc)

Type	Comments
504Q	Arctic expedition three-seat seaplane G-EBJD, first flown on 11 June 1924 and abandoned at Spitzbergen only two months later, on 18 August 1924.
504R 'Gosport'	Prototype G-EBNE was first flown in June 1926.
558 and 560	Respectively biplane and monoplane entries for the 1923 Light Aeroplane Trials. The Avro 558 G-EBHW achieved 13,850ft on 13 October 1923 to win the Duke of Sutherland's prize. The Avro 560 achieved a measured fuel consumption of 63.3mpg.
561 and 563 Andover	Large single-engine passenger transport and ambulance biplane. Avro 561 prototype J7261, three built.
562 Avis	Entrant for the 1924 Two-seat Light Aeroplane Trials, superficially similar to the Hawker Cygnet.
566 and 567 Avenger	A Napier Lion-powered fighter of exceptionally clean lines first flown on 26 June 1926 and modified from Avro 566 to Avro 567.
571 and 572 Buffalo	Private venture torpedo/bomber design of 1926; one Avro 571 only, G-EBNW, later modified to become Avro 572 N239.
Autogiro types	Built for The Cierva Autogiro Co. Ltd, see below.
Avian	Series of light aircraft, see additional comments below.

A number of Avro 504 were constructed at Hamble, for example 150 Avro 504J with serials from B3101; some Manchester-built Avro 504J/K were also erected and test flown here. G. Jenks indicates (in communication to the author) that there was official resistance to A.V. Roe & Co. Ltd making use of Hamble for production as well as test-flying. The official preference was for production to be contracted to other firms – much to the dissatisfaction of Mr A.V. Roe.

The Avro 534 Baby was a tiny biplane (25ft span, 20ft long) designed by Roy Chadwick to try to attract the private owner. The type is chiefly notable for a number of long-distance flights carried out in it by Bert Hinkler. One of these was a non-stop flight of 800 miles from Sydney to Bundaberg in Australia. On another occasion Hinkler flew non-stop from England to Turin in G-EACQ, whose tank capacity he had increased to twenty-five gallons.

Intended as a fighter, the Avro 529A was flown in October 1917. This was the second of two prototypes (the Avro 529 and 529A) both of which were destroyed in testing at Martlesham Heath. (BAE SYSTEMS plc)

Hamble was used for the development of floatplane versions of the Avro 504, including the 504L and 504Q. This aircraft is a 504O (floatplane version of the 504N) being tested at Hamble in 1925 prior to delivery to the Royal Hellenic Naval Air Service. (BAE SYSTEMS plc)

The Avro Avian marked the transition of flight testing back to Manchester from Hamble. This magnificently restored example was prepared to re-enact Bert Hinkler's famous flight to Australia. (Author)

As was the norm for Avro designs at the time, the Baby first flew at Hamble. Unfortunately, it crashed after take-off, and its replacement (the second Baby K-131/G-EACQ) flew, also at Hamble, on 10 May 1919. The two-seat Baby, G-EAUM, is quoted as achieving 82mph on its 35hp Green engine and cruising at 70mph at 2½gal/hr. Eight Avro Baby were assembled at Hamble (in addition to the original, unregistered and ill-fated prototype).

The Avro 552 was a Wolseley Viper-powered Avro 504, of which a number were built for export to Canada and Argentina. The prototype, G-EAPR, was used as a long-standing development aircraft by A.V. Roe & Co. Ltd, and had a most interesting career. First flown as a landplane, it was retained for experimental use and appeared in a number of guises before being transformed into the Cierva C.8V (or Avro 586) autogiro, in which form it was registered G-EBTX. As if to disown this as an aberration, it re-appeared at Hanworth as a conventional biplane in 1930 as Avro 552A G-ABGO.

One unsung but successful design was the Avro 555 Bison, a reconnaissance biplane, whose prototype (serial N153) flew in 1921 at Hamble. Production consisted of two prototypes and fifty-three production aircraft in two variants. The type was built at Newton Heath, production aircraft being delivered from Woodford. The Bison was one of the more successful new military designs of the 1920s.

The Avro 581 Avian prototype G-EBOV was built for the 1926 Two-seat Light Aeroplane Trials, powered by a 70hp Armstrong Siddeley Genet engine. The prototype was re-engined with an 85hp ADC Cirrus II to become the Avro 581A, and became the private aircraft of H.J. 'Bert' Hinkler, Avro's famous Australian test pilot. Hinkler's notable long-distance flights in this aircraft included a 1,200-mile non-stop flight to Riga, Latvia, from Croydon on 27 August 1927, and the even more spectacular flight to Darwin, Australia. In the course of 15½ days during February 1928, the aircraft was flown over 11,000 miles.

The Avian was subsequently developed to become second only in sales to the de Havilland Moth series. A total of 396 Avian were built, split between 194 wooden airframe Avian I to IV, and 202 metal airframe aircraft made up of 156 Avian IVM, sixteen Sports Avian, two long-range aircraft for Sir Charles Kingsford Smith, two Avian monoplanes and at least twenty-six aircraft constructed under licence in Canada and the USA. Production was at Newton Heath, and the early aircraft were flown at Hamble, the Avian production run covering the period when A.V. Roe & Co. Ltd were purchased by Armstrong Siddeley Developments Ltd, which resulted in the withdrawal of Avro test-flying from Hamble.

One of the last Avro types to make its first flight from Hamble was the Avro 604 Antelope J9183 of November 1928. The Antelope was a large conventional single-bay biplane resembling a stretched DH9A with a Rolls-Royce F.XIB V-12 liquid-cooled engine. The type was an unsuccessful competitor to the Hawker Hart.

A.V. Roe & Co. Ltd erected the **Vickers** Vagabond at Hamble in 1924 as an entrant in the 1924 Lympne Two-seat Light Aeroplane competition.

British Aerospace (BAe) took over from **Hawker Siddeley Aviation Ltd** the production facilities previously used by **Folland Aircraft Ltd**. BAe used this capacity for component manufacture, setting up a separate subsidiary, **Aerostructures Hamble Ltd**, in January 1989. BAe disposed of Aerostructures Hamble Ltd in April 1992, it thereafter operating as an independent concern. Aerostructures manufactured components for a wide range of civil and military aircraft, including the Boeing 737, 747, 757 and 777; C-17; MD-80/90; T-45 Goshawk; Harrier II; Hawk (centre and rear fuselage); Sea Harrier; Tornado; Nimrod; P-3 Orion; Canadair Regional Jet; Avro RJ; Raytheon Hawker 800; Saab 340 and 2000; and Airbus A300, A310, A330 and A340. A significant single item was the main cargo door for the Airbus (SATIC) Beluga transport. In 1994, the company became **Aerostructures Hamble Holdings plc**, this being itself taken over by **EIS plc** on 2 November 1995. EIS was taken over by TI Group in July 1998, the Hamble activity becoming part of the **Dowty Group**.

First of the experimental Cierva Autogiros to be built by A.V. Roe & Co. Ltd was the Avro 504K-based Cierva C.6C/ Avro574. (Via Westland)

The Blackburn Aeroplane & Motor Co. Ltd: the Blackburn Pellet entry for the 1923 Schneider Trophy race was assembled at Hamble in The Fairey Aviation Co. Ltd works in September 1923. Unfortunately it suffered from porpoising and was destroyed during its second test flight.

The Cierva Autogiro Co. Ltd was registered on 24 March 1926; substantial numbers of Cierva autogiros, both experimental and production versions, were constructed on behalf of Cierva by the A.V. Roe & Co. Ltd at Hamble and later (C.30A) in Manchester. The main versions produced by A.V. Roe & Co. Ltd are listed below.

Avro Type	Cierva Type	Serial or Registration	Comments
574	C.6C	J8086	Derived from Avro 504K. First flown 19 June 1926. Crashed due to loss of blade in flight at Worthy Down. The crash was due to Cierva failing to provide a lag hinge to relieve Coriolis loads due to flapping. Amazingly the pilot, Frank Courtney, survived the accident.
575	C.6D	G-EBTW	First two-seat Autogiro – flew 29 July 1926.
586	C.8V	G-EBTX	Modified from Avro 552 G-EAPR, flown Autumn 1926.
587	C.8R	G-EBTW	Derived from C.6D, flew in October 1926 with blade lag hinges.
576	C.9	J8931	Flown in September 1927, powered by a Genet radial. The fuselage design was based on that of the prototype Avian G-EBOV.
611	C.8L Mk I	J8930	Based on an Avro 504N fuselage. Flown in mid-1927.
617	C.8L Mk II	G-EBYY	Ordered for J.G. Weir who financed the Cierva Co. Flown in May 1928, it is notable for its cross-channel flight on 18 September 1928. Two further C.8L (Mk III and IV) were exported, the Mk IV becoming the basis of the American series of Pitcairn designs.
612	C.17	G-AABP	Based on Avian IIIA. Flown 23 October 1928 but underpowered. Second aircraft: G-AAGJ.
620	C.19 Mk I-IV	Production design	New ('clean sheet of paper') design. Total of twenty-nine built, all at Hamble. First aircraft G-AAGK flew in the late summer of 1929. Main production version was the Mk IVP, fifteen being built.

Avro Type	Cierva Type	Serial or Registration	Comments
671	C.30A	Production design	Genuinely successful design, widely licence built for civil and military use. The C.30A was built at Manchester and was derived from the C.19 Mk V G–ABXP via intermediate prototypes as follows: C.30 G–ACFI assembled at Hanworth by National Flying Services; C.30P first of which (G–ACKA) was built at Heston by Airwork Ltd, three others being built by Avro in Manchester. A total of sixty-six Cierva C.30A were built by A.V. Roe & Co. Ltd in Manchester and distributed by Cierva at Hanworth.

In November 1930, the company was advertising thus: 'The World's only Safe Flying Machine. All who drive a car can learn to fly an Autogiro!' Other copy included: 'The Autogiro constitutes the first practical solution to the problem of completely controlled flight. It ensures safety. It cannot stall. It can ascend and descend in a small area.'

With the construction of the C.30A, Cierva Autogiro activity was moved from Hamble to Hanworth in Greater London. Experimental construction of Cierva designs was also undertaken under license by other firms across the British industry, including **Parnall Aircraft Ltd, Westland Aircraft Works, Comper Aircraft Ltd** and **The de Havilland Aircraft Co. Ltd.**

The Fairey Aviation Co. Ltd was associated with Hamble from the formation of the company. Fairey's first contract in 1916 was to build twelve Short 827 seaplanes. These aircraft were constructed at Clayton Road, Hayes, and assembled in a shed provided by the Admiralty at Hamble Point. This shed was situated a short distance from the waterfront, immediately behind the hangar of the Hamble River, Luke & Co. Ltd.

Forty of the fifty Fairey Campania built at Hayes were erected at Hamble, this location being preferred due to the size of the aircraft. The Campania was a large and relatively clean two-bay, single-engine biplane seaplane with folding wings. A total of sixty-two aircraft were built, twelve being constructed by Barclay, Curle & Co. Ltd.

The hull of the N.4 Mk II Titania flying boat N129 was built by Fyffes, a firm of Clyde yacht-builders, and moved by road to Fairey Aviation at Hamble. Here it was united with its superstructure, which was manufactured by Fairey at Hayes, and moved piecemeal to Hamble. After erection, the whole edifice was moved, again by road, to the Isle of Grain for flight testing.

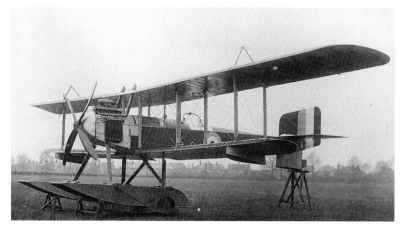

The majority of the fifty Campania seaplanes built by Fairey were erected at Hamble, the two prototypes being first flown at Hamble during 1917. (John W.R. Taylor)

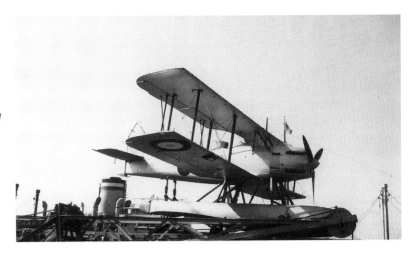

The Seafox naval reconnaissance seaplane was manufactured at Hamble. Two prototypes were followed by sixty-four production aircraft. (John W.R. Taylor)

During the inter-war years, Fairey mainly used Hamble for seaplane testing. The location of the Fairey slipway in the 1920s was at the very tip of the western side of the Hamble River estuary, at its junction with Southampton Water. A number of buildings were in use, these displaying the name FAIREY on their frontages and roofs.

Examples of Fairey types tested at Hamble are given below:

Type	Comments
Campania	Prototype F.16 Campania N1000 was first flown at Hamble on 16 February 1917. F.17 N1001 was flown on 3 June 1917.
Fairey IIIB	N2225, the first production Fairey IIIB seaplane, was first flown at Hamble on 8 August 1918. Fewer than thirty Fairey IIIB were built, the later aircraft in the original production batch being converted to Fairey IIIC.
Fairey IIIC, IIID	Prototypes of the Fairey IIIC and IIID were tested at Hamble. The IIIC was a general purpose seaplane powered by a 375hp Rolls-Royce Eagle. Thirty-six were built, the first aircraft, N2255, flying at Hamble in July 1918. The prototype IIID N9450 was flown at Hamble in seaplane configuration in August 1921. The IIID was flown by both the RAF and the Fleet Air Arm in landplane and seaplane configurations. A total of 227 were built, twenty of which were sold for export to Australia, Netherlands, Portugal and Sweden. The type made a number of notable long distance flights in RAF, Australian and Portuguese service, including an RAF flight from Cairo to the Cape and back.
Flycatcher	Single-seat naval fighter prototype N163 first flown (on wheels) at Hamble aerodrome on 28 November 1922. Second prototype flown on floats on 5 May 1923.
Freemantle	One only, N173, first flown on 28 November 1924. This large single-engine biplane seaplane was powered by a 650hp Rolls-Royce Condor and had a wingspan of 69ft (24ft more than a Swordfish).
Fairey IIIF	Prototype N198 first tested here in floatplane form on 20 April 1926, a month after its first flight.
Seal	The Fairey Seal prototype S1325 was flown at Hamble in seaplane configuration on 29 September 1932.
TSR II Swordfish	The TSR II K4190 was tested at Hamble on floats on 10 November 1936.
Seafox	The Seafox catapult-launched reconnaissance seaplane was produced at Hamble – the first of two prototypes, K4304, was flown on 27 May 1936, followed by K8569, the first of sixty-four production machines, on 23 April 1937.
Albacore	The prototype Albacore L7404 was tested at Hamble in floatplane configuration during 1940.

The Fairey Primer (which was developed from Tipsy M OO-POM) competed unsuccessfully with the Chipmunk for the post-war RAF basic trainer contract. Two Primer aircraft were built at Hamble in 1948 (in the midst of the Firefly aircraft then under repair in the factory). The first of these machines, G-6-4/G-ALBL, was built and flown in only ninety-eight days. The second aircraft was G-6-5/G-ALEW. The advertised design features were as follows: 'Fairey "Primer" designed for training, exceptional handling qualities, rugged construction, lowest cost, minimum maintenance.'

Five Firefly aircraft were converted at Hamble for target tug use by the Indian Navy.

Folland Aircraft Ltd of Sydney Lodge, Hamble, had its origins in **British Marine Aircraft Ltd** which was formed in February 1936 to provide maintenance for Imperial Airways' Empire flying boats, and also to act as agents for Sikorsky Manufacturing Corporation in the UK, including a licence to build their S42A flying boat. The company also took over the interests of the failed British Aircraft Manufacturing Co. Ltd. Henry Folland joined British Marine Aircraft Ltd after his departure from the Gloster Aircraft Co. Ltd.

Sir Ernest Petter sought to amalgamate Westland Aircraft, General Aircraft and British Marine Aircraft in early 1937. This project did not come to fruition, and the company was restructured in May 1937 under the direction of Henry Folland. Following a board meeting on 10 December 1937, the company changed its name to Folland Aircraft Ltd, George Handasyde becoming Production Director.

In 1938 the company was advertising: 'Designers and Manufacturers of Aircraft. What Folland did years ago, people are doing today.' Advertising at the end of the Second World War was in a style very similar to that used by many companies in the First World War: 'Designers and Constructors of Aircraft for all Purposes. Contractors to the Air Ministry.'

Folland Aircraft undertook extensive sub-contract work throughout its existence. During the Second World War this included construction of components for the Blenheim, Beaufort (nose sections), Beaufighter, Buckingham, Buckmaster, Mosquito, Hornet, Sunderland, Wellington and Spitfire. Other items included 5,299 bomb beams and 2,800 engine nacelles for the Wellington and Warwick, and more than 3,500 Spitfire and Seafire ailerons. Large quantities of Wellington engine nacelles and Seafire wings, tails and fuselage components were manufactured. All told, parts were made for no less than sixteen types of aircraft, and the company also operated a Civilian Repair Organisation. Folland operated a number of dispersed facilities during the Second World War, including sites at Eastleigh, Woolston, Exeter, Clevedon, Chipping Norton, Cheltenham and close to Romsey.

Spitfire V EP751 was one of three Spitfire Mk V and one Mk IX converted to seaplane configuration during the Second World War. The conversion of the aircraft was conducted by Folland Aircraft Ltd. (C. Hodson Collection)

Above and right: (Copyright: BAE SYSTEMS plc)

Folland built the floats for the seaplane Spitfire V W3760, which first flew from Hamble on 12 October 1942. Two more aircraft (EP751 and EP754) were converted by Folland, who constructed twelve float sets to allow additional aircraft to be converted. Spitfire LF. Mk IXb MJ892 was also converted. Twelve Folland F.43/37 aircraft were built for use as specialised engine test bed aircraft. For further details see Staverton and Southampton, Eastleigh.

Post-war sub-contract production included components for the Dove (wings), Vickers Viking and all of the flight control surfaces for the Brabazon 1. Bristol Brigand RH748 was fitted with arrester gear by Folland Aircraft, for trials at Farnborough and Filton. The post-war period also brought enforced diversification into a range of products including refrigerators, milk floats, beds, toolboxes, parts for Vincent motorcycles, the almost inevitable aluminium pre-fabricated housing and the aluminium-hulled Terrapin and Trollboat water craft. Other aircraft types for which components were manufactured included the Britannia, Canberra, Chipmunk (wings), Comet, Vampire (wings), Venom, Sea Vampire, Sea Venom and Sea Vixen. Folland Aircraft also constructed the tailplanes of the Hawker Hunter prototype WB188.

W.E.W. 'Teddy' Petter joined Folland from The English Electric Co. Ltd in October 1950, becoming Managing Director on 1 July 1951, taking on the additional role of Chief Engineer from 1954. Petter was responsible for the Midge and Gnat lightweight fighters, to follow his equally innovative and successful English Electric Canberra. His forward-looking approach was reflected in advertising of 1953: 'Follands of Hamble are forging the weapons of the future.' By 1957 the Gnat was a proven success and the advertising ran: 'Folland Gnat Light Jet Fighter – as a modern tactical fighter the GNAT is the right aircraft, for the right job, at the right time.'

The single-seat Midge was developed as a private venture to demonstrate the concept of a small, agile and low-cost fighter. Built at Hamble, the Midge was transported by road to Boscombe Down for its first flight. Owing to its small size, the Midge G-39-1 was conveyed

Above: *Gnat Trainers on the Hamble production line. This photograph emphasises the small size of the airframe and the easy access that this enabled from ground level.* (C. Hodson Collection)

Left: *Members of the workforce look on as the prototype Midge is moved within Folland's Hamble factory.* (C. Hodson Collection)

Opposite: *The Hamble River, Luke & Co. Ltd HL-1 seaplane was displayed at the 1914 Olympia Aero Show.* (C. Hodson Collection)

in one piece (save for the wing tips) and flew for the first time on the same day, 11 August 1954. Despite lack of official support for the type, it was greeted with considerable enthusiasm for its handling when tested at Boscombe Down. As an illustration of cost savings, it was reported that five Gnat aircraft could be built for the man hours required to build a single Hunter or Swift, for one third to one quarter of the cost.

The Folland Gnat was the production variant of the Midge. The first Gnat F.1 G-39-2 was flown at Boscombe Down on 18 July 1955. As a single-seat fighter, it was exported to Finland (thirteen), Yugoslavia (two) and India (twenty-five aircraft and twenty sets of components). A further 195 were subsequently produced under licence by Hindustan Aeronautics Ltd (HAL) at Bangalore, India. Two Gnat aircraft built by HAL were modified to become prototypes for the further developed Ajeet (the first flying on 6 March 1975). A further seventy-nine production Ajeet followed, the type remaining in service until 25 March 1991. (Other figures can also be found.)

After evaluation of six single-seat Gnat F.1, the type was ordered into production for the RAF in two-seat trainer form. The prototype Gnat T.1 XM691 was flown for the first time on 31 August 1959 and 105 Gnat T.1 were built for the RAF. Folland Aircraft Ltd was taken over by **Hawker Siddeley Aviation** in September 1959. Midge/Gnat test-flying was initially conducted at Chilbolton, with Gnat T.1 test-flying subsequently moving, under Hawker Siddeley, to Dunsfold. Production Gnat T.1 aircraft were transported from Hamble to Dunsfold by road to enter the flight test programme.

Hamble River, Luke & Co., yacht builders and engineers, erected two Farman hydro-biplanes for B.C. Hucks, in June 1912. At this time Hucks was trading as Frank Hucks Waterplane Co. Ltd, the company later amalgamating with the Eastbourne Aviation Co.

Hamble River, Luke & Co. advertised themselves as 'Manufacturer of seaplanes' and produced a large pusher design, the HL1, for the 1914 Olympia Aero Show. This aircraft was designed by Mr F. Murphy, previously of The British & Colonial Aeroplane Co. Ltd, and *The Aeroplane* reported that 'it strikes one at once as being undoubtedly for use, and not for ornament'. This aircraft was test flown by E.C. Gordon England. Hamble River, Luke & Co. had a notable telephone number and telegraphic address – Telephone: No.1 Hamble, Telegrams: 'Engineering', Hamble.

In July 1914, the Hamble River, Luke & Co. Hydro-Aeroplane Station was advertised for sale. The station covered 8¼ acres and included a slipway, two 70ft by 80ft sheds, one 55ft by 44ft shed, and other items and facilities. The buildings and machinery were subsequently auctioned off at the beginning of June 1915.

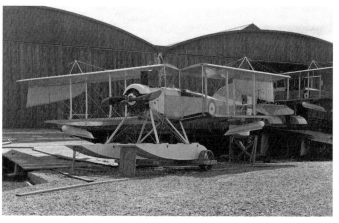

Above: *This evocative photograph shows Short 166 floatplanes built by Westland Aircraft Works whist under test at Hamble. The main subject of the photograph is 9751, the first Short 166 to be built by Westland.* (Westland)

Left: (Copyright: BAE SYSTEMS plc)

Hawker Siddeley Aviation Ltd took over the Folland factory, which subsequently passed into British Aerospace (see above). Under Hawker Siddeley, the factory completed Gnat T.1 production before transferring to airframe components for a number of types including Harrier (front and rear fuselage, and tail surfaces for the GR.1 and T.2); Trident wings and tailplanes; Avro 748 wings; canopies for the Harrier T.2 and Hawk; and Airbus A300 and A310 sub-assemblies.

H.J. 'Bert' Hinkler, test pilot for A.V. Roe & Co. Ltd at Hamble, designed and built a light aircraft, the Hinkler Ibis, in 1929. The sole example (registered G-AAIS, but flown un-marked) was first flown in May 1930 and was powered by two Salmson radial engines mounted in a tractor/pusher arrangement over the wing centre section. A side-by-side two-seat cockpit was positioned forward of the wing leading edge, the wing being situated on top of the boat-like fuselage. Mr Hinkler formed a company, **Ibis Aircraft Co.** – with offices at his home address in Sholing, Southampton – to build the prototype, and the wing was designed by Basil Henderson and built by **Hendy** at Shoreham.

Liberty Aircraft plc, of Kings Avenue, Hamble-le-Rice, announced in mid-2000 the Liberty XL-2 two-seat light aircraft. The XL-2 visually closely resembles a Europa with a fixed tricycle undercarriage. Indeed, members of the Europa team formed Liberty Aircraft plc in 1997, specifically to develop the XL-2.

Unlike the all-composite Europa, the XL-2 is of mixed construction with a composite fuselage, steel rolling chassis carrying the undercarriage loads, and aluminium wing and flight control surfaces. Power for the prototype is provided by a 100hp Rotax 912S, providing an estimated cruise speed of 120kt and a range of 500nm. Production aircraft for the US market will be powered by the 125hp Teledyne Continental 10F-240. The Rotax-powered version is now designated XL-2R.

The initial press release showed an aircraft (believed to be the company's 'static demonstrator') carrying the marking G-LBTY. The first flight of the XL-2 prototype, N202XL, took place on 2 April 2001. Aircraft are to be built by STW Composites Inc., also of Montrose, Colorado, and the programme now appears to be focused primarily on the US general aviation market.

Two **Royal Aircraft Factory** CE1 (Coastal Experimental) Flying Boats were built at Farnborough and tested at Hamble, the first, N97, flying in January 1918.

Simmonds Aircraft Ltd: This company was established in September 1928 and built the Simmonds Spartan biplane in a factory at Weston Shore just to the north of Hamble. The company's founder was Mr Oliver E. Simmonds, who left Supermarine in mid-1928 to set up the firm. (Oliver Simmonds was also Chairman of the Hampshire Aero Club.)

The prototype Simmonds Spartan two-seat biplane, G-EBYU, flew in mid-1928, competing in the King's Cup Air Race in July of that year. This first aircraft was constructed by Mr Simmonds at his own home at 65 Portsmouth Road, Woolston, and assembled at the Rolling Mills in Archers Road, Southampton. Production aircraft were moved by road to the airfield at Hamble for test-flying.

A feature of the Simmonds Spartan was the use of physically interchangeable aerodynamic surfaces of symmetrical section. Thus the four half wings, their ailerons, the rudder and elevators, and the fin and each half tailplane were interchangeable with their counterparts to ease production. Even the two halves of the split-axle undercarriage could be fitted to either side of the aircraft.

The aircraft was built in both two-seat and three-seat configurations, the latter having an elongated front cockpit opening. A Cirrus III engine powered the prototype, and production aircraft used a range of engines, including the Hermes I, Hermes II, Gipsy I and Gipsy II. At least forty-nine Simmonds Spartan were constructed, a creditable number in the face of competition from the de Havilland Moth, Avro Avian and Blackburn Bluebird.

Following the acquisition of a controlling interest by Whitehall Securities Corporation, the company was renamed **Spartan Aircraft Ltd**, being registered as such in April 1930 with a share capital of £110,000, 'acquiring the issued share capital of the Simmonds Interchangeable Wing Co. Ltd, and the whole undertaking and assets (including the trademark "Spartan") of Simmonds Aircraft Ltd.' Spartan Aircraft Ltd moved from Weston Shore to East Cowes in February 1931, making use of Somerton Aerodrome. For further details, see East Cowes, Isle of Wight.

The Sopwith Aviation Co. Ltd tested some floatplanes at Hamble, including the initial (unsuccessful) test of the modified Sopwith 'Schneider' Tabloid on a single central float in 1914. Sopwith Greek Navy pusher seaplanes are also reported to have been under test from Hamble in early March 1914. Eight of these aircraft were subsequently diverted to the RNAS as the Type 880.

The Sopwith Bat Boat was flown to success in the Mortimer Singer prize on 8 July 1913, operating from the Portsmouth side of the Hamble River.

The Supermarine Aviation Works Ltd: The Supermarine Sparrow built for the 1924 Lympne competition was first flown at Hamble on 11 September 1924, piloted by Henri Biard. The sole example of the Sparrow, G-EBJP, was initially flown as a biplane, being later converted to parasol monoplane configuration as the Sparrow II. The Sparrow was powered by a Blackburn Thrush engine, and suffered no less than nineteen engine failures in two weeks! In 1927, the Bristol Cherub-powered Sparrow II was used for trials with different wing sections, flying from RAF Worthy Down, and remained active until 1933.

The Supermarine Aviation Works (Vickers) Ltd also used Hamble for the flight testing of the Vickers Viastra. Five Vickers Viastra were constructed at Woolston and taken by barge to Hamble. The first aircraft, G-AAUB, was flown on 1 October 1930, the last in April 1933.

Westland Aircraft Works (Branch of Petters Ltd): Short 166 and Short 184 aircraft built by Petters were flight tested at Hamble by Ronald Kemp and/or Sydney Pickles on behalf of Short Brothers.

The immaculate Kittiwake G-BBRN displays its naval ancestry as XW784. (Author)

Aquila Airways were based at Hamble and operated Shorts flying boats, which were mainly taken over from the BOAC fleet. Aquila also acquired Sunderland V PP162 for conversion to Hythe standard as G-ANAK, and the Seaford prototype NJ201/G-AGWU for conversion to Solent 3 G-ANAJ. These modifications were carried out at Hamble in 1953. The company operated twelve Hythe and one Solent, and used the telegraphic address 'Boating, Hamble'. Maintenance services were provided to Aquila by AST Ltd.

Hamble airfield was closed following the closure in 1984 of the College of Air Training and the site was sold to developers. Much of the Hamble site has now been given over to housing and, as with many other such locations, an acknowledgement of the site's past heritage has been made in the selection of appropriate street names; these include Aquila, Ensign, Spitfire, Pegasus and Tutor.

King's Somborne

John Fairey's Flycatcher Replica G-BEYB/S1287 was completed by John Hall and Maurice Gilbank on John Fairey's estate at King's Somborne, and first flew in July 1979. Construction had been started by Robinson Aircraft at Blackbushe, Hants. See also Lands End, Cornwall.

Lasham

Air Tows Ltd: The Beagle-Auster Terrier sprang from a less refined glider-towing aircraft, the Auster 6A or Tugmaster. F. Horridge/Air Tows Ltd of Lasham initially developed the Tugmaster conversion in August 1960, the prototype flying as G-25-9/G-ARCY. Air Tows continued to carry out a number of additional Auster 6A and Terrier conversions, G-ATHU being an example of the latter.

General Aircraft Ltd, based at Hanworth, used Lasham as a test centre from late 1946; among other types, Hamilcar gliders were tested here. Many Hamilcar were constructed by a production group managed by the furniture manufacturers **Harris Lebus** of Tottenham; the companies involved including **Birmingham Carriage and Wagon Works, The Co-operative Society, A.C. Cars, Peerless Furniture** and others. A similar consortium including **Harris Lebus, Wm Lawrence & Co.** and **Waring & Gillow**, constructed some 600 General Aircraft Hotspur.

The prototypes of the twin-engine Hamilcar X, LA704 and LA728, were built at Feltham, and LA704 was moved by road to Lasham for assembly and first flight in February 1945. Like many such episodes, the journey was marked by a familiar saga of trees being cut down and traffic lights being negotiated.

The GAL 56 experimental tailless gliders were tested at Lasham during 1947 and 1948. The aircraft identities were GAL 56/01 TS507, GAL 56/03 TS513B and GAL 56/04 TS510D. These gliders featured wings with different sweep angles and were used to investigate low-speed aerodynamics, stability and control of swept wing tailless configurations. The experiments came to a tragic end with the crash of TS507 on 12 February 1948, in which the great sailplane pioneer Robert Kronfeld lost his life.

GAL conversions of the de Havilland Mosquito to TT39 configuration were test flown from Lasham.

Mitchell-Procter Aircraft Ltd: The Mitchell-Procter Kittiwake I was flown at Lasham, having been designed from the outset as a single-seat glider tug. Two aircraft were built, the first, G-ATXN, flying on 23 May 1967. The design gave rise to a number of derivatives, including the Kittiwake II (see Blackbushe) and the Procter (later Nash) Petrel. The twenty-six-year-old Kittiwake I G-BBRN (which was first flown at Lee on Solent on 21 October 1971 as XW784) was flying from Henstridge in 1997 and was at that time in immaculate condition. The company name was subsequently changed to **Procter Aircraft Associates**.

Southdown Aerostructures Ltd built a small number of composite construction microlights known as the Pipistrelle. The Pipistrelle was of high-wing pusher configuration with butterfly tail surfaces. By 1994 G-MNPI, a Pipistrelle 2C, was believed to be the last of its type still flying. In 2002, **Southdown Aero Services Ltd** were advertising their capabilities as follows: 'Rebuilding, repairing gliders and light aircraft for over fifty years. – Aircraft worked on include Tiger Moth – Moth Minor – Rapide – SE5 Replica – Pfalz Replica – Turbulent – Jodel D9 – 120 – 140 – Condor – Slingsby Firefly – J3 Cub – RF3, 4 & 5 – Steen Skybolt – Quickie – LongEze – VariEze – Europa. Be it composite, wood, steel tube and fabric – WE CAN REPAIR OR REBUILD IT!'

Marwell (near Winchester)

Cunliffe-Owen Aircraft Ltd set up a satellite airfield in Marwell Park (now Marwell Zoo), Marwell Hall being owned by Mr R. Hayes, the Managing Director of Cunliffe-Owen. The location was chosen because it lay to the north of the Southampton balloon zone, which considerably hampered operations at Eastleigh. Two or three fields were joined together to make a landing strip, which was crossed by a road and bordered for the most part by trees. Aircraft were distributed around the edge of the field, there being twenty hangars dispersed among the surrounding woods, each able to house four Spitfires. Initial operations were of Spitfires and Blenheims, then Tomahawks, Bostons, Hudsons, Airacobras and Halifax. Halifax aircraft were modified at Marwell to take the H2S surface mapping radar. The strip was rather narrow for a Halifax, and rather short for an Airacobra. The peak of activity was in 1943 with Seafires, Venturas and Liberators (!).

Flying ceased from this site when the risk of bombing declined in 1944. Marwell was by intent difficult to find from the air, the only real clue being a small pond (Fisher's Pond) near the west end of the strip. There were often problems with turbulence due to the nearby trees, particularly in cross-wind conditions.

Middle Wallop Airfield

Somerton Rayner: Capt. Mike Somerton Rayner modified a number of Auster aircraft to non-standard configurations. The most notable example was the Auster 9M G-AVHT (previously WZ711) which was re-engined with a 180hp Lycoming O-360-A1D and cleaned up aerodynamically. The Auster 9M was first flown on 4 January 1968. A less highly modified example of Capt. Somerton Rayner's work was Auster 5/150 G-ALXZ, modified in 1966 with a 150hp Lycoming O-320-A2B.

Portsmouth

Portsmouth Municipal Airport was opened on 2 June 1932, and was active for just over forty years, the last aircraft to land at Portsmouth doing so on the last day of 1973. The airfield is now a housing and industrial estate.

Airspeed Ltd moved to Portsmouth from York during 1933, whilst the first Airspeed Courier was under construction. The company was renamed **Airspeed (1934) Ltd** in August 1934 when Swan Hunter and Wigham Richardson became associated with Airspeed Ltd. In May 1940, **The de Havilland Aircraft Co. Ltd** acquired Swan Hunter and Wigham Richardson's shares and on 1 January 1944 the company name reverted to **Airspeed Ltd.**

The first type to be built at Portsmouth was the six-seat Courier low-wing monoplane, the prototype G-ABXN flying for the first time on 10 April 1933. The type was the first British design to be fitted with flaps and an undercarriage which retracted into the wings. Sixteen were built.

The next Airspeed design was the twin-engine Envoy. The first Envoy, G-ACMT, flew at Portsmouth on 26 June 1934; a total of eighty-two were built. The type was advertised in February 1936 as 'The Fastest Machine on the Dawn Service'. The subsidiary text continues: 'With the newspapers the Envoy has done Paris-Croydon (205 miles) in 68 minutes, in a following wind, and two weeks ago the one with metal airscrews did Hatfield-Newcastle in 1hr 40min. The Airspeed Envoy is fast and thoroughly reliable.'

In September 1936 the success of the type was becoming apparent, and this added an air of authority to the advertising: 'Airspeed Envoy – Amongst the countries to which exports have been made recently are: South Africa, India, Australia, Czechoslovakia, Japan. Envoy aircraft are being manufactured at the Airspeed factory at Portsmouth for delivery at 7-8 weeks from

Airspeed's Portsmouth factory and its confined grass airfield are well shown in this aerial view. The airport area has now been developed for housing, having been active as an airfield from 1932 until 1973. (BAE SYSTEMS plc)

The Auster 9M was a refined version of the Auster AOP9, produced by Mike Somerton-Rayner at Middle Wallop. (Author)

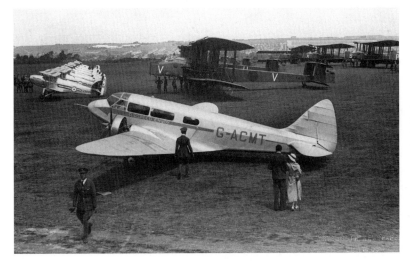

Envoy prototype G-ACMT shows off its strikingly modern lines at Portsmouth Airport. Eighty-two were built, but the type's real significance was as the progenitor of the Oxford navigation trainer. (Ken Ellis Collection)

The Oxford was Airspeed's most important product and a total of 8751 were built. PH318 was built by Airspeed Ltd at Portsmouth. It is seen here after a mishap at Exeter. (H.E. North)

the receipt of order of one aircraft, and then one machine each week until completion of order. In order to keep abreast of the increasing demand for the Airspeed Envoy it has been necessary to greatly enlarge the factory.'

The Envoy was developed into the Oxford, which was used for pilot, navigation and radio operator training, and brought large-scale production success to Airspeed Ltd. The prototype L4534 flew from Portsmouth for the first time on 19 June 1937 and the type remained in RAF service until 1954. Ultimately 8,751 were built, 4,411 at Portsmouth and 550 at Christchurch, supplemented by production by de Havilland (1,515 at Hatfield), Percival (1,525 at Luton) and Standard Motors (750).

Airspeed built seven examples of the Queen Wasp, an attractive Cheetah-powered cabin biplane intended for use as a target. The Queen Wasp prototype K8887 was first flown on 11 June 1937. In early 1939, Bulldog K3183 was used for the testing of the new Alvis Leonides engine, the tests being undertaken by Airspeed Ltd.

The Aeroplane Spotter of 11 January 1945 reported that, at the 1945 AGM of Airspeed Ltd, Mr Alan Butler had reviewed Airspeed's war effort. Besides building the Horsa and Oxford, modifications were carried out on C-47s for the RAF, and large numbers of Spitfires had been converted into Seafires, together with the manufacture of a quantity of Mosquito (comprising 300 FB VI and 122 B35). The reference to the C-47 reflects the fact that Airspeed acted as sister design authority for the type in the UK. The reference to Seafire conversions is at odds with most references, which do not ascribe any responsibility for this activity to Airspeed Ltd.

Mr Butler gave further details at the 1946 Ordinary General Meeting (reported in *The Aeroplane*, 8 February 1946). These included the statements that the peak production rate of the Oxford was seventy-five per month in the spring of 1942. A total of 3,655 Horsa assault gliders were built, 695 of these at Christchurch.

Perhaps, however, a veil should be drawn over the unlovely AS39 Fleet Shadower. This aircraft was designed, together with its competitor, the General Aircraft GAL 38, to a specialised requirement which sought six hours endurance, low stalling speed and shipboard operation – more or less a 1940s equivalent of the EH101. With its high wing, four Pobjoy engines and a carrot-shaped fuselage terminating in an empennage with three tiny fins and rudders, the AS39 was not a thing of beauty. Folding wings and a bay window in the nose added their own character to this extraordinary device. The prototype N1323, mercifully the only one built, flew at Portsmouth on 17 October 1940.

Another unsuccessful product was the Airspeed AS45 Cambridge trainer, which first flew in February 1941 (T2449); only two were built.

The Consul was a civil conversion of the Oxford, the prototype G-AGVY (previously V3679) flying in March 1946. Airspeed Ltd carried out 161 conversions at Portsmouth and Christchurch, and forty-six other Oxford aircraft were also registered for civil use. Some Consul aircraft were supplied to the Government of Burma for military use, and one aircraft was used for the flight test of Alvis Leonides engines.

Airspeed Division of The de Havilland Aircraft Co. Ltd: From 1951, following reorganisation, Airspeed Ltd traded under its new parent's name.

The **Hampshire Aircraft Co. Ltd** of Southsea was registered in November 1916, but nothing else is known of this firm.

Hants & Sussex Aviation Ltd built a single-seat monoplane, the Hants & Sussex Herald, in 1953. The aircraft was registered G-ALYA and it was powered by a JAP engine. The Herald was abandoned in 1954 due to its wholly inadequate performance.

Hants & Sussex Aviation built three Antoinette replicas for the film *Those Magnificent Men in their Flying Machines*, two of which were flown. These aircraft were built initially with

The Portsmouth Aerocar offered 'airline comfort for the first time in a small twin'. Only the single prototype G-AGTG was flown, and plans to build the type in India came to nothing. (Portsmouth Aviation via Ken Ellis)

wing warping for lateral control, as was the original design. This was quickly abandoned in favour of ailerons as a result of concern over the aircraft's handling and structural safety. A final Hants & Sussex project was the installation in 1966 of a 116shp Rover 1S/90 gas turbine in de Havilland Chipmunk G-ATTS.

Portsmouth Aviation Ltd was initially registered in 1932 under the name of the Portsmouth, Southsea & Isle of Wight Aviation Co., flying air services from Portsmouth. The firm, which changed its name to Portsmouth Aviation in 1943, repaired and flight tested around 5,000 aircraft during the Second World War. These included the Airspeed Horsa glider, the Oxford navigation trainer and a number of other training types.

Whilst most reference sources omit Portsmouth Aviation's activity in support of the Oxford, the fact that they played a role of some significance is at least suggested by the presence of a photograph in the company's present boardroom captioned: 'The Last Oxford, October 1946', with company personnel standing in front of the aircraft. See also Christchurch.

The company's own product, the Portsmouth Aerocar, was a twin-engine high-wing monoplane with twin tail booms, fins and rudders. The Major and Minor variants were intended to be powered by Cirrus Major and Cirrus Minor engines respectively. The following two advertisements from 1946 sum up the aims of the design:

Aerocar: Airline comfort for the first time in a small twin – VP propellers – retracting pneumatic tricycle undercarriage – excellent visibility – easy access – full utility – high cruising speed – low operating costs.

Special features: 3 models, each seating in comfort five to six persons. The Major and Minor with full equipment for serious day and night flying – the Junior with simplified equipment to minimise initial cost and permit increased payload, for flying by day at the lowest possible cost. Good single-engine performance. Steerable tricycle undercarriage which simplifies landings and makes ground handling as easy as driving an automobile. Variable pitch and feathering airscrews giving high cruising speed for low power, enhanced take-off climb, and minimum fuel consumption with resultant increased range. Engineered streamlined comfort – deluxe seating – air conditioning – super sound proofing – perfect all-round pilot and passenger view. Automobile-type access by 4 separate doors – 9 inches from ground-floor level – opening rear end to cabin for admission of stretchers and bulky freight. Minimum maintenance costs, one hour powerplant change, backed by efficient round-the-clock spares service.

The two prototypes were registered G-AGNJ and G-AGTG, but only the latter flew (and it is reported to have been significantly overweight). Capt. F.L. Longmore first flew G-AGTG, powered by two 155hp Cirrus Major engines, on 18 June 1947.

The company announced in 1947 that they had negotiated an agreement for the aircraft to be produced in India, with works and plant planned for Port Sika. There are also consistent rumours among company employees that two aircraft were shipped, crated up in component form, to India for local production, which was planned to be at Jamnagar. One of these airframes may have been the unassembled Aerocar Minor, G-AGNJ.

Portsmouth Aviation manufactured an experimental nose section that was grafted on to Lincoln RF533 during 1952 for radar gun sight and other experiments. The company continues to trade from the same site, conducting specialist machining and fabrication operations, and producing a range of defence equipment including weapon handling devices, practice bombs, the Paveway III laser-guided bomb, and transportation and packaging equipment for its products.

Southampton Area

The various factories of **Vickers–Armstrongs Ltd (Aircraft Section) (Supermarine Works)**, and its predecessors, dominate aircraft construction in the Southampton area. The Supermarine activity is supplemented by a varied collection of enterprises at Southampton Airport, Eastleigh.

Southampton Area – City of Southampton, Docks and Southampton Water

BOAC operated twenty-five Sunderland III and converted eighteen to civil standards with passenger interiors as the Hythe class; four additional aircraft were converted by Short & Harland at Belfast. The first of type was G-AGJM, *Hythe*. A BOAC flying boat terminal was operated from Pier 50 in Southampton Docks, this being opened on 14 April 1948. (This terminal replaced facilities at Berth 108, used from 1938, and a pontoon terminal at Berth 101, used for the South African services of Imperial Airways from 29 June 1937.) The last flying boat service from Southampton Docks was flown on 2 September 1958.

May, Harden & May was a subsidiary of the Aircraft Manufacturing Co. (AIRCO), and was established during the First World War to manufacture flying boats and their hulls. The company had works on Southampton Water at The Seaplane Base, Hythe, which were said (in an article published in 1928) to be 'just where the Power Boat Co. now is at Hythe'. The site is reported to have been on Shore Road at grid reference SU429077. The company also had works at Kingston Bridge Boathouse, Hampton Wick. During the First World War the company built hulls for a number of flying boats, including eighty Felixstowe F.2A and Felixstowe F.5 (from N4480) erected by AIRCO, two Phoenix Cork, and hulls for twenty-one Porte Baby. May, Harden & May also built the hull for the N.4 Mk I Atlanta flying boat.

In the inter-war years, the company built the wooden floats initially used by the Gloster III Schneider racer. The May, Harden & May sheds were taken over by Supermarine in 1927 to provide expanded production capacity for the Supermarine Southampton flying boat.

Moonbeams Ltd of Moonbeam Works, Wool House, Royal Pier Gate, Southampton, carried out modifications to Patrick Hamilton's Deperdussin two-seater in 1912, including structural strengthening and duplication of flying wires. This aircraft was flown from Beaulieu. The Moonbeam Works was the factory of E.R. Moon of The Wool House, Southampton, who styled himself as 'Hampshire's first aircraft manufacturer'. The Moon

Moonbeam monoplane was flown from Eastleigh in 1910. The **Canute Airplane Co.**, of Royal Pier Gate, Southampton took over the works of **Moonbeams Ltd** in October 1916. The company advertised its ability to supply 'Seaplanes, land machines, fittings and engine parts.'

The **Sopwith** Schneider floatplane was flown for the first time from Hythe on Southampton Water on 10 September 1919. In the event, fog prevented the successful completion of the event, and the 1919 race was declared null and void.

Vickers-Armstrongs Ltd: The Supermarine Seagull was a spectacular amphibian erected at Woolston and first flown (in the shape of PA143) from Southampton Water on 14 July 1948. Notable features were the complexities of the variable incidence folding wing with its full-span flap system, and the centre section-mounted Griffon engine driving a six-blade contra-rotating propeller immediately to the rear of the cockpit. This aircraft was, in effect, a Sea Otter writ large. Only two aircraft were built, the second being PA147. This aircraft set a 100km speed record for its class of 241.88mph on 22 July 1950.

Southampton Area – Eastleigh (Southampton Airport)

During the First World War, Eastleigh operated as an Aircraft Acceptance Park.

British Burnelli: The Cunliffe-Owen OA-1 (see below) was a British design based on the concept of the American UB14 'lifting fuselage' design. Licence building of the UB14 was initially proposed in July 1936 by **Scottish Aircraft & Engineering Ltd**, with the civil variant of the aircraft to be called the Clyde Clipper. Although this company was based in London, its unsuccessful efforts to launch a British version of the Burnelli design are described here because of its close linkage to the later efforts of Cunliffe-Owen at Eastleigh.

In September 1936, the company was advertising a military version: 'British Burnelli Bomber Transport – Lifting fuselage. Performance with Rolls-Royce Kestrel XVI 245mph maximum speed and 15,000lb all up weight. Delivery 6 months, ex-works. Scottish Aircraft & Engineering Co. Ltd, Shell-Mex House, Strand WC2, and Scotia Works, NW10.'

For the Clyde Clipper itself, a more expansive style was adopted:

Evolution of the Lifting fuselage – A lifting fuselage is better than a subsidy. British Clyde Clipper advantages:
- *Accessible multiple engine compartment allowing inspection and minor repairs in flight.*
- *Reduced turning movement on one engine.*
- *Increased capacity of fuselage.*
- *Superior safety in operation. Protection afforded by engines and propellers being well forward of pilots and passenger cabin.*
- *Extensive reduction of head resistance.*
- *Fuselage lift reduces landing speed.*
- *Practical landing gear retraction.*
- *Structural efficiency and simplicity (loads of engines, propellers and landing gear are not imposed on wing structure).*

Scottish Aircraft & Engineering Ltd failed to get the UB-14, or any of its proposed projects, into production and receivers were appointed on 26 July 1937. The Burnelli concept was, however, then taken up by Cunliffe-Owen Aircraft Ltd (see below).

The Cierva Autogiro Co. Ltd. 'Pioneers of Rotating Wing Aircraft'. By the end of the Second World War, the Cierva company had turned its attention to helicopters with the unconventional W-9 (with its ducted jet torque compensation) and the triple rotor, Merlin-powered W-11 Air Horse. The W-9 PX203 was built as a joint effort with G. & J. Weir Ltd and flew at Henley, possibly in early 1945.

The W-11 Air Horse VZ724/G-ALCV was the largest helicopter in existence when it first flew at Eastleigh on 8 December 1948. H.A. Marsh's log book indicates that there were three flights that day totalling 50 minutes and one of 20 minutes on 17 December (information provided by Elfan Ap Rees). The Air Horse was destroyed in a fatal accident on 13 June 1950. Testing of the second prototype, WA555, was limited to tethered hover trials and a flight of 1 hour on 23 March 1950. Four Cierva C.30A Autogiro were also re-furbished at Eastleigh by Cierva in the spring of 1946.

The company's more conventional project, the diminutive W-14 Skeeter G-AJCJ first flew on 10 October 1948, and was subsequently developed and produced by **Saunders-Roe Ltd**, who took control of the Cierva company in January 1951.

The triple-rotor W-11 Air Horse was the largest design to be built by The Cierva Autogiro Co Ltd. Unfortunately, it was destroyed in a fatal accident in 1950. (Ken Ellis Collection)

A busy scene in the Cierva works at Eastleigh, probably in early 1950. Both Air Horse helicopters, two Skeeter prototypes, three incomplete Skeeter airframes and a C.30A Autogiro can be seen. (Ken Ellis Collection)

Cunliffe-Owen Aircraft Ltd was formed in 1935 and was initially involved in the project to build a version of the Burnelli UB14 lifting fuselage transport (see above). Cunliffe-Owen stepped in after the failure of the Clyde Clipper, and built a single example of a wholly new variant, the OA-1, G-AFMB, which first flew from Eastleigh in January 1939.

The mayor of Southampton opened a new factory for Cunliffe-Owen Aircraft Ltd at Eastleigh on 23 January 1939. During the Second World War the company designed, built or repaired over 6,000 aircraft 'from the lightest two-seater to the heaviest bomber'. Cunliffe-Owen built some 554 Seafire (Mark III (350), XV (184), and XVII (twenty)) and specialised in repairs and modifications to US aircraft. Types worked on by Cunliffe-Owen included the Tomahawk, Kittyhawk, Hudson, Ventura, Boston, Havoc, Baltimore, Marauder, Blenheim and Walrus. A range of other types – Liberator, Halifax, Airacobra, etc. – were modified at Marwell Park, which was the estate of Marwell Hall, owned by Mr R. Hayes, managing director of Cunliffe-Owen (see Marwell for further details).

Peter Weston (who worked at Cunliffe-Owen, and whose brother-in-law was manager of the experimental hangar at Eastleigh) describes the operation thus: 'The experimental department evaluated American Lend-Lease aircraft, and designed modifications to conform to RAF requirements. The aircraft concerned were mainly the Hudson, Ventura, Baltimore and Marauder. The Airacobras were delivered to us from Southampton Docks in large wooden containers and lined up in the flight shed for assembly alongside Hudsons and Tomahawks. The Havocs and Bostons flew in direct from the squadrons, only a few of each, for quick modifications to certain parts.' (Private communication to author.)

The development of a lifeboat that was suitable for dropping from the air, designed by the yachtsman Uffa Fox, was assisted by trials on a Hudson Mk III, Cunliffe-Owen developing the necessary modifications. In July 1946, a number of Avro Lancaster III aircraft were modified at Eastleigh to ASR. Mk 3 configuration, carrying airborne lifeboats. The author has not been able to ascertain the company responsible for this work, which was probably carried out by Cunliffe-Owen in the light of their role in the development of the air-droppable lifeboat.

After the Second World War, Cunliffe-Owen attempted to enter the civil aircraft market with a twin-engine passenger aircraft of their own design called the Concordia. The Concordia featured a tricycle undercarriage and was powered by two Alvis Leonides LE4M nine-cylinder radial engines of 500hp. Two examples were built, the prototype Y-0222 which was first flown on 19 May 1947, and G-AKBE.

The objectives of the design are indicated by the contemporary advertising:

Filling a vital gap ... The Cunliffe-Owen Concordia – now in production – fills that vital gap between the high capacity long distance airliner and the small feeder-type aircraft. Its 10-12 passenger capacity (with adequate luggage allowance) makes it the right aircraft for shorter and medium-distance hauls up to 1,000 miles, where the large aircraft would be unprofitable and the smaller aircraft offers insufficient passenger accommodation to meet traffic requirements. The CONCORDIA gives passenger comfort and luxury equal to that of the largest airliners – and incidentally smoking is permitted. Operating either as a wholly passenger or part passenger-freight, or in its full freighter version, the CONCORDIA will prove a dividend paying proposition to operators on scheduled routes, charter services, or cargo lines.

Construction of a production batch of six aircraft was begun, but the end of the Concordia project came with the following announcement, made in May 1948:

By order of The Cunliffe-Owen Aircraft Ltd: Offer for sale by tender, as a whole or in lots, the aircraft and component parts, jigs, drawings and patterns lying at Eastleigh, and including 'Concordia' prototype and production aircraft, fuselage shells, engines, drawings, prints and technical data, partly completed aircraft and components, jigs, tools, and templates, castings, forgings and consumable stores. Tenders by 12 noon, 29 May 1948.

Undoubtedly the Concordia could not compete with war surplus DC-3 aircraft.

One of last aviation projects undertaken by Cunliffe-Owen was the construction of the second prototype Cierva Air Horse WA555/G-ALCW, which was delivered to store after the crash of the prototype G-ALCV. Cunliffe-Owen pulled out of aviation-related activities early in 1948, with the plant being purchased by The Ford Motor Co. Ltd and subsequently used for Transit Van production.

R.H. Eggleton of Eastleigh designed and built a very practical glider of Caudron configuration, but with increased wing span. Over 100 flights were made, the majority being towed. This design was Eggleton's third glider and it was flying successfully during 1913.

Folland Aircraft Ltd assembled the first two of the F.43/37 specialist engine test bed aircraft (P1774 and P1775) at Eastleigh. The fuselages of these aircraft were built in Cheltenham, with the wings being sub-contracted to **Oddie, Bradbury & Cull** (see below). The factory continued to be used by Folland after the Second World War, and was used for the manufacture of single-seat Gnat forward fuselages.

The Cunliffe-Owen team stand proudly in front of the brand-new Concordia. (Via R. Davidson)

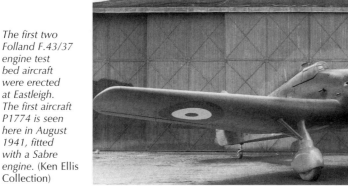

The first two Folland F.43/37 engine test bed aircraft were erected at Eastleigh. The first aircraft P1774 is seen here in August 1941, fitted with a Sabre engine. (Ken Ellis Collection)

The Roe triplane IV was the last of A.V. Roe's triplane developments before his adoption of the tractor biplane configuration. This replica was built by The Hampshire Aero Club at Eastleigh. (Author)

Foster Wikner Aircraft Co. Ltd: The Foster Wikner Wicko single-engine, high-wing light aircraft was initially built in Bow Common, London and flown (G-AENU) at Stapleford Tawney, Essex in September 1936. A total of eleven airframes were completed, of which ten were flown; eight of these were impressed for wartime communications duties. G.N. Wikner, the designer, was the cousin of Capt. Edgar Percival. The company moved its operations to Eastleigh from London/Stapleford during 1937, the first aircraft to be built here being G-AEZZ.

The **Hampshire Aero Club** built two Currie Wot aircraft, G-APNT and G-APWT, which were flown in various exotic configurations as follows: with floats (Wet Wot), gas turbine power (Whiz Wot) and Walter Mikron-powered (Hot Wot). The Currie Wot design was revived in 1958 whilst its original designer J.R. Currie was working as chief engineer for the Hampshire Aero Club at Eastleigh. The first of these aircraft, G-APNT, was flown on 11 September 1958, G-APWT following on 20 October 1959. The emergence of these two aircraft was followed by a revival of the type in the hands of home-builders all over the UK. John Currie was also Chief Engineer of the Wiltshire School of Flying and was much involved in the development of the Thruxton Jackaroo.

The Hampshire Aero Club also constructed three Avro Triplane replicas for *Those Magnificent Men in their Flying Machines*, the first flying on 9 May 1964. A further film replica built at Eastleigh in 1965 was the Pfalz D.III replica G-ATIJ/EI-ARD for the film *The Blue Max*.

The Currie Wot was developed by John Isaacs into the Isaacs Fury, which has become a popular home-built aircraft. (Author)

The Kay Gyroplane is seen here undergoing trials at Eastleigh. (Via Author)

John Isaacs, a Hampshire Aero Club member, designed the very successful Isaacs Fury as a development of the Currie Wot. By 1988, eighteen Fury aircraft were flying world-wide (UK, Canada, US, New Zealand). The prototype G-ASCM and the later Isaacs Spitfire scale replica G-BBJI were both built in Southampton, and both were first flown from Thruxton. G-ASCM first flew on 30 August 1963; G-BBJI flying in May 1975.

Kay Gyroplanes Ltd: This company was formed in 1934 to continue the development of a promising autogyro designed by David Kay. The resultant Kay Gyroplane Type 33/1 G-ACVA first flew at Eastleigh on 18 February 1935. The Pobjoy 'R'-powered G-ACVA was built by **Oddie, Bradbury & Cull** of Portswood Road, Southampton and is noteworthy for the incorporation of collective pitch control in the rotor head. Early design and testing had taken place in Scotland, with an experimental machine, the Kay Type 32/1, being flown at RAF Leuchars in 1932.

The **Moon** Moonbeam monoplane of 1910 was tested at Eastleigh, flying from meadows near North Stoneham Farm. The aircraft was built in works at The Wool House, Royal Pier, Southampton, which were later taken over by the Canute Airplane Co. The monoplane used a steel tube fuselage and was of Demoiselle configuration – that is with the pilot seated low between the aircraft wheels, beneath the wing and the engine, both of which were mounted directly on the fuselage top longerons. *British Aircraft before the Great War* suggests that Moon carried out experimental flying at a number of other locations in the Southampton area, including Fawley, Beaulieu and Ower.

Oddie, Bradbury & Cull Ltd, Portswood Road (the company was registered as a limited company on 26 July 1935) had previous experience of Cierva Autogiro rotor construction, and, in 1938, built components and assemblies for the nine Cierva C.40 built by **British Aircraft Manufacturing Ltd** at Hanworth. In December 1936, the company was advertising: 'Oddie, Bradbury & Cull Ltd, Southampton Airport. Manufacturers of complete aircraft, wood or metal. Special designs and experimental work undertaken in strictest secrecy.'

By 1947, the company was offering a more restricted range of products, as follows: 'Oddie Fasteners & Quick Release Pins. The Oddie fastener, which has been standardized by the Ministry of Aircraft Production for use on all aircraft, has been fitted to most aircraft produced during the war, and is being used on commercial aircraft now.'

In February 1946, **W.A. Rollason Ltd** were reported as taking over the factory vacated by Saunders-Roe Ltd at Eastleigh. Rollason were to use this facility for the repair, modification, maintenance and resale of ex-RAF and other aircraft.

Saunders-Roe Ltd set up a small factory at Eastleigh in 1937 for component manufacture, this being sold to W.A. Rollason in 1946. The Saunders-Roe connection with Eastleigh was re-established in January 1951 when the company took over The Cierva Autogiro Co. Ltd. Saunders-Roe continued their own helicopter development activities at Eastleigh until the company was, itself, taken over by **Westland Aircraft Ltd** in 1959.

Saunders-Roe Ltd developed the Skeeter to production status (eighty built) and subsequently produced the P.531. The P.531 was developed by Westland into the long-serving Scout and Wasp for Army and Navy use, respectively. The first P.531, G-APNU, flew on 20 July 1958; two Saunders-Roe-built examples were flown prior to the Westland takeover. Production of both the Scout and Wasp was undertaken at Hayes. During 1959, the company was involved in the production of a one-man helicopter designed by the Hiller Corporation. This led to the first flight of a Hiller YROE-1 Rotorcycle, G-APYF, at Eastleigh on 15 October 1959. Information from Hiller indicates that Saunders-Roe built ten Hiller Rotorcycles, in two batches of five. The first batch was shipped to the USA for evaluation, the second batch, completed in December 1961, was delivered to Hiller's European agents, Helicop-Air, in Paris.

The Skeeter was built by the Helicopter Division of Saunders-Roe Ltd at Eastleigh, following that company's takeover of The Cierva Autogiro Co. Ltd. G-BLIX/XR809 is seen here at the PFA Rally. (Author)

The Spitfire prototype K5054 at Eastleigh in 1936. (Via Author)

The Supermarine Aviation Works (Vickers) Ltd and **Vickers-Armstrongs Ltd (Aircraft Section) (Supermarine Works)**: Eastleigh is, perhaps, best known for its association with Supermarine and the Spitfire. The relationship between Vickers and Supermarine was somewhat complex, being subject to several re-organisations. In summary (and to the extent that this author has been able to unravel the corporate arrangements): **Vickers Ltd (Aviation Dept)** became in July or August 1928 **Vickers (Aviation) Ltd**, and then **Vickers-Armstrongs Ltd** in October 1938.

The 1928 change in designation to Vickers (Aviation) Ltd was associated with a merger of the heavy engineering (i.e. non-aviation) interests of Vickers Ltd and Sir W.G. Armstrong Whitworth Ltd to form Vickers-Armstrongs Ltd. (Sir W.G. Armstrong Whitworth Aircraft Ltd were not affected by this merger, having passed into the control of John Siddeley in December 1926.) Vickers-Armstrongs Ltd were the parent company for Vickers (Aviation) Ltd, and also of The Supermarine Aviation Works (Vickers) Ltd, which was acquired in November 1928.

Examples of contemporary styling from November 1930 advertising are (i) The Supermarine Aviation Works Ltd, proprietors: Vickers (Aviation) Ltd and (ii) Vickers (Aviation) Ltd, Vickers House, Broadway Westminster. In September 1935 the Supermarine concern was using the style: The Supermarine Aviation Works (Vickers) Ltd, Southampton.

The 1938 reorganisation saw Vickers-Armstrongs Ltd take direct control of its two subsidiaries. After this date the company was generally known only as Vickers-Armstrongs Ltd, the subsidiaries being generally distinguished as Vickers-Armstrongs Ltd (Aircraft Section) (Weybridge Works) or Vickers-Armstrongs Ltd (Aircraft Section) (Supermarine Works).

To complete this saga one should also note that, in December 1954, the aircraft business was again reorganised to form **Vickers-Armstrongs (Aircraft) Ltd**, with the subsidiary interests trading as the Supermarine Division and Weybridge Division.

It is not surprising that a confusing array of names and titles is to be found in various reference sources.

The remainder of this section provides a convenient location to discuss the development and evolution of the Supermarine Spitfire. The combination of stressed skin monoplane with a liquid-cooled engine of minimum frontal area came together with the S.4, S.5 and S.6 Schneider Trophy racers. These factors, together with exotic fuels and supercharging, allowed speeds to be achieved that were virtually double those of the Service fighters of the day. This practical experience of the problems of high-speed flight no doubt gave the Supermarine design team additional confidence in the design of the Spitfire.

Supermarine tendered for the official monoplane fighter specification F.7/30 with their gull-wing Type 224 prototype K2890, which was first flown on 19 February 1934. Performance was unsatisfactory and none of the F.7/30 types tendered was ordered. Supermarine then proceeded with the private venture development of a new design, the Type 300. Later re-named Spitfire, the prototype K5054 was first flown at Eastleigh on 5 March 1936.

During 1937, Spitfire production was rapidly expanded by the use of many sub-contractors. Supermarine built fuselages, **Folland Aircraft Ltd** the empennage, **Westland Aircraft Ltd** wing ribs, **General Aircraft Ltd** and **Pobjoy Air Motors & Aircraft Ltd** the wings, and **Singer Motors Ltd** the engine mounting. Other companies involved (by December 1938) included: **Aero Engines Ltd, The Airscrew Co. Ltd, Heston Aircraft Co. Ltd** and **J. Samuel White & Co. Ltd**. There were, however, very significant production difficulties, and in mid-1938 the supply of fuselages had greatly outstripped that of wings (by around 7:1 at the best estimate, and 25:1 at the worst). Supermarine blamed the sub-contractors, and the sub-contractors blamed Supermarine, for late delivery of (or at least inability to 'freeze') drawings. At the official level, Supermarine were criticised for their 'chaotic' sub-contracting arrangements. Perhaps the desire for high performance had taken too high a priority over ease of production in the initial design.

More than 20,000 Spitfires were manufactured. The total production total is the subject of considerable variation between different references, with a number of sources quoting 22,759 (both Spitfire and Seafire) and others 20,334 Spitfire plus 2,556 Seafire (including a number of Spitfire conversions). Alfred Price suggests a likely figure of around 20,400 for the Spitfire in *The Spitfire Story*.

Production quantities for most marks are shown in the following table (typical variations in the production figures for individual marks are also shown). Note that many of the prototype aircraft were flown from Worthy Down.

Mark	Number Built	Comments
Prototypes and limited production	• Single prototype K5054	• Flown 5 March 1936
	• Two Mk III	• One Mk III from Mk I, one from Mk V
	• Two Mk IV	• First Griffon Spitfires, first DP845, flown 27 November 1941
	• Six Mk XIV development aircraft, JF316-JF321	• Griffon-powered Mk VIII used to develop Mk XIV, first flown 20 January 1943
	• Two Mk XX	• Re-designated Mk IV supported development of F. Mk 21
Mk I	1,556–1,566	Initial production standard
Mk II	920–921	750 or 751 Mk IIA, 170 Mk IIB

The early development of the Spitfire is represented here by Westland-built Spitfire 1b, AR213. (Author)

Supermarine Spitfire PR.XIX PS915 poses over Lancashire after its 1986 rebuild at Warton. The PR.XIX here illustrates the highly developed Griffon-engined versions of the Spitfire. (BAE SYSTEMS plc)

Mark	Number Built	Comments
PR Mk IV	Two prototypes and 229 production	Prototype conversion P9551 flown 15 September 1940. Built by Supermarine, initially as PR 1D.
Mk V	6,464-6,479 (some 6,500)	Most numerous version, built with different armament and wing planforms – including ninety-four Mk VA; 3,411 Mk VB; 2,467 Mk VC; and fifteen PR Mk V (other break-downs of individual variants can also be found).
Mk VI	100	Pressurised high altitude version
Mk VII	140	As above, often fitted with extended wing tips
Mk VIII	1,652-1,658	Merlin 61, 63, 66 or 70-powered
Mk IX	5,656-5,665	Merlin 61 in Mk V airframe. 282 further conversions from Mk V.
PR Mk X	16	Based on F Mk VII
PR Mk XI	471	Some conversions of Mk IX, first flown 21 November 1942
F Mk XII	100	Initial Griffon Spitfire production
PR Mk XIII	29 (conversions only)	Low altitude photo reconnaissance
F Mk XIV	957	Griffon 65-powered
Mk XVI	1,054	Canadian-built with Packard Merlin 226
Mk XVIII	300	Strengthened and with lengthened fuselage
PR Mk XIX	225	Final photo-reconnaissance version with Griffon 65
F.21	120	Prototype Spitfire XX (from Spitfire IV) DP851 flown on 8 August 1942. Later used in the initial development of the Mk 21, see Worthy Down. Mk 21 prototype PP139 flown 24 July 1943.
F.22	278-287	Cut-down rear fuselag
F.24	54	Last production variant. Twenty-seven additional aircraft converted from F.22.

The figures above suggest a total of between 20,300 and 20,400 aircraft built. Whatever the precise totals, there can be no doubt that the Spitfire was truly a prodigious design.

The main contractor for Seafire production was **Westland Aircraft Ltd**, who built more than half the total, other companies involved being Supermarine (prototypes and late model aircraft), **Air Service Training** (initial Seafire IB conversions) and **Cunliffe-Owen Aircraft Ltd**. Although there is some variation in quoted production numbers, a consensus view is presented under the entry for Westland at Yeovil. This shows, for comparison with the figures quoted above, total Seafire production to be made up of fourteen prototypes, 538 Spitfire conversions and 2,094 new-build aircraft.

In late 1940, both the Itchen and Woolston works were bombed, with severe effects upon Spitfire production. As a result, an extensive dispersed production system was bought into effect. Administration, design and prototype manufacture were moved to Hursley Park, and around thirty-five manufacturing sites were established based upon local control centres in Trowbridge, Newbury, Southampton, Salisbury and Reading, in addition to the large shadow factory at Castle Bromwich. The Southampton production group concentrated on the Spitfire Marks V, VI, VII, VIII, IX and XIV.

Smaller towns with factories participating in the scheme included Wonston (north east of Chilbolton), Hungerford, Botley and Westbury. Southampton production included wings built at the **Hants & Dorset Bus Garage** and fuselages built at **Hendy's Garage**. **Sewards Garage**, Southampton, produced vital production tools and jigs. Other dispersed sites were also used for the production of details and to provide toolrooms, stores, machining capacity and other functions.

In August and September 1938, **Vickers-Armstrongs Ltd** used Eastleigh to conduct high all-up weight trials of the first production Wellington L4212, its normal base at Brooklands being too small for this purpose. During the early 1950s, Vickers-Armstrongs Ltd built parts for the Swift at Eastleigh, including wings and some fuselages. This work was carried out in the hangar that was subsequently converted into the terminal building.

Southampton Area – Hursley Park

Vickers-Armstrongs Ltd: The Supermarine Works used Hursley Park, to the north of Southampton as head office and drawing office, and for prototype construction, following the bombing raids at Woolston and Eastleigh in September and October 1940. Supermarine occupied Hursley Park in December 1940, with pre-production build being carried out for a time at Hendy's Garage, Chandler's Ford. Hursley Park remained the centre for design queries, prototype design and production drawing throughout the Second World War. A well-camouflaged hangar in the grounds was used for prototype assembly.

Hursley Park was used by Supermarine as its head office and for the construction of experimental prototypes. (Alan Curry via Ken Ellis)

One Hursley Park product was the Supermarine 392 (or E.10/44), which was later developed into the Attacker. The E.10/44 was built at Hursley Park, assembled at High Post and first flown from Boscombe Down. Subsequent company flight testing was carried out at Chilbolton.

The novelty represented by the use of swept wings on another Hursley Park prototype, the Supermarine 510, is reflected in contemporary advertising: 'The Supermarine 510 adapted from the Attacker has swept back wings and tail unit to delay the onset of compressibility effects. The superb finish on all surfaces ensures a high aerodynamic efficiency which makes full use of the thrust of the Rolls-Royce Nene engine.' 'Vickers-Armstrongs Limited, Aircraft Division, Weybridge and Supermarine Works.' The final prototype to be built at Hursley Park was the unflown Type 545, XA181, which strikingly resembled the F-100 Super Sabre.

Southampton Area – Itchen

Vickers–Armstrongs Ltd: After Vickers took over Supermarine in 1928, an additional production factory was built at Itchen to supplement the existing Supermarine works at Woolston. Both the Woolston and Itchen plants were heavily bombed in September 1940, leading to the Spitfire dispersed production scheme.

Southampton Area – Woolston

The most important activity at Woolston was that of the Supermarine Aviation Works and its predecessor, Pemberton-Billing Ltd. This is presented below chronologically, followed by a review of other activities in this area. Note that Mr Pemberton Billing's name was not hyphenated, whereas the name of his company is hyphenated.

Pemberton-Billing was founded in 1912, and became **Pemberton-Billing Ltd** just prior to the First World War, being registered at Oakbank Wharf, Woolston, in July 1914. *Flight* reported that Mr Pemberton Billing's new works were underway at Woolston in April 1914. One early achievement was the building, in August 1914, of the PB 9 Scout. This was a small (26ft span) biplane, which resembled the Sopwith Tabloid. It was designed, constructed and flown in the space of a single week and became known as the '7 day bus'.

The distinctive Pemberton-Billing PB25 Scout. Twenty were ordered, but the number of these completed is not clear. (Philip Jarrett)

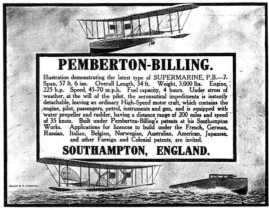

(Copyright: BAE SYSTEMS plc)

The 'bus' was first flown from a small field in the Netley area and was subsequently also flown at Brooklands, earning much publicity for Pemberton-Billing. The aircraft was accepted into RNAS service, flying at Hendon and Chingford until mid-1915 with serial number 1267.

Prior to the establishment of the company, Mr Pemberton Billing had experimented, from 1908 onward, with three pusher monoplanes: the PB 1, PB 3, and PB 5. These were all unsuccessful. The PB 7 was an elegant and futuristic flying boat shown at the 1914 Olympia Aero Show. Although the PB 7 was also unsuccessful, this was the design that sparked the formation of the company, later to become famous as **The Supermarine Aviation Works Ltd**. The company telegraphic address was 'Supermarine', this being reputed to have been chosen by Mr Pemberton Billing as representing the opposite of submarine.

First World War deliveries included one PB Boxkite, one PB 23 pusher Scout biplane (serial 8487), at least four PB 25 Scout (a production version of the PB 23) from an order for twenty, and one PB 29E quadruplane. The PB 29E had two pusher propellers, driven by engines mounted at part-span on the second lowest of its four wings, and featured a 'crow's nest' or 'pulpit' gunner position in the upper-wing centre section. The type was first flown at Chingford on 16 January 1916.

Pemberton-Billing Ltd was re-named **The Supermarine Aviation Works Ltd**, when Mr Pemberton Billing stood for and entered Parliament in March 1916, selling his shares to Mr Hubert Scott-Paine. The Supermarine Aviation Works Ltd was registered on 20 September 1916. The company's advertising styling from 1917 was: 'The Supermarine Aviation Works Ltd. Designers and Constructors of Aircraft. Flying water and slipways, Woolston. Seaplanes and flying boats, pusher and tractor scouts, observation and patrol machines, battleplanes. Speciality rapid production of experimental machines. Speed boats and all kinds of racing craft. H. Scott-Paine, General Manager.'

The Supermarine Southampton was the company's most successful flying boat of the inter-war period. The type was also used for a number of notable long distance flights. (Philip Jarrett)

Mr Noel Pemberton Billing famously learned to fly in a single day (following a bet with Handley Page) in September 1913. Pemberton Billing was an outspoken MP who, with C.G. Grey of *The Aeroplane*, orchestrated a campaign against the Royal Aircraft Factory at Farnborough. Hubert Scott-Paine was later to be well known in the field of powerboat racing, and for the design of motor torpedo boats. Among the craft that he designed, built and raced were *Panther I, II* and *Miss Britain I, II* and *III*.

During the First World War, some twenty-nine AD flying boats were built by The Supermarine Aviation Works Ltd, with five more delivered as spares. The company also received orders for the Supermarine Nighthawk (sometimes referred to as the PB 31). This quadruplane followed the same concept as the PB 29E, but had tractor rather than pusher propellers and a fully enclosed cockpit. One example (No.1388) was built, with a second example being cancelled.

Reginald Mitchell was appointed Chief Engineer and Designer in 1921. The Channel, a developed version of the AD flying boat, was the first design to be given the name Supermarine. In August 1922, the company's Sea Lion II G-EBAH (powered by a 450hp Napier Lion) was entered to represent Great Britain in the Schneider Trophy race at Naples. The Sea Lion won the event, at a speed of 145.7mph. The Supermarine S.4 monoplane for the 1925 Schneider contest (G-EBLP/N197) was first flown at Woolston on 25 August 1925. Although it subsequently crashed at Baltimore, the S.4 set a world speed record of 226.752mph at Calshot on 13 September 1925.

For the 1927 event the company produced the Supermarine S.5, still powered by the Napier Lion, but combining a thin, wire-braced, low-wing, all-metal construction and the use of radiators integrated into the skinning of the fuselage sides as part of the engine cooling system. This formula was retained with the successful S.6 (1929) and S.6B (1931), the Lion being replaced by the Rolls-Royce R engine. First flight details, and information on the speeds achieved by these superlative machines, can be found under the entry for Calshot Castle.

In parallel to the Schneider Trophy developments described above, Supermarine continued their development of the flying boat for RAF service. The Seal, Sea Eagle, Sea King, Seagull, Scarab, Sheldrake and Swan met with only limited success, but led to production success with the Supermarine Southampton series. The Southampton I was first flown in 1925. The type was a twin-engine biplane, initially produced with a wooden hull, but later adopting all-metal construction. The Southampton I and II were used for a number of well-publicised long-distance flights, for example a tour in 1927-1928 by four Southampton II aircraft from

England to Singapore, with an onward extension consisting of the complete circumnavigation of Australia thrown in for good measure! A total of sixty-eight were built for the RAF, with additional aircraft being exported to Argentina (eight), Turkey (six) and Japan (one).

In 1928 the company became **The Supermarine Aviation Works (Vickers) Ltd**, later becoming **Vickers–Armstrongs Ltd (Aircraft Section) (Supermarine Works)**. (See Eastleigh for further details of the evolution of the company and for Spitfire production details.) After Vickers took over control, the Woolston works were used to construct Vickers Viastra II aircraft and Vildebeest wings, in addition to the following Supermarine products:

- The Supermarine Scapa, originally known as the Southampton IV, was an intended replacement for the Southampton. The Scapa was a 75ft-span biplane all-metal flying boat powered by two Rolls-Royce Kestrel IIIMS engines in clean nacelles mounted on the upper wing. The prototype was first flown in 1932 (K3991) and a total of fourteen production machines were built.
- The Walrus (Seagull V, N-1/K4797) first flew on 21 June 1933. Production consisted of the prototype; twenty-four Seagull V for Australia; 281 Walrus I built by Supermarine; and Saunders-Roe Ltd production of 272 Walrus I and 190 Walrus II, for a grand total of 768. Of these, about eleven were not delivered, probably being destroyed by enemy action whilst under construction. Other production figures can also be found.
- The Supermarine Stranraer prototype K3973 first flew on 27 July 1934; the Stranraer was one of the company's more successful types of the inter-war years. Seventeen production aircraft were built for the RAF and an additional forty aircraft of this type were built in Canada.
- The Sea Otter, which was intended as a replacement for the Walrus, was first flown (K8854) on 23 September 1938. A total of about 290 Sea Otter were built by Saunders-Roe Ltd. Amphibians (such as the Walrus and Sea Otter) were usually tested at Woolston off the water, and then flown to Eastleigh for landplane testing.

The Woolston factory was largely destroyed by an air raid on 26 September 1940. After this, Spitfire production was largely dispersed; details of Southampton area production are summarised under Eastleigh. The planning of the dispersed production scheme was carried out from a requisitioned floor of the Polygon Hotel in the city centre. Woolston was abandoned as a production facility after this raid.

Production of the Walrus was split between Supermarine and Saunders-Roe. The type served with unglamorous distinction throughout the Second World War. (Ken Ellis Collection)

Simmonds Aircraft Ltd: The prototype Simmonds Spartan G-EBYU was constructed at 65 Portsmouth Road, Woolston, and assembled at the Rolling Mills, Archers Road, Southampton, prior to its first flight during the summer of 1928. Production aircraft were built at Weston Shore, near Hamble, with assembly and test-flying at Hamble, which see for further details.

In 1920, there was a shed immediately to the north of the Woolston Chain Ferry, on the roof of which was written '**The Sopwith Aviation Co. Ltd**.' Sopwith seaplane testing at Woolston included testing of the Sopwith 860 (1914), Sopwith Schneider and Gunbus float-planes. These aircraft were test flown by the Sopwith pilot Victor Mahl, who unfortunately succumbed in April 1915 to an attack of appendicitis at the early age of twenty-five.

Thruxton Airport

The **Isaacs** Fury G-ASCM was first flown at Thruxton on 30 August 1963. The Isaacs Spitfire G-BBJI was assembled here prior to its first flight in May 1975, the author being among the party that helped to move the aircraft from Southampton to Thruxton.

Leisure Sport: The Supermarine S.5 wooden replica G-BDFF was built at Thruxton for Leisure Sport. First flown at Calshot on 28 August 1975, the aircraft was destroyed in a fatal accident on 23 May 1987 caused by structural failure of the tail surfaces in flight. The aircraft had been rebuilt at Bodmin following an accident on 23 September 1982, when it crashed into the lake at Thorpe Water Park. It flew again in October 1986, with only the original rear fuselage being used in the rebuild.

Jackaroo Aircraft Ltd: The Wiltshire School of Flying developed a Tiger Moth variant with a wider fuselage and enclosed cockpit, which was produced as the Thruxton Jackaroo by Jackaroo Aircraft Ltd. The aircraft was equipped with four seats, and the type could also be adapted for crop spraying with a hopper installed in the widened cockpit area. The Jackaroo prototype was G-AOEX, and the type made its first flight on 2 March 1957. The Jackaroo was available in 1957 for £1,095 complete, and was said to be the cheapest four-seat aircraft in the world. Twenty-six aircraft were converted at Thruxton, with one further aircraft (G-APOV) converted at Croydon by **Rollason Aircraft & Engines Ltd**. The company name was changed in 1961 to **Paragon Aircraft Ltd**, the unfulfilled intent being to produce a light aircraft called the Thruxton Paragon.

Thruxton Aviation & Engineering Co. Ltd built the single Gadfly HDW1 two-seat autogyro, G-AVKE, in 1968, but it is believed never to have been flown successfully.

Whitway

Geoffrey de Havilland carried out early experiments at Seven Barrows Field near Beacon Hill to the south of Newbury, assisted by Frank Hearle. The actual site of these experiments was close to the village of Whitway. The second machine, which was tested in the summer of 1910, flew here very successfully, making a flight of ¼ mile on 10 September 1910. To quote *The Newbury Weekly News* of 22 September 1910 (headline: 'The All-British Biplane. The de Havilland Aeroplane flies at Beacon Hill') there was 'nothing very novel in the aeroplane itself, it being a combination of various designs which have been found to fly successfully.' Nevertheless, this machine marked the first success of a man who was to become a major force in the British aircraft industry. One notable feature was that the aircraft was powered by an engine that was also designed by Mr de Havilland. Many of his future company's products were similarly to be powered by engines of de Havilland manufacture.

The sole example of the Isaacs Spitfire G-BBJI is seen here in its 'photo-reconnaissance' colour scheme at the Cranfield PFA Rally. (Author)

The cockpit modifications required to produce a Thruxton Jackaroo from a de Havilland Tiger Moth are readily apparent in this view of G-AOIR. (Author)

G-AVKE is the unlovely and unlikely Gadfly HDW-1, here seen at Thruxton. (Author)

Geoffrey de Havilland's first successful machine was flown for the first time on 10 September 1910 at Seven Barrows Field near Whitway. (BAE SYSTEMS plc)

This machine was purchased by the Balloon Factory at the end of 1910 and tested at Farnborough, where it was found to fly entirely successfully, 'the pilot showing very good control over the machine and all landings were accurately made'. Shortly thereafter, de Havilland joined the staff of the Royal Aircraft Factory as a designer, subsequently being responsible for the BE2.

The field at Seven Barrows was used because J.T.C. Moore Brabazon had previously erected a suitable aircraft shed there. De Havilland and Hearle often stayed at the nearby Carnarvon Arms public house in Whitway.

Winchester

The **Blake** Bluetit was a parasol monoplane constructed using the upper wings of an Avro 504K (purchased for £5) and the rear fuselage and tail surface components from two Simmonds Spartan aircraft G-AAGN and G-AAJB (purchased for a few shillings). The wings were reduced in span and both Spartan fuselage sections were incorporated in the fuselage. The total construction cost was £26. The Bluetit flew, unregistered, on 19 October 1930 from the Blake farm (Woodhams Farm), adjoining Worthy Down. All flights were deliberately of short duration, and the Bluetit continued in use until it suffered storm damage whilst parked in the open in 1932. It was donated to the Shuttleworth Trust in 1968, where, in recent years, it has been the subject of a lengthy restoration programme.

Worthy Down, Winchester

This airfield had been the old Winchester Racecourse and was subsequently used as a flight test airfield by Supermarine.

A.V. Roe & Co. Ltd: The Avro C.6C Autogiro was flown at Worthy Down, when first modified with stub wings, on 1 January 1927.

The Supermarine Aviation Works Ltd: The Supermarine Sparrow was flight tested at Worthy Down for the Air Ministry with a number of different wing sections during 1927. The move of Supermarine (**Vickers-Armstrongs Ltd**) experimental flight testing to Worthy Down followed the bombing raids at Eastleigh in July 1940 and Woolston in September and October 1940.

A separate Experimental Flight Department was needed to ensure that parallel development and improvement of the Spitfire could proceed independently of production flight testing. Spitfire Mk I R6700 (the second Spitfire to be fitted with a Merlin 61 with two-stage, two-speed supercharger) was first flown in this form from Worthy Down on 7 January 1942.

The first Griffon Spitfire IV, DP845, first flew here on 27 November 1941. DP851 was modified from Spitfire IV to become the prototype Mk XX, flying on 8 August 1942. This same aircraft was then fitted with a two-stage two-speed supercharged Griffon 61, to conduct transitional development flying for the Mk 21, flying in this form on 1 December 1942. A more fully developed Mk 21 prototype, PP139, was flown from Worthy Down on 24 July 1943. The prototype Supermarine Type 322 'Dumbo' R1810 also flew for the first time at Worthy Down on 6 February 1943. Only two examples of this single-engine, high-wing, variable incidence monoplane were built. From 1944, the Supermarine flight test activity was transferred to High Post, Wiltshire.

Isle of Wight

Bembridge

Bembridge Airfield has been the home of Britten-Norman throughout the company's existence (in its various guises). The history of this company is presented chronologically below, followed by entries for two further companies which were formed at Bembridge to exploit the designs of John Britten and Desmond Norman. Historical information relating to Britten-Norman activities has been drawn from a number of sources, including the B-N Group internet site.

John Britten and Desmond Norman established **Britten-Norman Ltd** in 1953. The company carried out Tiger Moth conversions for agricultural use by its sister company Crop Culture (Aerial) Ltd. The first Britten-Norman design to be built was the BN-1F single-seat parasol monoplane G-ALZE, which was first flown on 26 May 1951 and is now on display in the Southampton Hall of Aviation.

Having been involved in agricultural operations all over the world, Britten-Norman identified the need for a rugged, reliable utility aircraft capable of operation from short unprepared airstrips. The result was the hugely successful BN-2 Islander, the prototype of which, G-ATCT, was first flown on 13 June 1965. The production prototype G-ATWU flew on 28 August 1966, subsequently becoming the prototype Trislander. Still in production more than thirty years later, the Islander has been a worthy successor to the de Havilland Rapide. To increase production capacity, a manufacturing agreement was signed with IRMA of Romania in 1968, the first Romanian-built aircraft, G-AXHY, flying on 17 May 1969. The 100th Romanian-built aircraft (BN-2A-26 G-BBFG) was flown on 21 November 1973; the 500th aircraft was BN-2T G-BVFK, flown on 12 June 1995.

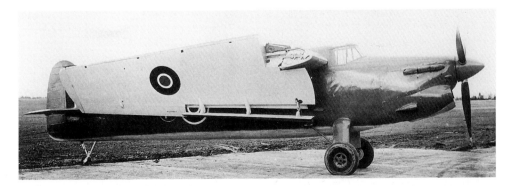

The two Supermarine Type 322 'Dumbo' prototypes conducted variable incidence wing trials. (Philip Jarrett)

The two Islander prototypes fly in formation. The aircraft to the rear was subsequently modified to become the prototype Britten-Norman Trislander. (Britten-Norman via Ken Ellis)

A three-engine derivative of the Islander, the BN-2A Mk III Trislander, first flew on 11 September 1970, the prototype, G-ATWU, being a modification of the second prototype Islander. The Trislander is distinguished by its fin-mounted third engine.

The Islander has been the subject of continuous development through its production life. Variants included the sole BN-2A-41 Turbo Islander, G-BDPR, flown on 6 April 1977; the BN-2T Turbine Islander (prototype G-BCMY flown on 2 August 1980); and the single experimental Dowty Rotol-Ducted Propulsor-powered Islander G-FANS, flown at Shoreham, West Sussex, on 10 June 1977. The most recent derivative is the BN-2T-4S Defender 4000 (prototype G-SURV, first flown on 17 August 1994).

The company sought to diversify its product line with the single-engine high-wing BN-3 Nymph, the prototype of which (G-AXFB) was first flown on 17 May 1969. The BN-3 was built and flown in just fifty-three days.

During the 1970s, Britten-Norman suffered a series of financial crises, each of which led to the restructuring of the company. A receiver was appointed to manage Britten-Norman Ltd on 22 October 1971, **Britten-Norman (Bembridge) Ltd** being formed on 23 November 1971 to manage the company assets whilst awaiting a purchaser. Its successor, **Fairey Britten-Norman Ltd** was formed on 31 August 1972, when Britten-Norman (Bembridge) Ltd was purchased by the Fairey Group. Further difficulties resulted in Britten-Norman (Bembridge) Ltd entering receivership on 3 August 1977, leading to the takeover of Britten-Norman by the Swiss firm Pilatus. **Pilatus Britten-Norman Ltd** was established on 19 June 1978 (in anticipation of acceptance of the Pilatus Aircraft bid). Pilatus Britten-Norman continued to build and develop the Islander and its derivatives for nearly twenty years before announcing the sale of the company to Litchfield Continental Ltd on 21 July 1998. The name of the company then reverted to its original, **Britten-Norman Ltd**. By September 1998, sales of the Islander and its derivatives had reached 1,219 aircraft.

By the end of 1998, it was announced that a further new owner had been found, in the form of the Isle of Wight company Biofarm Inc. In February 1999, it was announced that Britten-Norman Ltd were broadening their production base by the purchase, upon its privatisation, of the Romanian aircraft manufacturer Romaero of Bucharest.

This promising development proved somewhat illusory, with the company entering a further period of receivership in early 2000. On 4 May 2000, the company was sold to the

Oman-based group Zawawi, being re-named **B-N Group Ltd**. As a result of this purchase, Britten-Norman Ltd went into liquidation on 19 May 2000. Further instability was introduced by the surprise announcement in July 2000 of the intention of their landlords to evict B-N Group from the Bembridge factory. This move would also have prevented B-N Group from carrying out flight operations from Bembridge. The situation was resolved in early 2001, with B-N Group fully re-opening the airfield on 21 April 2001. Deliveries continue of both the Islander (BN-2B-20 and BN-2B-26) and Defender (BN-2T-4S).

Above: *The prototype BN3 Nymph was built and flown in only fifty-three days.* (Britten-Norman via Ken Ellis)

Right: *An early production scene on the Islander production line at Bembridge. G-AVCN is the first production aircraft.* (Britten-Norman via Ken Ellis)

Aircraft Designs (Bembridge) Ltd: This company was established to develop the Britten Sheriff, following the death of Mr John Britten in 1977. A light, twin-engine aircraft with twin fins, the Sheriff could be characterised as a modern, metal Gemini. The prototype reached an advanced state of construction, but was not flown. The company was jointly owned by Air Bembridge and Crop Culture (Aerial) Ltd.

NDN Aircraft (UK) Ltd was formed by Desmond Norman in 1976, developing the Firecracker trainer at Goodwood. The company also took over development of the BN-3 Nymph, flying a revised prototype, G-NACI, as the NAC-1 Freelance on 29 September 1984. A third venture was the Fieldmaster agricultural aircraft. These aircraft, together with the Optica, have been marketed with limited success by a range of companies including **Norman Aeroplane Co. Ltd**, **NDN Aircraft Ltd**, **Croplease Ltd** and **Brooklands Aircraft Co. Ltd**, (later **Brooklands Aerospace Ltd**) at (variously) Barry, South Glamorgan; Goodwood, West Sussex; Old Sarum, Wiltshire; and Sandown, IoW.

East Cowes

Auster Aircraft Ltd: Auster VI VF517 was tested on floats from the Saunders-Roe slipway at Cowes from January 1947. In February 1955, Auster J/5G Autocar G-AMZV was under test, fitted with a Saunders-Roe hydro-ski undercarriage.

S.E. Saunders Ltd had its origins as a firm of boatbuilders that was established in 1830 at Streatly-on-Thames, moving to Goring and then, in 1906, to East Cowes to manufacture fast motor launches. Initially a private company, on 16 May 1908 it became a public company as S.E. Saunders Ltd. The company's boat building skills led to an early involvement in aircraft construction when they produced the hull for the famous Sopwith Bat Boat.

First World War Production

During the First World War, the company built a remarkable variety of aircraft including the following types: BE2A (one); Avro 504A/J (200); Short 184 (eighty); Norman Thompson flying boat (at least fifteen NT2B); Felixstowe F.2A (at least 100, some completed as Felixstowe F.5, some delivered to store without engines); the Saunders T1 X14; and two A4 Medina. Aircraft production was supplemented by 116 flying boat hulls, plus seaplane floats, aircraft parts and airship gondolas.

The incomplete SA1 Sheriff G-FRJB is seen here at Castle Donington. (Author)

Production of Felixstowe F.2A and F.5 flying boats in the S.E. Saunders factory at Cowes during the First World War. (Via Norman Barfield)

The significant amount of flying boat work, which included hulls for White & Thompson, arose from Saunders' invention and use of 'Consuta' wire-sewn plywood construction. Early advertising material reflects the marine origins of the company: 'Designers and constructors of Air and Marine craft'. Later advertising (April 1917) focused more on aircraft products: 'Saunders for Speed and Stability', 'Erecting and Testing: Seaplanes Osborne Works, East Cowes. Land machines – West Medina aerodrome.'

Collapse and Rebirth between the Wars (1919-1939)

After the First World War, the company was less successful in aircraft construction, although they did receive a contract for the rebuild of eighteen DH9A. The importance of Consuta plywood to the company is reflected in the prominent role that it played in their advertising material in the years immediately after the end of the First World War. The complex and unsuccessful Saunders Kittiwake G-EAUD was flown on 19 September 1920, testing continuing into Spring 1921. The company was also contracted to build the unsuccessful Isacco Helicogyre K1171 of 1928.

Saunders–Roe Ltd was formed in 1929 after A.V. Roe purchased a controlling interest in S.E. Saunders Ltd on 23 November 1928. The company built a range of flying boat and amphibian designs in modest numbers during the 1930s. The company sometimes adopted the style 'SARO' in its advertising material. Early Saunders-Roe products are summarised in the following table:

Type	First Flight	Comments
A.17 Cutty Sark	4 July 1929	Prototype G-AAIP. Four-seat amphibian, the first product of Saunders-Roe Ltd. Twelve built with various engine types.
A.19 Cloud	16 July 1930	Prototype G-ABCJ. Eight to ten-seat amphibian. Twenty built as the Saunders-Roe A.19 and A.20, flown with several different types of engine.
A.21 Windhover	16 or 17 Oct 1930	Two aircraft, prototype ZK-ABW built for Dominion Airways Ltd. Six-seat amphibian powered by three Gipsy II. (Contemporary reports in *Flight* of October 1930 give the first flight date as 17 October, the aircraft having been launched for the first time on the previous day.)

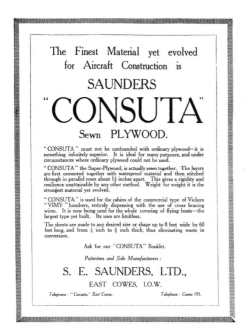

Type	First Flight	Comments
A.27 London	March 1934	Twin-engine general reconnaissance all-metal biplane flying boat. Prototype K3560 to R.24/31, followed by thirty production aircraft for the RAF – Saunders-Roe's most successful design of this period.
Lerwick	Nov 1938	A stumpy twin-engine flying boat which proved not to be a success operationally. Prototype L7248, twenty-one built.

In addition to the above, Saunders-Roe built fifty-five all-metal Blackburn Bluebird IV during 1930-1931, the wings being sub-contracted to Boulton & Paul Ltd in Norwich. The large assembly hangar at East Cowes was built for Saunders-Roe by Boulton & Paul Ltd to meet the needs of SARO London production. This hangar has a frontage of 210ft, and a floor area of 50,000sq.ft.

Saunders-Roe Ltd adopted a somewhat high-flown and wordy advertising style, as reflected in the following advertisements for the Cutty Sark:

Long years have passed since the Cutty Sark, famous old time clipper, battled for supremacy over the world's trade routes. Today, inheriting that famous name, comes a new Cutty Sark, carrying the speed, grace of line and seaworthiness of its predecessor to a higher pitch, and adding to them the final virtue of flight.

The 'Cutty Sark' is the ideal light amphibian flying-boat, designed to meet every possible requirement of civil flying. Its sphere of utility embraces pioneer work over land or water; in the service of private owners; mails or freight carrying; survey and aerial photography; fire patrol, as a training unit; and popular flights. … She cruises at 90mph and seats four in a silent and vibrationless cabin. Her absence of wire bracing indicates that maintenance has been kept to a minimum. Produced at Cowes by a firm with a hundred years of constructional experience behind it.

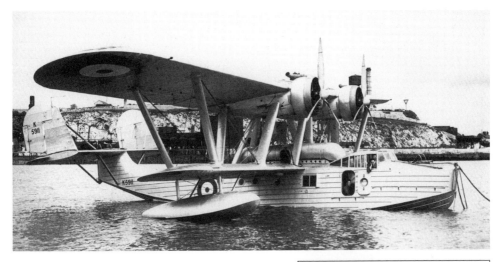

Above: *K5911 is a Saunders-Roe London II fitted with a long-range fuel tank over the fuselage.* (Ken Ellis Collection)

Right: (Copyright: BAE SYSTEMS plc)

Below: *Saunders-Roe Cutty Sark G-AEOH in the company of an Air Service Training Ltd motor launch. Twelve aircraft were built with a number of different engine types.* (Rolls-Royce via Ken Ellis)

The SARO 'Cutty Sark' gives you choice! Flying in the 'Cutty Sark' saloon amphibian is a matter of extreme pleasure both to the private owner and to the pilots of the civil flying service. There is no other craft quite equal to the comfort, the convenience, or the degree of usefulness of the SARO 'Cutty Sark'. It is unsurpassed as a coastal airliner, cheap to operate and economical to maintain. ... It is the craft that enables you to fly where you wish; the 'Cutty Sark' can alight and take off wherever there is sufficient space, be it the surface of a land-locked harbour or the turf of a local aerodrome. It takes but 40 seconds to operate the land undercarriage. ... The cosy cabin of 'Cutty Sark' comfortably accommodates four people; no need at all of any special flying kit.

To cap it all, the company offered this understated exposition of their experience and capability: 'Built by Saunders-Roe Ltd. Contractors to the Air Ministry, Admiralty, War Office, Crown Agents, Royal National Lifeboat Institution and leading marine undertakings. Constructors of all types of aircraft; of lifeboats; yachts, motor craft, and all marine auxiliaries. Manufacturers of plywoods; sewn, waterproof and metal plys.' This advertisement refers to the company's continued interest in boat building. Prestigious examples included the world record-breaking *Miss England III* for Sir Henry Segrave in 1930 and the 130.9mph *Bluebird* for Sir Malcolm Campbell in 1938.

Saunders-Roe Ltd also built the prototype of the twin-engine Segrave Meteor G-AAXP on behalf of the Aircraft Investment Corporation (AIC), this aircraft being flown for the first time on 28 May 1930. This type was subsequently put into production by Blackburn at Brough with an all-metal monocoque fuselage replacing the wooden fuselage of the attractive prototype. The linkage between Saunders-Roe and Blackburn in the case of the Meteor (and Saunders-Roe production of the Blackburn Bluebird IV) reflects significant investment by AIC in both firms.

Saunders-Roe Ltd, despite the landplane production noted above, were always primarily flying boat manufacturers, this being reflected in their December 1936 advertising: 'SARO – Specialists in high performance marine aircraft.' Spartan Aircraft Ltd, having been actively collaborating with Saunders-Roe Ltd, merged with them in Spring 1933.

Second World War Production

During the Second World War Saunders-Roe Ltd manufactured 462 Supermarine Walrus and 290 Sea Otter (built between July 1943 and July 1946). The company prepared 195 Catalina aircraft for RAF service at Beaumaris, the aircraft being received via Scottish Aviation Ltd, after their transatlantic ferry flights.

The SR.A/1 and Princess typify the prepared-ness of Saunders-Roe to explore unconventional design solutions, albeit without securing production contracts for their designs. (Via Ken Ellis)

The ten-engined Saunders-Roe Princess was a true flying ship. Unfortunately, it also proved to be at the end of an evolutionary cul-de-sac. (BAE SYSTEMS plc)

The Saro A.37 Shrimp was powered by four Pobjoy engines and was a reduced scale experimental aircraft used for the development of flying boat hull shapes. Registered G-AFZS (later TK580), it first flew at Cowes in October 1939 and was based at Beaumaris, Anglesey from 1940, moving in August 1940 to Helensburgh.

Saunders-Roe Ltd were involved in the design and manufacture of the **Short** Shetland, their workshare including such items as the flaps, ailerons, engine mountings and floats. In fact, in 1946, the Shetland was being advertised as follows: 'Shetland Flying Boat. Short Brothers: Makers of Fine Aircraft. Designed and Constructed by Short Brothers and Saunders-Roe in collaboration.'

Post War (1945-1960)

Saunders-Roe Ltd is noted for the rather 'extreme' nature of its post-war projects. These included the largest British flying boat, the Princess; the first jet flying boat fighter, the SR.A/1; and the SR.53 mixed power interceptor.

After the takeover of **Short Brothers (Rochester & Bedford) Ltd** by the Government, test pilot Geoffrey Tyson, and the designer Sir Arthur Gouge, moved to Saunders-Roe Ltd. Tyson's display of the SR.A/1 jet fighter flying boat TG271 at the 1948 Farnborough show is still remembered as one of Farnborough's finest. The aircraft was one of the first to provide the pilot with a 'g-suit', and it could pull 6 g. The SR.A/1 prototype, TG263, first flew at Cowes on 16 July 1947, three prototypes being built. Design and component manufacture was at Beaumaris, Anglesey, with assembly and flight test at East Cowes.

By 1950, Saunders-Roe Ltd had joined Shorts in fighting a rearguard action for the flying boat. Advertising copy for the Saunders-Roe Princess illustrates this:

> *Water is and must continue to be the ideal runway material. It is unbreakable, and can never wear out or need strengthening, and it is provided by nature free of charge. The Saunders-Roe 'Princess' flying boats will displace some 140 tons, but few existing concrete runways in the world would take an aircraft of this weight.*

The prototype Princess G-ALUN, with its ten Proteus engines, first flew on 22 August 1952. This giant aircraft, with its wing span of nearly 220ft, accumulated less than 100 hours of test-flying in the forty-seven flights made up to June 1954. The prototype was cocooned at Calshot Castle with the two other airframes which had been built, all three being progressively scrapped from 1967 at Burseldon, on the Hamble River.

The Spartan Arrow was a development of the Simmonds Spartan. G-ABWP is the last flying example of the type. (Ian Frimston/ Fuji Labs)

The SR.53 mixed-power interceptor was of tailed delta configuration and was propelled by a 1,750lb-thrust Viper turbojet augmented by an 8,000lb-thrust Spectre rocket. Two prototypes were built, the first, XD145, being flown at Boscombe Down on 16 May 1957. Performance was spectacular, with climb rates in excess of 50,000ft/min being achieved. A total of forty-two test flights were flown, but the programme was marred by a fatal accident to the second prototype on 5 June 1958.

Saunders-Roe Ltd was taken over by **Westland Aircraft Ltd** in 1959 (see below).

The Sopwith Aviation Co.: In May 1913, H.G. Hawker was test-flying the Sopwith Bat Boat at Cowes, operating from the S.E. Saunders sheds. The Sopwith Type C (serial 138) was also operating from Cowes in early 1914.

Spartan Aircraft Ltd developed improved versions of the Simmonds Spartan (see Hamble) which were produced as the Spartan Arrow and the Spartan Three-Seater. The company took over as production facilities, the works at Somerton previously used by J. Samuel White & Co. Ltd. The Spartan Arrow, which was first flown (as G-AAWY) in May 1930, was less successful than the Simmonds Spartan, despite a change from the Simmonds symmetrical aerofoil to the more docile Clark 'Y' section. Fifteen Spartan Arrow and twenty-six Spartan Three-Seater were built.

The first Spartan Three-Seater, G-ABAZ, was flown during June 1930. The Three-Seater was more successful than the Spartan Arrow, in part because it was ideally suited to joy-riding and therefore appealed to a commercial, as well as a private owner, market. The Three-Seater Mk I (nineteen built) sat the passengers ahead of the pilot, this configuration being reversed in the Three-Seater Mk II, seven of which were built. The Mk II also featured a change of engine from the upright Gipsy II or Hermes II, to the inverted Hermes IIB/IV.

Spartan Aircraft advertising extolled the robust virtues of the Spartan Arrow and Spartan Three-Seater as follows:

The Spartan Arrow is a robust light aircraft of good performance and easy flying qualities. The cockpits are planned to give a maximum of comfort and protection from draught, together with a good range of view. A high degree of interchange-ability is a feature of the construction.

The Spartan three-seater is unique among British light aircraft; its success is due to an ingenuity of design which enables it to provide exceptional comfort and protection with little sacrifice in performance, and none of strength. The pilot is in a single aft cockpit and the passengers' cockpit is so designed that the two passengers can both face forward, or travel facing each other...

The ideal joy-riding machine – the short landing and take-off runs reduce taxiing between flights to a minimum, and the ease of ingress and egress still further cuts down the time spent on the ground.

British Spartan Aircraft: Light aeroplanes of robust construction and high performance. Distinctly 'Spartan' are the virtues of rugged strength, short take-off run, economy of mainte-nance, and pleasant well-balanced flying controls. Every Spartan aircraft possesses them.

Spartan also produced the Spartan Clipper: a Pobjoy-powered single-engine monoplane with a long slim fuselage, which used the outer wings of the twin-engine Monospar ST4. The sole example of the Clipper, G-ACEG, was first flown on 14 December 1932.

The final production type was the Spartan Cruiser, which had its origins in the form of the Saro-Percival Mailplane G-ABLI of 1931, in collaboration between **Edgar Percival** and **Saunders-Roe Ltd**. Spartan Aircraft Ltd adapted the Mailplane to a passenger configu-ration, this flying in May 1932 as the Spartan Cruiser, G-ABTY. The Cruiser featured a metal fuselage, with a cabin containing six passenger seats instead of the cargo compart-ment of the Mailplane. After the first aircraft, production consisted of thirteen Cruiser II, one of which (YU-SAP) was built in Yugoslavia, and three Cruiser III, the variants having different cabin arrangements. An early (and local) user of the type was Spartan Airlines Ltd, who operated a total of ten of these aircraft between 1932 and 1937, together with Spartan Three-Seater G-ABTR. Towards the end of their flying days, a number of the Spartan Cruiser aircraft were used by Northern & Scottish Airways (later Scottish Airways) on routes in the Hebrides, elsewhere in Scotland, and in northern England.

Spartan Aircraft Ltd, having been actively collaborating with Saunders-Roe Ltd, merged with them in Spring 1933.

Westland Aircraft Ltd took over Saunders-Roe Ltd in 1959. In 1966, the Saunders-Roe Division became the British Hovercraft Corporation. Saunders-Roe Ltd constructed the rear fuselage and loading ramp for the Short Belfast freighter.

The Cowes-based **GKN Westland Aerospace** division has established a role as a specialist manufacturer of large composite structures. Example products include a 12ft composite air intake duct for the centre engine of the MD-11, the inner fixed structure of the A340 thrust reverse system, more than 1,000 composite trailing edge panels for the Boeing 737, components for the Lockheed C-130H/J, Boeing C-17 flap vanes and more than 500 wing-tip fences for the Airbus A320/A321.

J. Samuel White & Co. Ltd were a long established firm of shipbuilders who decided to set up an aviation department in 1912. The designs of the aviation department, which were mainly seaplanes, were sold under the name **Wight**. Howard T. Wright joined J. Samuel White in November 1912, at the end of his contract with Coventry Ordnance Works, to set up the aviation department, which opened on 1 January 1913. The company advertising slogan was: 'Aeroplane and Warship Builders' or (1916) 'Warship & Aeroplane Constructors', and the location of the works was the 'Gridiron Shed' on the bank of the River Medina. The first Wight seaplane was designed and built in six weeks – it crashed on its first flight.

The same fate awaited the Wight No.2. This aircraft was, however, rebuilt with a rede-signed tail section and flew successfully in August 1913. It proved capable of leaving the water with a take-off run of 60yds, and could operate safely from choppy water. By October 1913, the machine had flown twenty hours, and showed great promise, with both good

THE "WIGHT" SEAPLANE
CONSTRUCTED BY

Telegrams:
White,
East Cowes

Telephone:
No. 3
COWES

J. SAMUEL WHITE & CO., LTD., EAST COWES
Warship and Aeroplane Constructors

Left: *A replica of the diminutive Wight Quadruplane can be seen in the Southampton Hall of Aviation.*

handling and seaworthiness. It was also tested as a landplane from a field at Three Gate Cottages, Cowes. In February 1914 the Wight seaplane was being tested at Cowes, flown by E.C. Gordon England.

Several large 'Navyplanes' and 'improved Navyplanes' followed, fourteen of these machines being built. These were followed by the even larger Twin Landplane and Twin Seaplane of 84ft span with a twin-fuselage layout reminiscent of the Lockheed P-38 Lightning. Moving even further up in scale, the company then built (in 1916/1917) two extremely large and ungainly Admiralty AD1000 biplanes, of similar configuration to the Twin Seaplane. These had a span of 115ft (49ft when folded) and a tailplane span of 40ft. Empty weight was 22,000lb.

Wight's most successful design was the Type 840 tractor seaplane for the RNAS. Forty-two were built at Cowes of which eight were delivered as spares, with a further thirty-two by **Wm Beardmore & Co. Ltd** (twelve of which were delivered as spares) and at least eight by **Portholme Aerodrome Co.**, which were also delivered as spares. Fifty-one examples of the Wight Landplane Bomber/converted seaplane were also constructed, some aircraft being delivered to storage without engines.

Sub-contract work included 110 Sunbeam Maori-powered Short 184 aircraft. In 1916, White built a diminutive quadruplane N546 of only 19ft span, a replica of which can be seen in the Southampton Hall of Aviation. Aircraft construction ceased on 21 January 1919.

During the Second World War, J. Samuel White & Co. Ltd are reported to have manufactured Spitfire, Mosquito and Lancaster components. The East Cowes yards were sold to Saunders-Roe/British Hovercraft Corporation/Westland, the West Cowes engineering shops remaining in use by White's to manufacture air conditioning components.

Ryde

Britten-Norman Ltd had a workshop in the former Labour Party Committee Rooms at the rear of the Commodore Cinema in Star Street, Ryde. These cramped facilities were used in 1956/1957 for the construction of Druine Turbi G-APFA. Mr A.W.J. Ord-Hume (see also Sandown) was involved in the completion of G-APFA, which was first flown (unofficially) on 24 April 1957, and (officially) on 13 May 1957.

This particular example was tail heavy when first flown with a Coventry Victor engine. Although subsequently re-engined with a Continental A65, the aircraft remained rather tail heavy, as the author can attest, having flown in this aircraft with its owner Fred Keitch.

Sandown

ARV Aviation Ltd was set up by Richard Noble, holder of the World Land Speed Record, in December 1983 to manufacture the two-seat ARV Super 2 light aircraft. The ARV1 Super 2 prototype, G-OARV, first flew at Sandown on 11 March 1985 and eighteen aircraft were built up to 1988. The aircraft showed excellent handling and performance, but has not been blessed with commercial success. Problems occurred with the crankshaft of the novel Hewland AE75 three-cylinder two-stroke engine. As a result, a number of aircraft have been re-engined with Rotax and similar engines. A further consequence of these difficulties was that ARV Aviation Ltd stopped production of the aircraft, entering administration on 17 June 1988. A succession of companies has since been involved in the design, including: **Taurus Aviation**; **Island Aircraft** (a subsidiary of Taurus) set up in 1984 but failed in 1991; and **Aviation Scotland Ltd** which took over the assets of Island Aircraft and were based at Burnbank near Glasgow.

NDN Aircraft Ltd: Following on from the Firecracker, NDN developed a turbine version, the NDN-1T Turbo Firecracker. The NDN-1T was powered by the Pratt & Whitney PT6A–25A of 550shp and the prototype, G-SFTR, first flew on 1 September 1983. A new company, **Firecracker Aircraft (UK) Ltd**, was set up to produce the type.

G-SFTR is the prototype NDN-1T Turbo-Firecracker, which competed unsuccessfully with the Embraer Tucano to become the next primary trainer for the Royal Air Force. (NDN Aircraft Ltd via Ken Ellis)

ARV Super 2 G-BMWJ has been re-engined with a Rotax engine in place of its original Hewland. (Author)

The purposeful Norman NDN-6 Fieldmaster failed to achieve market success in the hands of a series of companies. This photograph shows the first two production aircraft. (NDN Aircraft Ltd via Ken Ellis)

The NDN-1T (promoted by Hunting Group) was unsuccessful in the AST412 competition for a trainer for the RAF, the competition being won by the Shorts-built Embraer Tucano. However, although unsuccessful in the RAF competition, the Turbo Firecracker was used briefly by Specialist Flight Training at Carlisle for foreign military pilot training. The existing airframes, rights, tooling and spares were eventually sold to the discus thrower and shot-putter Mr Richard Slaney in the USA, G-SFTR becoming N2157C in October 1989.

The first NDN.6 Fieldmaster, G-NRDC, flew at Sandown on 17 December 1981. The company became **Norman Aeroplane Co. Ltd** (NAC) in July 1985, simultaneously moving production to Barry in South Wales. The first production aircraft, G-NACL, flew on 29 March 1987. This aircraft flew in Firemaster configuration at Old Sarum, Wiltshire, on 28 October 1989. Subsequent companies involved with the Fieldmaster project include **Brooklands Aircraft Ltd**, **Croplease Ltd** and **Croplease plc**.

Mr A.W.J. Ord-Hume of 'Mirador', Rose Mead Lane, Sandown, has produced a number of derivatives and modifications of existing designs for home-building. Mr Ord-Hume was, in particular, responsible for producing an 'anglicised' version of the French Minicab, all UK-built examples of the type (at least five aircraft) being to this standard. This activity operated under the name **Southern Aircraft Co**.

Mr Ord-Hume also co-founded Phoenix Aircraft Ltd (of Cranleigh, Surrey and Denham, Bucks) which extensively redesigned the Luton Minor, leading to its post-war success as a home-built aircraft. Recently, Mr Ord-Hume published a comprehensive history of British light aircraft construction, entitled *British Light Aeroplanes – Their Evolution, Development and Perfection 1920 – 1940*.

Somerton (also known as West Cowes)

The aeronautical usage of Somerton airfield is presented chronologically below.

J. Samuel White & Co. Ltd used Somerton as a factory and flight test airfield from 1916, the Wight Landplane Bomber being built at Somerton. After one example for the RNAS, a revised version was flown in 1916, crashing on its second flight due to failure of the outer portion of its 76ft-span upper wing. Five aircraft were built with a reduced wing extension, and these formed the basis of a seaplane derivative, the 'Converted' Seaplane, forty of which were built.

In July 1919, the **Selsdon Aero & Engineering Co. Ltd** commenced work at Somerton Works, Cowes, IoW. The works were subsequently used by the Vectis Bus Co., and then by **Spartan Aircraft Ltd,** and have survived relatively unchanged.

Saunders-Roe Ltd: Somerton was used for test-flying of the Saunders-Roe-built Segrave Meteor G-AAXP, which first flew here on 28 May 1930. Supermarine Walrus aircraft built by Saunders-Roe Ltd were also flown here during the Second World War.

Ventnor

Newman, Crinage & Co., of Ventnor, advertised their ability to supply 'Wood and metal component parts for all types of aircraft'. Nothing else known.

Whiteley Bank

F. Warren **Merriam**, who was Chief Instructor of the Bristol flying school at Brooklands prior to the First World War, constructed a glider at Whiteley Bank for the 1922 Itford glider trials. The glider was later converted to a two-seat configuration and was still flying in 1930.

Somerset

Banwell

The **Bristol Aeroplane Co. Ltd** established a dispersed production factory at Banwell, which was used for production of the Hawker Tempest II. The first Bristol-built Tempest II, MW374, flew on 4 October 1944. The Banwell shadow factory was located at Elborough between Banwell and Hutton, to the south east of RAF Locking (Weston-super-Mare). The Old Mixon shadow factory, which was subsequently used by Bristol's Helicopter Division and Westland Helicopters Ltd, is located immediately to the west of RAF Locking. See also Old Mixon.

Bath

Bath Aircraft Ltd, of Flight Works, Lower Bristol Road, Bath advertised their capabilities as 'Manufacturers of planes, propellers, struts, fuselages, etc. to the highest possible quality'; nothing else known.

The **Bush** Motorplane was built in 1912 by the Bush brothers, after a series of glider experiments, and was briefly tested at Keynsham. The Motorplane was a single-seat tractor biplane of unequal span and workmanlike appearance. The overhung top wing gave the machine the distinct air of a Caudron design.

W. & T. Lock, of Bristol Road, Bath is included as an aircraft manufacturer in *The Aviation Pocket-Book 1919-1920*; nothing else known.

Clevedon

Folland Aircraft Ltd had dispersed capacity at Clevedon during the Second World War.

Glastonbury

Whittaker MW6 Microlights were distributed by **Skysports Ltd** of The Vestry Hall, High Street, Glastonbury.

Martock

Sparrows Yard at Bower Hinton was used to manufacture Spitfire/Seafire assemblies in support of **Westland Aircraft Ltd**.

Merryfield

Merryfield airfield was constructed during the Second World War for American use. In the 1950s, the airfield was used as an RAF Operational Conversion Unit (OCU) for the Canberra and Vampire. Merryfield was also used by **Westland Aircraft Ltd** for fixed-wing flight test activity of the Seafire and, in particular, the Wyvern. The sole Welkin NF.2 was scrapped at Merryfield.

One of the last fixed-wing aircraft developments contracted to Westland Aircraft Ltd was the modification of Meteor RA490 for deflected jet pipe trials. RA490 was first flown at

Like many other manufacturers, Westland used local workshops for dispersed production, in this case for fuselage assembly at Sparrows workshop at Bower Hinton, Martock. (Westland)

Boscombe Down on 15 May 1954. Some fifteen hours of contractor trials were carried out at Merryfield. The engine tailpipes permitted jet deflections of up to sixty-three degrees, and the trials demonstrated a reduction in stall speed of up to 40kt.

Old Mixon, Weston-super-Mare

The Bristol Aeroplane Co. Ltd: Old Mixon was a shadow factory set up by the Ministry of Aircraft Production and used for the construction of 3,336 Bristol Beaufighter, built with a heavy reliance on local sub-contractors. The first Weston-built aircraft flew in February 1941. Bristol also constructed at least thirty-six Tempest II at nearby Banwell. A separate assembly building on the airfield was also used, and referred to as the Hutton Moor factory.

From mid-1945, the Bristol Aeroplane Co. produced prefabricated aluminium houses at Weston-super-Mare, alongside the Beaufighter production line, at a rate of some 1,200 houses per month. In 1953, the Bristol Aeroplane Co. was referring to this factory as **The Bristol Aeroplane Co. (Weston) Ltd**.

Bristol Helicopter Division: Bristol purchased the patents and assets of the **ARIII Construction Co. Ltd** partnership in September 1944, Raoul Hafner joining the company as Chief Engineer of the helicopter activity. The helicopter division worked initially at Filton, but subsequently took over the Weston-super-Mare factory, helicopter development being transferred from Filton to Weston in 1955. Production designs were the single-rotor Sycamore and the twin-rotor Belvedere, which was eventually successful following protracted development. The Sycamore was the first post-war helicopter to be built in the UK. Some 180 were produced before production finally ended in 1959, many of these having been built at Filton prior to the move of the helicopter activity to Weston-super-Mare. 1948 advertising copy emphasised their potential for commercial operation: 'Bristol Type 171 Helicopter – providing the inter-urban links for international air travel.' The first production Bristol 192 Belvedere, XG544, was flown for the first time at Weston-super-Mare on 5 July 1958.

Hafner's designs are technically interesting because they represent an entirely independent line of development (as opposed to the Westland designs based upon Sikorsky licences). Hafner's control system principles and blade retention tie rods can still be found today in the

Merryfield was used by Westland for fixed wing flight test activity and is much associated with the Wyvern, seen here in the form of the TF.2 prototype, VP109. (Westland)

Left: *Belvedere development aircraft XG451 is seen here undergoing external load trails with an early empennage configuration.* (Via author)

Below: *Bristol's helicopter division took over the Old Mixon shadow factory. Some 180 Sycamores were built, these examples being preserved at the Newark Air Museum.* (Author)

Lynx, whose design benefited from ideas contributed from both Bristol and Fairey Aviation, once these companies' helicopter interests had been absorbed into Westland Helicopters Ltd.

Westland Helicopters Ltd took over the Weston site from Bristol Helicopters in March 1960 and used it to provide additional production capacity to supplement that at Yeovil. The initial Westland usage was the completion of the production batch of Bristol 192 Belvedere helicopters, the last example being delivered in June 1962. Weston was then used for the turbine conversion of large numbers of Whirlwind helicopters. The Gazelle production line was moved to Weston-super-Mare in the mid-1970s due to the high volume of production at Yeovil of the Sea King and Lynx. Puma repair and modification has also been carried out at Weston-super-Mare.

Westland Industrial Products Ltd (WIPL) manufactured aerospace components (particularly aircraft doors) for a number of programmes. This includes more than 100 airstair doors for the Jetstream 31, together with the fin and tailplane for this aircraft. The company was the sole supplier of passenger doors for the BAe 146 and supplied passenger, baggage and cargo doors, and escape hatches for the Jetstream 41.

The decision by **AgustaWestland** to close its factory at Weston-super-Mare was announced on 10 January 2002, to be effective by the end of May 2002.

Western Airways Ltd: During the Second World War, **Western Airways Ltd** at Weston-super-Mare managed a Civilian Repair Organisation which handled the repair of Lend-Lease Curtiss Tomahawk aircraft. The company subsequently carried out conversions of Anson aircraft to civil use, as reflected in the following advertisement from December 1948: 'Western Airways Ltd can arrange early delivery of passenger versions of Anson 1. Recognised to be the best civil version of this type available today. Anson freighters and navigational trainers available for early delivery.'

Yeovil

Petters Ltd: Petters were initially famous for their domestic ironware made at the Nautilus Works, and were later well known for their diesel engines.

One of the twelve Short Admiralty Type 184 seaplanes to be built by Westland Aircraft Works in 1916. (Westland)

First World War Production

Petters' aviation department was formed on 3 April 1915 by the Petter twins – Percy and Ernest. The aircraft department was styled **Westland Aircraft Works (Branch of Petters Ltd)**, with telegraphic address 'Aircraft, Yeovil'. Typical advertising from around April 1916 included: 'Aircraft Constructors to The Admiralty', 'Orders can be accepted for complete machines, propellers, parts.' Robert Bruce joined the company from The British & Colonial Aeroplane Co. Ltd and was joined by Arthur Davenport from Ruston, Proctor & Co. Ltd. The company built a variety of types during the First World War including the following:

- Short 184 seaplane: twelve aircraft, first aircraft delivered January 1916
- Short Admiralty Type 166 seaplane: twenty, first aircraft delivered July 1916
- Sopwith 1½ Strutter: seventy-five, delivery from late 1916
- AIRCO DH4: at least 125 (some sources state 140 or 150)
- AIRCO DH9
- AIRCO DH9A
- Vickers Vimy: twenty-five aircraft
- Westland N1b Scout
- Westland Wagtail
- Westland Weasel

Early Westland-built aircraft, including the Short 184, Short 166 and 1½ Strutter, were delivered by rail prior to the establishment of an airfield next to the works, the airfield coming into use in April 1917. At the time of its construction, the Vimy production shed at Yeovil was said to be the largest single-span hangar (140ft width) in Britain.

The Westland N1b was a Bentley AR1-powered single-seat seaplane fighter first flown in August 1917; two were built with serials N16 and N17. The Wagtail was an ABC Wasp-powered single-bay biplane, the first of five prototypes flying in April 1918. The last two prototypes were used for testing of the Armstrong-Siddeley Lynx engine. The Weasel was a two-seat fighter powered by the ABC Dragonfly and originally intended as a potential replacement for the Bristol Fighter. Four were built, the prototype F2912 flying in November 1918. These aircraft were used at Farnborough, mainly for engine testing of the 350hp Armstrong Siddeley Jaguar II (in F2914) and the 400hp Bristol Jupiter II (in J6577).

Westland was responsible for the DH9A, which was transformed from the AIRCO DH9 by the use of the American Liberty engine. AIRCO would normally have carried out this

N5972 is a
Rolls-Royce
Eagle-powered
AIRCO DH4,
one of a batch of
fifty constructed
by Westland
Aircraft Works
for the RNAS.
(Westland)

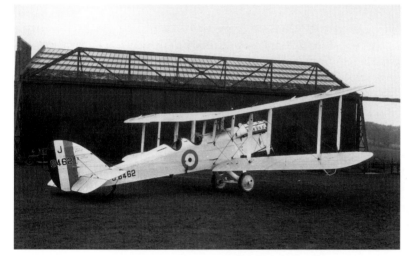

Westland was
responsible for
the development
of the DH9A,
here represented
by a late model
dual control
machine,
J8462, which is
parked outside
Westland's
'Vimy hangar'.
(Westland)

The Westland
Weasel was
a potential
replacement
for the Bristol
Fighter. F2913
was the
second of three
proto-types. A
single additional
aircraft was
ordered at the
end of August
1919. (Westland)

development, but were too busy with contracts for the DH10. The first Liberty-powered Westland-built DH9A, C6122, flew at Yeovil on 19 April 1918. Up to the end of 1918, no less than 865 DH9A had been built by a number of contractors.

The Westland production numbers for the DH9 and DH9A quoted in different sources vary markedly. The figures are undoubtedly confused by a number of post-war rebuilds of DH9A, and conversions between DH9 and DH9A. A *Flight* article celebrating forty years of Westland stated: '...the Yeovil works got underway with their own contract for 423 machines of the type. Of these 390 were completed before the Armistice.' The Westland Aircraft volume published by Putnam indicates a total of 355 DH9A, together with the majority of the 300 DH9 that were ordered from the firm.

Production between the Wars

In 1922, the company was using the following (trilingual) advertising copy: 'Westland: the word needs no translation. The world over it is known for the super aircraft designed and constructed by Petters Ltd. Correspondence invited in any of the principal languages.'

The fact that Westland held contracts for DH9A production, development and repair (and was subsequently to develop the type into the highly successful Wapiti) protected the company from the worst of the lean years after the First World War. Even so, the company did find it necessary to produce products for other markets, leading, for example, to the production of relatively small numbers of Westland-built pianos.

An early DH9A derivative produced at Yeovil was the cumbersome Walrus of 1920. This machine was intended for naval use and featured a plethora of additional equipment including folding wings, flotation bags, undercarriage and fuel jettison, etc. All this required the power of a 450hp Napier Lion II. Although Westland are often attributed the dubious privilege of having designed this edifice, the true glory belongs to the RAE. Armstrong Whitworth built the prototype, to the design of the RAE, as the Tadpole J6585. The thirty-six production Walrus were constructed by Westland.

The Westland Limousine and Six-seater Limousine were single-engine biplanes with passenger cabins for three and five passengers, respectively. The Limousine Mk I K-126/G-EAFO flew in July 1919, with the first Mk II, G-EAJL, following in October of the same year. The aircraft was initially marketed as an executive aircraft with the combined character-istics of 'a luxurious motor and a yacht'. In contrast to this glowing description, Ord-Hume provides a less complimentary opinion, saying that the aircraft had a 'strong visual affinity to a tried and tested railway carriage'. The Six-seater Limousine prototype, G-EARV, won the £7,500 prize as the best 'small aeroplane' in the 1920 Air Ministry Commercial Aircraft competitions at Martlesham Heath. Production comprised a single Mk I, five Mk II, and two of the much larger Mk III Six-seater Limousine.

In September 1926 Westland flew the Westbury J7765, a twin-engine heavy fighter to Specification 4/24 which was designed to use the Coventry Ordnance Works (COW) 37mm gun as its armament. Only two prototypes were built.

Westland developed the DH9A into the Wapiti – the quintessential long-serving (and unglamorous) general-purpose aircraft of the inter-war years. The Wapiti prototype J8495 was first flown on 7 March 1927, the main production variant being the Wapiti IIA, 413 of which were built for the RAF. The *Flight* article celebrating forty years of Westland cites 565 Wapiti aircraft, including 517 for the Air Ministry, thirty-eight for Australia, four for China and four for South Africa. Twenty-seven additional aircraft were licence-built in South Africa. Other sources cite a production total of 558 aircraft.

In 1930 Westland were advertising:

> *The Wapiti general purpose two-seater. Wherever Service aircraft are called upon to operate under arduous conditions; where reliability and performance are vital factors – over the arid wastes of Iraq and Arabia; above Indian jungles; across the African veldt and Australian desert – the WESTLAND WAPITI is the standard chosen by the Air Forces both at home and abroad. Westland Aircraft Works (Branch of Petters Ltd), Yeovil.*

This was nothing less than a true reflection of the operational use and value of this robust machine. At one time, the RAF had more Wapiti aircraft in service than any other type.

The Wallace was a refined development of the Wapiti, which first flew, as the Westland PV6 K3488/P6, on 31 October 1931 (the prototype being a converted Wapiti V). The PV6 (as G-ACBR) was used as the back-up aircraft to the Westland-Houston PV3, G-ACAZ, which made the first flight over Mount Everest on 3 April 1933.

The Wapiti prototype J8495 is seen here in early 1927 prior to its fuselage being covered. This aircraft used DH9A wing and tail components. (Westland)

Source	Prototypes	New build	Conversions from Wapiti	Total
1	2	8 Wallace I	57 Wallace I	67 Wallace I
	–	104 Wallace II	3 Wallace II	107 Wallace II
2	1	–	68 Wallace I	69 Wallace I
	–	104 Wallace II	–	104 Wallace II
3	1	Total of 113 Mk I and II	12 initially	*not specified*
4	–	–	68 Wallace I	68 Wallace I
	–	104 Wallace II	–	104 Wallace II
5	1	8 Wallace I	58 Wallace I, plus 1 ex-civil conversion from G-ACJU	68 Wallace I
	–	107 Wallace II	–	107 Wallace II
6	1	8 Wallace I	57 Wallace I, plus 1 ex-civil conversion from G-ACJU	67 Wallace I
	–	104 Wallace II	3 Wallace II	107 Wallace II

Sources

1 *British Aircraft at War 1939-45*, Gordon Swanborough.
2 *British Aircraft of World War II*, David Mondey.
3 'Wings from the West – Forty years of Westland', *Flight* article by H.F. King. (Source 3 does not list Wapiti conversions subsequent to initial batch of twelve Wallace I.)
4 *World Encyclopaedia of Aircraft Manufacturers*, Bill Gunston.
5 *Westland Aircraft since 1915*, Derek James.
6 *Westland 50*, J.W.R. Taylor and Maurice F. Allward.

Wallace production comprised a mix of new–build aircraft and Wapiti conversions, with quoted production quantities being subject to considerable variation, dependent upon the reference source. (See above table.)

Like many of the country's major manufacturers, Westland participated in the Air Ministry Two-seat Light Aeroplane Trials of 1924, entering the Woodpigeon biplane and the Widgeon monoplane. Two examples of the Woodpigeon were built, the first (G-EBIY) flying on 17 September 1924. The second aircraft (G-EBJV) featured a significant increase in wingspan and area in an attempt to improve the marginal flying performance of the type.

Westland's only entry into the private aircraft market to reach production status was with the Widgeon. Originally an entrant into the 1924 Lympne Two-seat Light Aeroplane Trials, the 1096cc Blackburn Thrush-powered Widgeon I first flew at Yeovil on 22 September 1924. The type was a parasol monoplane with folding wings, the prototype using the same fuselage design as the Woodpigeon biplane. The wings were of 'lozenge' planform with

The prototype Wallace II, K3488, at Yeovil. This machine was initially G-AAWA, the Wapiti V demonstrator, before becoming the Westland PV6 G-ACBR. It was the back-up aircraft for the Everest flight, and the prototype for the Wallace series. (Westland)

This immaculately polished Wallace I is taking part in the RAF Pageant at Hendon. (Westland)

pronounced compound taper, a feature subsequently adopted on the Lysander. The low-installed power proved to be the downfall of the design, and the aircraft was badly damaged during the Lympne competition.

The Widgeon II, G-EBJT, was powered by a 60hp Genet I engine and was a re-built version of the Widgeon I. This proved to be a wholly practical machine and pointed the way to the Widgeon III, which was placed in full production.

The first Widgeon III, G-EBPW, was flown at the end of March 1927 and featured revised fuselage lines and a conventional constant chord wing planform. The Widgeon III/IIIA were variously powered by the Cirrus II, Cirrus III, Genet II, Gipsy I, Cirrus Hermes I/II and ABC Hornet engines. Production comprised the prototype Widgeon I (subsequently converted to Widgeon II), a prototype Widgeon III, and twenty-five production machines (Widgeon III and IIIA). The Widgeon IIIA sub-variant differed in having a steel tube fuselage construction and a split-axle undercarriage arrangement. A number of Widgeon III aircraft were subsequently converted to this standard.

The Westland IV civil airliner was a wooden passenger transport powered by three Cirrus III engines. The prototype, later to be registered G-EBXK, flew at Yeovil on 22 February 1929. The second machine, G-AAGW, featured Cirrus Hermes engines and introduced metal construction for the rear fuselage. The Westland IV was followed just over a year later by the more powerful Genet Major-powered Wessex, which flew in May 1930. Seven production machines followed the Wessex prototype P-1/G-AAAJI/G-ABAJ. The last of these, G-ABVB, was a larger eight-seat machine for Portsmouth, Southsea & Isle of Wight Aviation Co. Ltd featuring metal wings, a raised cockpit and larger tail surfaces.

The Westland IV was advertised in September 1929 as:

> *The Westland 3-engined Limousine (Three Hermes engines). The ideal machine for regularity of service, all weather comfort and care-free travel – for business or pleasure. Carries four passengers in cabin with additional seat for a fifth alongside the pilot. The only medium powered commercial vehicle that possesses all the advantages of multi-engined machines, combined with extremely low maintenance and running costs.*

The Wessex received its own publicity:

> *Announcing the Westland Wessex – 3 Armstrong Siddeley Genet Major engines. Pilot, 5 passengers, luggage and lavatory (7 passengers if no lavatory installed). Luxuriously equipped cabin, with Triplex sliding windows, turn indicator and wheel brakes. If any engine of the three fails, the remaining two will maintain the Wessex at 4000ft altitude with full load. For Air Lines, Taxi Work, and the Private Owner.*

A notable, though ultimately unsuccessful, venture was the series of striking Pterodactyl tailless aircraft. These aircraft were originated by Professor G.T.R. Hill, the first aircraft being flown as a glider by the then Capt. Hill in 1924, and as a powered aircraft (Pterodactyl 1a J8067) at Farnborough, Hampshire, on 3 December 1925. Capt. Hill joined Westland in 1928, Westland taking over the subsequent development of the Westland-Hill Pterodactyl in its various forms. Professor Hill was the brother of Air Chief Marshal Sir Roderic Hill and worked at the Royal Aircraft Factory before joining Handley Page Ltd as chief test pilot in 1919.

The Pterodactyl Mk IV was a Gipsy III-powered three-seater, which was flown in March 1931 with serial number K1947. This aircraft was used to develop the control system for the type and proved to be remarkably successful. During its test programme, this model performed aerobatics and was extensively spun. The final Pterodactyl was the large and powerful Mk V K2770, which was flown at Andover in May 1934. This ambitious type was intended as a fighter, which would have mounted a rear turret exploiting an exceptionally large field of fire. The Pterodactyl Mk V was powered by a 650hp Rolls-Royce Goshawk and had the large span of 46ft 8in, but had a fuselage length of only 20ft 6in. The Pterodactyl V proved capable of 190mph, and was regarded as being comparable in performance to in-service designs such as the Hawker Demon.

Westland had an early involvement in rotating-wing aircraft with the construction of two autogiros: the Cierva C.29 and the CL.20. The C.29 was unsuccessful due to ground resonance and vibration, and was not flown. The CL.20 (C for Cierva and L for Lepère) was a two-seat cabin machine powered by the 90hp Pobjoy Niagara S. The sole example, G-ACYI, was flown successfully at Hanworth, the first flight being on 4 February 1935.

Other Westland designs of the inter-war years are summarised below:

- Yeovil: A large Rolls-Royce Condor-powered single-engine biplane to specification 26/23. Three prototypes were built, the first being J7508, initially flown from Yeovil on 3 April 1925, continuing its flight test programme at Andover. The Yeovil competed unsuccessfully with the Hawker Horsley.
- Wizard: Flown as a private venture, the Wizard was an elegant single-seat parasol monoplane powered by a Rolls-Royce F.XIA in a streamlined installation. The type was initially of all-wooden construction, but was subsequently rebuilt as the Wizard I with a steel tube fuselage structure. The machine was further remodelled as the Wizard II with a revised centre section, an all-metal (wing and fuselage) structure and a Rolls-Royce F.XIS engine. The Wizard II was allocated the serial J9252. A

The Cirrus Hermes-powered Westland IV, G-AAGW, is seen here at Yeovil. The type was later developed to become the Genet Major-powered Wessex. (Westland)

The Pterodactyl Mk IV was probably the most successful of this series of tailless aircraft. K1947 is seen at Yeovil, showing clearly its bicycle undercarriage, elliptical tip-mounted rudders and a rather splendid Pterodactyl motif on its nose. (Westland)

The clean installation of the Rolls-Royce F.XIS is emphasised in this photograph of the Wizard II, devoid of virtually all its covering. The rectangular object behind the under-carriage is the retractable cooling radiator lowered to its maximum extent. (Westland)

relatively high performance was achieved by this aircraft, as indicated by a maximum rate of climb in excess of 2,000ft/min.

- Witch: A large parasol monoplane of more than 60ft span, which was designed to specification 23/25 and first flown in 1928. The Witch was intended as a day bomber, or for use as a coastal defence torpedo bomber. The sole prototype, J8596, was used for parachute development testing at Henlow.
- F.20/27: This aircraft was a low-wing wire-braced monoplane, serial J9124, which was powered initially by a Bristol Mercury and subsequently a Bristol Jupiter radial engine. The type was first flown in August 1928 and competed unsuccessfully with the Hawker F.20/27.
- F.29/27: Developed around its planned armament of an upward-firing COW 37mm gun, the F.29/27, J9565, resembled the smaller F.20/27 but for its longer, slimmer fuselage. The F.29/27 was first flown in December 1930.
- F.7/30: The sole F.7/30, K2891, was a Goshawk-powered biplane, which was distinguished by its mid-fuselage engine installation. The fuselage spanned the gap between the wings and the pilot was sat high and well forward (ahead of the gull-wing upper-wing centre section), this position providing a superlative view over the nose.

Westland built all 178 production examples of the Hawker Hector, the aircraft being assembled in the Vimy hangar. Components of at least fifteen aircraft can be seen in this photograph, which was taken on 1 October 1937. (Westland)

The Whirlwind production line, with around a dozen aircraft visible. Note the prominent outboard automatic slats on the wing of the aircraft in the foreground. (Westland)

In addition to their own designs, Westland built the Hawker Hector Army co-operation type as an Audax replacement for the RAF. The Hector, of which Westland built all 178 production machines, was noted for the smoothness of its twenty-four-cylinder engine and its beautifully harmonised controls. The first Westland-built machine, K8090, was flown in February 1937, with the entire production run being completed within ten months. Westland had also constructed forty-three Hawker Audax and the prototype Hendy 3308 Heck G-ACTC, which was flown in July 1934.

During 1935 Westland Aircraft Works separated from Petters Ltd, becoming **Westland Aircraft Ltd** on 4 July 1935.

Second World War Mass Production

Westland Aircraft Ltd came into being just before the expansion schemes prior to the Second World War. In 1938 Petters Ltd sold their interest in Westland to John Brown & Co. Ltd, the Petters engine business also being sold and moved to Loughborough, thereby freeing additional production capacity at Yeovil. Wartime products such as the Lysander, Spitfire and Seafire dominate the company's subsequent history, prior to the post-war decision to focus on helicopter production.

Westland's most famous product, the Lysander, was first flown (K6127) at Boscombe Down on 15 June 1936. The type was used for Army co-operation, target towing and (most famously) for special duties (the delivery and collection of SOE personnel to and from occupied Europe). The 1947 edition of *Jane's All the World's Aircraft* indicates Westland production of 1,426 Lysander, suggesting a production total of 1,651 aircraft, including the 225 built in Canada (other production totals can also be found). Seventeen of the UK total were built in the Westland works at Doncaster, which were subsequently used as a repair organisation for Westland-built aircraft.

The Westland Whirlwind was a twin-engine, four-cannon fighter designed to meet Specification F.37/35, and was first flown (L6844) on 11 October 1938, also at Boscombe Down. The Whirlwind was hampered by its under-developed Peregrine engines; production was limited to 114 aircraft plus the two prototypes. Operationally, the aircraft was found to be restricted by relatively poor endurance and performance at altitude, despite it being an excellent, heavily-armed gun platform. As a result it was mainly used for convoy escort patrols.

The Lysander is best known for its use in clandestine operations to occupied Europe during the Second World War. Fairfield Aviation of Watford and Elstree were responsible for carrying out special operations modifications to the Lysander. (Westland)

Welkin production, with cockpit sections in the foreground and wing centre sections to the rear. The cockpit sections are being built back-to-back in pairs on a common central jig. (Westland)

The last of Westland's wartime designs was the Welkin, which was intended for use as a high altitude interceptor against specification F.4/40, having been selected for production in preference to the Vickers Type 432. The Welkin was a large aircraft with a 70ft wing span and an armament of four 20mm cannon. The first prototype, DG558/G, was first flown at Yeovil on 1 November 1942. A total of 101 Welkin production aircraft were built, but the type never entered service, with most aircraft being delivered to storage and eventually scrapped. The last twenty-six Welkin were delivered without engines. A single Welkin II night fighter prototype, PF370, was built, being flown on 23 October 1944. Work on the pressure cabin for the Welkin led to the formation of Normalair Ltd, this company being registered on 15 March 1946.

Other Westland wartime contracts included the construction of 685 Spitfire (Mk IB, VB and VC), and eighteen Fairey Barracuda (source: 1947 *Jane's All the World's Aircraft*).

Westland was also the major manufacturer of the Seafire, but actual production quantities are the subject of some uncertainty. The table below indicates a consensus view of overall Seafire production, which, in addition to Westland, was undertaken by AST Ltd (conversions of Spitfire to Seafire IB), Supermarine (prototypes and late model production) and Cunliffe-Owen. Note that there may have been additional activity at Airspeed Ltd. Mr Alan Butler, the Chairman of Airspeed Ltd is reported in *The Aeroplane Spotter* of 11 January 1945 as telling the Annual General Meeting of Airspeed Ltd that 'large numbers of Spitfires had been converted into Seafires' by the firm. However, no other evidence has been found to support this assertion.

Seafire Mark	Quantity by Manufacturer				
	Vickers-Armstrongs Ltd (Aircraft Section) Supermarine Works)	**AST Ltd**	**Cunliffe-Owen Aircraft Ltd**	**Westland Aircraft Ltd**	**Total**
IB: conversions from Spitfire VB	Prototypes AB205, AD371, BL676 and thirty at South Marston	136	–	–	169
IIC: conversions from Spitfire VC	Prototype AD371 and 262 conversions	–	–	110	373
III: new-build with folding wings	Prototype MA970	–	350	913	1,264
XV: Griffon-powered	Six prototypes	–	184	250	440
XVII: cut-down rear fuselage	Prototype NS493	–	20	213	234
F.45: naval Spitfire F.21	Prototype TM379 and fifty production	–	–	–	51
F.46: Contra-props	Twenty-four production	–	–	–	24
F.47: modified wing fold	Prototype TM383 and ninety production	–	–	–	91
Total	Fourteen prototypes, 456 production = 470	136	554	1,486	2,646

The total Seafire production figures quoted above are made up of fourteen prototypes, 538 Spitfire conversions and 2,094 new-build aircraft. Of these, Westland was responsible for 1,376 new-build aircraft and 110 Spitfire VC conversions to Seafire IIC. These figures exclude the possible activity at Airspeed Ltd, referred to above.

For a short period Westland was also involved in the assembly, armour and armament installation and testing of lend–lease Mohawk and Tomahawk aircraft. Other wartime activity included production of Albemarle centre sections and Spitfire and Seafire repair.

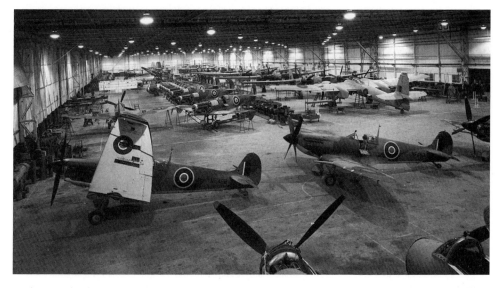

A photograph taken in February 1944, showing the final assembly of Seafire and Welkin aircraft. (Westland)

Post War (1945-1960)

The last Westland fixed-wing design was the troublesome Wyvern. This impressive, not to say imposing, naval strike aircraft suffered a protracted seven years of development involving sixteen prototypes. Wyvern development testing was carried out at Merryfield as well as at Yeovil. The production aircraft served with the Fleet Air Arm for only four years. Wyvern development and production is summarised below:

Model	Number built	Comments
TF. Mk 1 prototypes	6	RR Eagle powered. TS371 first flown at Boscombe Down on 16 December 1946. (12 December 1946 is quoted in *Westland 50*.)
TF. Mk 1 pre-series	10	Four of these aircraft were not flown.
TF. Mk 2 prototypes	3	Turbine-powered prototypes. VP120 (Clyde) flew 18 January 1949, with Python-powered VP109 flying on 22 March 1949 and VP113 on 30 August 1949.
T. Mk 3	1	Dual control trainer, one only, VZ739, flown 11 February 1950.
TF. Mk 2 pre-series	13	First aircraft flown on 16 February 1950. Seven additional aircraft converted to pre-series S. Mk 4.
S. Mk 4 pre-series	7	Converted on production line from last seven pre-series TF Mk 2.
S. Mk 4 production	87	The operational production machines.

The troubled development of the Wyvern marked a period of transition for Westland; initial license production of Sikorsky helicopters followed an agreement concluded on 10 January 1947 and was to lead to Westland becoming the company around which Britain's helicopter industry was to crystallise. The first helicopter to be built by Westland, a WS-51 G-AKTW, flew at Yeovil on 5 October 1948.

One of the last fixed-wing aircraft developments contracted to Westland was the modification of Meteor RA490 for deflected jet pipe trials. This aircraft, which had previously been used as a trials aircraft for the Beryl turbojet, was first flown at Boscombe Down on 15 May 1954. Contractor trials were carried out at Merryfield.

During the immediate post-war period, Westland decided to enter the field of helicopter manufacture, initially on the basis of the licence production, and subsequent development, of established Sikorsky products. The main Westland helicopter products that were flown during the period prior to the reorganisation of the industry in 1960 are listed in the following table:

Type	Comments
Dragonfly	Sikorsky S-51 produced as WS-51 Dragonfly, powered by Alvis Leonides or Pratt & Whitney Wasp Junior. Some sources state that 139 were built, although a total of 133 is also widely quoted. In addition to UK Service aircraft and British civil machines, the type was exported for service in Ceylon, France, Iraq, Japan and Yugoslavia. The first development WS-51, G-AKTW, flew on 5 October 1948 and Sikorsky supplied an additional six aircraft as part of the licence agreement. These six aircraft may be responsible for the production number discrepancy noted above.
Widgeon	Civil derivative of the Dragonfly with revised cabin arrangements. The Widgeon made use of a Whirlwind rotor head to provide an extended centre of gravity range. The prototype G-ALIK was first flown on 23 August 1955. Fifteen were built, three of which were conversions from the WS-51 Dragonfly, including the original WS-51 G-AKTW.

This fine
photograph of
the prototype
Wyvern TF.
Mk 2 VP109
emphasises
its clean lines
and the field of
view from its
high-set cockpit.
(Westland)

Testing of the
WS55 Whirlwind
included trials of
XJ398 fitted with
barn door-like
drag plates.
(Westland)

The prototype
Widgeon G-ALIK
is seen here
on Westland's
airfield at Yeovil.
(Westland)

Type	Comments
Whirlwind	Sikorsky S-55 produced with various engines, including Leonides Major piston engine and Gnome gas turbine. A Sikorsky-built demonstrator, G-AMHK, was flown at Westland on 6 June 1951 and was later allocated the serial WW339. The first Westland-built WS-55 Srs 1, G-AMJT, was flown on 12 November 1952. The same aircraft was allocated the military serial XA862 and re-designated Westland WS-55 Whirlwind HAR.1, flying in this guise at Yeovil on 15 August 1953. Some 296 Whirlwind were built for the UK armed services in nine different marks, the most important versions being the HAS.7 (129), and HAR.10 (sixty-eight). A total of sixty-eight civil WS-55 were built in three versions, with additional conversions of ex-military machines. Total production exceeded 400 machines. The last RAF Whirlwind was retired from service on 30 November 1981.
Westminster	Crane/transport helicopter using Sikorsky S-56 dynamic components, powered by two Napier Eland. Only two built; prototype G-APLE first flown on 15 June 1958, the second aircraft G-APTK following on 4 September 1959.
Wessex	Derived from the Sikorsky S-58 and converted to turbine power with either a single Napier Gazelle or two Gnome turbo-shafts. The Sikorsky-built S-58 (HSS-1N) pattern aircraft, XL722, was re-engined with a Napier Gazelle and flown on 17 May 1957. The Westland-built pre-production prototype XL727 first flew on 20 June 1958. 382 Wessex were built, the most important versions being the Mk 1 (128), Mk 2 (seventy-four) and Mk 5 (101). The first coupled-Gnome Wessex was flown on 18 January 1962. The main Gnome-powered production types were the HC. Mk 2 flown on 5 October 1962 and the HU. Mk 5 Commando assault variant flown on 31 May 1963.

Many of the above products were referred to as Westland Sikorsky designs, this description being used in Westland advertising material as early as 1948. As an example, in 1950 we find: 'Westland Sikorsky S-51. The first and only British-built helicopter with a Full Certificate of Airworthiness.'

Rationalisation and Modern Times

Saunders-Roe Ltd was purchased by Westland in 1959. Shortly after this came the major consolidation of the helicopter sector. On 23 March 1960, the **Bristol Helicopter Division** was acquired, followed on 2 May 1960 by the aviation interests of **The Fairey Co. Ltd**. Of the six helicopter division sites – Yeovil, Cowes, Eastleigh, Weston-super-Mare, Hayes and White Waltham – only Yeovil and Cowes remain in use today. **Westland Helicopters Ltd** was formed when the company reorganised on 1 October 1966, **Westland Aircraft Ltd** then becoming the name of the holding company. Subsequent helicopter products are tabulated below:

Type	Comments
Scout	Army general-purpose light helicopter derived, like the Wasp, from the Saunders-Roe P.531. The Scout prototypes were the two P.531-2 aircraft G-APVL and G-APVM. The Westland-built, Nimbus-powered G-APVL (later XP166) was flown on 9 August 1959, followed by Gnome-powered G-APVM (later XR493) on 3 May 1960. The first pre-production Scout AH.1, XP165, was flown at White Waltham on 4 August 1960. Eight development aircraft (one being the ex-G-APVL) and 141 production machines were built at Hayes for UK service, with limited additional aircraft exported. The first production aircraft, XP846, was flown in 1961.

This photograph, showing the Westminster prototypes G-APTK (flying) and G-APLE, was probably taken in September 1959. The type was unsuccessful and only these two examples were built. (Westland)

A Wessex equipped with a special amphibious float system hovers menacingly during testing. (Westland)

Type	Comments
Wasp	Naval small ship observation and anti-submarine helicopter developed from Saunders-Roe P.531. The first P.531 prototype, G-APNU, was flown at Eastleigh, Hants on 20 July 1958. A second prototype, G-APNV, was also flown at Eastleigh (on 30 September 1958) and later became XN332. The naval development aircraft (P.531-0) were XN332, XN333 and XN334. The first Wasp HAS1, XS463, was flown at White Waltham on 28 October 1962. The two pre-production aircraft (XS463 and XS476) were followed by ninety-eight production machines built for the Royal Navy at Hayes, with aircraft exported to Brazil (three), the Netherlands (twelve), New Zealand (three), South Africa (seventeen) and Indonesia.

The Lynx AH Mk 9 was the last production version for British Army use, being distinguished by its wheeled undercarriage. (Author)

The Westland Sea King has, in addition to the production of large numbers for the Royal Navy, been widely exported. The type has been extensively and progressively developed from the Sikorsky SH3. (J.S. Smith)

A footnote to Lynx development is provided by the sole example of the Lynx 3, ZE477. The wheeled undercarriage developed for this machine was also applied to the British Army Lynx AH Mk 9. (Westland)

Type	Comments
Sea King	Anti-submarine, search and rescue, troop transport and early warning helicopter adapted from the Sikorsky SH-3. A pattern S-61D-2 aircraft, G-ATYU/XV370, was imported from Sikorsky, followed by four aircraft in component form. XV370 was first flown from Avonmouth Docks on 8 September 1967, following its shipment from the USA.

Westland production began with XV642, first flown on 7 May 1969. Throughout its Westland production run, the Sea King has been substantially developed and grown in capability and maximum all-up weight. Some 328 examples of all marks have been built; many for export customers that include Australia, Belgium, Egypt, Germany, India, Norway, Pakistan and Qatar. The first Commando troop transport variant, G-17-1, flew on 12 September 1973; about eighty have been built, half of which have been exported. In 1996, production came to an end with six Mk 3A search and rescue aircraft for the RAF and two Mk 43B for Norway.

| Bell 47G3B | The Sioux, a licence-built version of the Agusta-Bell 47, was used for Army basic training and observation. Fifty AB47G-3B-1 were supplied by Agusta, with a further 250 AB47G-3B-4 assembled by WHL as the Sioux AH. Mk 1. The first British-assembled aircraft was XT151, which flew at Yeovil on 9 March 1965. |
| Lynx | Army utility/anti-tank helicopter and a very successful naval helicopter optimised for small ship operation. The army and naval variants share common dynamic systems and many airframe components. Produced in collaboration with Aérospatiale (70% Westland, 30% Aérospatiale). XW835, the first of thirteen development aircraft, flew on 21 March 1971. A total of more than 380 had been sold by mid-1995, the type being particularly successful in the small ship role. Export customers have included Brazil, Portugal, South Korea, West Germany, Nigeria, the Netherlands, Denmark, France, Norway, Qatar and Argentina. In November 1998, South Africa announced its intention to procure four Super Lynx. The single Gem 60-powered Lynx 3 ZE477 (first flown on 14 June 1984) failed to enter production. |

The type continues in production and development, with AgustaWestland announcing the sale of sixteen Super Lynx 300 to Qatar in a contract signed on 19 January 2002. This version features a glass cockpit and is powered by the CTS800 engine. Six aircraft were sold to Malaysia in 1999 and two to the Royal Thai Navy in August 2001.

Gazelle	Training and observation helicopter: UK aircraft were built by WHL as part of the Anglo-French helicopter agreement. 262 were built for all three of the UK Armed Services, with a limited number of civil machines. The main user was the Army with 197 Gazelle AH.1. The first production machine was XW842, which was flown at Marignane on 28 January 1972.
Puma	Transport helicopter, designed by Aérospatiale and built by Westland at Hayes under the Anglo-French helicopter agreement. Forty-eight aircraft were built for the RAF, the first production aircraft, XW198, flying on 25 November 1970.
Westland 30	An unsuccessful attempt to enter the civil transport helicopter market. Forty aircraft were built, the prototype G-BGHF flying on 10 April 1979. The prototype was followed by an additional development aircraft, twelve WG30 Srs 100, twenty-four uprated Srs 100-60, a single GE CT7-powered Srs 200 G-ELEC, and a single prototype of the heavier Srs 300, which featured a five-bladed main rotor.

EH101 Merlin   Three-engine anti-submarine military and civil transport helicopter developed jointly
with Agusta of Italy. The prototype EH101, ZF641/PP1, first flew at Yeovil on
9 October 1987. Production commitments to date include a total of nine prototypes,
forty-four Royal Navy Merlin, twenty-two Merlin HC.3 RAF utility transports,
sixteen for Italy (with eight options) and fifteen Cormorant search and rescue aircraft
for Canada. The first production Merlin, ZH821, flew on 7 December 1995. The
Merlin Intensive Flight Trials Unit (IFTU), 700M Naval Air Squadron, was commis-
sioned at Culdrose on 1 December 1998.

In September 2001, it was announced that Denmark had also selected the EH101
to meet its requirements for SAR and troop transport, ordering fourteen aircraft.
This order was followed in December 2001 by the announcement of a further twelve
aircraft ordered by Portugal for use in SAR and fishery protection roles. In January
2002, the Italian government exercised four of their options, with their requirement
standing at eight ASV, four AEW, four Utility, and four amphibious support, with
four further options remaining.

The Westland Lynx demonstrator G-LYNX was used to break the world helicopter speed
record on 11 August 1986, achieving a speed of 249.09mph. This remarkable speed was
achieved using BERP blades, Gem 60 engines and reduced area rearward-facing exhausts to
give a degree of residual jet thrust, which allowed the full thermodynamic performance of the
engines to be exploited, without exceeding the main gearbox torque limits. The airframe was
subjected to careful drag reduction measures, a larger low-set tailplane was fitted and local
strengthening of the tail cone was required.

Attempts to market the Sikorsky Black Hawk as the WS-70 were unsuccessful. WHL
acquired a WS-70 demonstrator, ZG468/G-RRTM, which was first flown on 1 April 1987,
it being reported as having been sold to Bahrain in the spring of 1996.

The company's latest production design is an anglicised Boeing Apache, the WAH-64,
with RTM322 engines and other adaptations, sixty-seven having been ordered on 13
July 1995 to meet the British Army attack helicopter requirement. The first eight were
initially flown at Mesa, Arizona, the remainder being assembled from kits by WHL. The
first Boeing-assembled aircraft was delivered in April 2000, the first Westland-assembled

Ship compatibility trials with HMS Norfolk demonstrate how a folded Merlin fills the available hangar space. (Westland)

machine, ZJ172, being flown for the first time on 18 July 2000. Twelve Apache are allocated to each of four squadrons, with the remaining nineteen allocated either to training or as attrition reserve. The Apache AH. Mk 1 achieved its Release to Service (with nine aircraft operational) on 16 January 2001.

In addition to the helicopter activities outlined above, the company is an important supplier (through **GKN Westland Aerospace** and **Westland Industrial Products Ltd (WIPL)**) of aerospace components to the industry at large. Westland Aerospace has manufacturing facilities at Yeovil and Cowes. The Yeovil group has manufactured Saab 2000 rear fuselage structures and propulsion system packages (consisting of nacelle, engine mounting and internal fittings) and engine nacelles for the Saab 340B, Bombardier Dash 8 (more than 400 ship sets), Dornier 328 and Jetstream 41. For WIPL information, see Weston-super-Mare (Old Mixon).

The defence and motor engineering company **GKN plc** purchased Westland in 1994 to create **GKN Westland Helicopters Ltd**. GKN has its origins in the mechanical engineering supply company Guest, Keen & Nettlefolds, the initials of these parties giving rise to the present company name. In April 1998, it was announced that GKN plc and Finmeccanica SpA of Italy had signed a Memorandum of Understanding to negotiate arrangements for the combination of their helicopter interests, GKN Westland Helicopter Ltd and Agusta. At the 2000 SBAC Show, the company announced management arrangements for the merged company, to be known as **AgustaWestland**. The merged company became operational on 21 February 2001.

Yeovilton

Westland Aircraft Ltd (and **Westland Helicopters Ltd**) operated a small experimental site on the south side of RNAS Yeovilton at Ilchester, used to support intermittent test and trials activities. During the Second World War, this facility was used for both Lysander and Spitfire conversion and modification work.

Wiltshire

Boscombe Down Airfield

Boscombe Down has been the site of many first flights of British aircraft, particularly after the Aircraft and Armaments Experimental Establishment (A&AEE) moved here at the start of the Second World War. The table below provides a listing of first flights, and also serves to illustrate the pace of experimental flying in the immediate post-war years.

Type	Serial	Date	Comments
Supermarine 392 (E.10/44)	TS409	27 July 1946	Developed into Attacker
Hawker P.1040 (N.7/46)	VP401	2 Sept 1947	Developed into Sea Hawk
Armstrong Whitworth AW52	TS363	13 Nov 1947	Flying wing – further comments below
Gloster E.1/44	TX145	9 March 1948	
Hawker P.1052	VX272	19 Nov 1948	Swept wing Sea Hawk
Supermarine 510	VV106	29 Dec 1948	Swept wing Attacker – precursor to the Swift
Avro 707	VX784	4 Sept 1949	Destroyed in a fatal accident within a month of its first flight. Vulcan sub-scale test aircraft
707B	VX790	6 Sept 1950	
707A	WD280	14 July 1951	

Type	Serial	Date	Comments
Supermarine 528	VV119	27 March 1950	Effectively the second prototype Supermarine 510, later modified to Type 535
Hawker P.1081	VX279	19 June 1950	With a swept wing, fin and tailplane, and single jet pipe, the P.1081 continued progress from the P.1052 to the Hunter
Supermarine 535	VV119	23 Aug 1950	Modified Type 528 with afterburning Nene, longer nose, tricycle undercarriage. Precursor to the Swift.
Boulton Paul P.111	VT935	6 Oct 1950	Experimental delta, flown as the P.111A on 2 July 1953
Fairey Delta 1	VX350	12 March 1951	Small experimental tailed delta, span 19ft 6½in, length 26ft 3in
Hawker Hunter	WB188	20 July 1951	First prototype of the outstanding fighter from Hawker Aircraft Ltd
Supermarine 541	WJ960	1 Aug 1951	First of two prototypes for the Swift
Supermarine 508	VX133	31 Aug 1951	Thin unswept wing and butterfly tail
Boulton Paul P.120	VT951	6 Aug 1952	Destroyed within a month of its first flight
Supermarine 529	VX136	29 Aug 1952	Second prototype Type 508 with minor modifications
Short SB5	WG768	2 Dec 1952	Research in support of the English Electric P1
Handley Page Victor	WB771	24 Dec 1952	Handley Page's crescent-winged bomber
Supermarine 525	VX138	27 April 1954	Derived from the Type 508/529 with a swept wing and conventional tail – but for its rotund lines close to the Type 544 Scimitar development aircraft
English Electric P1A	WG760	4 Aug 1954	Developed into the Lightning
Folland Midge	G-39-1	11 Aug 1954	Private venture lightweight fighter
Fairey Delta 2	WG774	6 Oct 1954	High-speed research aircraft, breaking the world absolute speed record on 10 March 1956, attaining 1,132mph. Subsequently adapted as the BAC221
Folland Gnat F. Mk 1	G-39-2	18 July 1955	Developed Midge
Supermarine Type 544	WT854	19 Jan 1956	Scimitar prototype. First flight also quoted as 20 January.
Fairey Delta 2	WG777	15 Feb 1956	Second aircraft. Exceeded Mach 1.0 on first flight.
Short SC1	XG900	2 April 1957	Direct lift VTOL research aircraft – first conventional flight
Saunders-Roe SR.53	XD145	16 May 1957	Mixed power (jet and rocket) interceptor
BAC TSR.2	XR219	27 Sept 1964	Low-level penetration bomber whose construction and later cancellation has shaped Britain's military aircraft industry

Avro 707B VX790 displays its dorsal NACA intake. This was the second Avro 707 to fly, taking to the air in September 1950. (Ken Ellis Collection)

The Armstrong Whitworth AW52 TS363 seen at Bitteswell in December 1947, one month after its first flight at Boscombe Down. (BAE SYSTEMS plc via Ken Ellis)

Folland Midge G-39-1 at Boscombe Down. Other aircraft visible include Fairey Delta 1, Valetta, Swift, Provost and two Hunters. (C. Hodson Collection)

Every new service type is flown at Boscombe Down for CA (Controller Aircraft) Release and Armament trials, and these efforts have been supported over the years by a number of experimental and trials support aircraft. A selection of the types used by the A&AEE (now the Air Test and Evaluation organisation of QinetiQ) is indicated below. This list is by no means comprehensive:

- English Electric Canberra B.2 WV787 modified to B(I). Mk 8 configuration and used as an icing spray rig
- Two Avro Lincoln B.2 (RF560, RF561), modified with elongated nose and tail fairings, for radar work
- An extensive fleet of Meteor T.7 aircraft used in photo-chase and calibration roles
- Javelin FAW.9, XH897, which served in an instrument calibration role until 1975 before being retired to Duxford
- Blackburn Beverley XB261, which spent fifteen years at Boscombe Down
- A fleet of North American Harvard aircraft, a number of which spent more than twenty years at Boscombe Down in the photo-chase/observer role

The Short SC1 research aircraft was the first British VTOL aircraft to complete a full transition between wing-borne and jet-borne flight. Its first conventional flight was made at Boscombe Down in April 1957. (Bombardier Aerospace, Belfast)

TSR-2 XR219 banks over the Wiltshire countryside, possibly during its first flight in September 1964. (BAE SYSTEMS plc via Ken Ellis)

The sleek lines of the prototype Westland Whirlwind are emphasised in this photograph, taken prior to its first flight, which demonstrates the smooth surface finish achieved and the closely-cowled Rolls-Royce Peregrine engines. (Westland)

The Wyvern TF.1 prototype TS371 photographed at Yeovil prior to its first flight. (Westland)

Moving the **Armstrong Whitworth** AW52 flying wing to Boscombe Down by road proved to be something of an expedition. The road convoy was more than half a mile long, and progress required bridge strengthening, tree surgery and the removal of shop and road signs.

In 1957 **The Fairey Aviation Co. Ltd** used a dynamic system test rig at Boscombe Down to support the development of the Fairey Rotodyne.

In early 1940, **Flight Refuelling Ltd** used their Armstrong Whitworth AW23, G-AFRX, to carry out the first experimental night refuelling flights from Boscombe Down. G-AFRX was destroyed at Ford in a German air raid on 18 August 1940.

Boscombe Down, like Andover, was sometimes used by **Westland Aircraft Ltd** for first flights. Notable examples are Lysander K6127 on 15 June 1936, Whirlwind L6844 on 11 October 1938 and the Rolls-Royce Eagle-powered Wyvern I prototype TS371 first flown on 16 December 1946. The Clyde-powered Wyvern VP120 followed on 18 January 1949, with Python-powered VP109 flying on 22 March 1949. The last Westland prototype to make its first flight from Boscombe Down was the modified jet deflection Meteor RA490, flown on 15 May 1954. For further details, see Yeovil and Merryfield, Somerset.

Wing Cdr K.H. Wallis: The first autogyro of Ken Wallis' own design, Wallis Autogyro G-ARRT, was first flown from Boscombe Down on 2 August 1961. (The first autogyro to be built by Ken Wallis, Bensen B7 G-APUD, was first flown at Shoreham on 23 May 1959.) Ken Wallis continued the development of the Wallis Autogyro at Reymerston Hall, Norfolk.

Dilton Marsh (near Westbury)

Designability Ltd constructed the prototype **CMC** (Chichester Miles Consultants Ltd) Leopard G-BKRL at Dilton Marsh. The aircraft was first flown at RAE Bedford on 12 December 1988, and has undergone flight test development at Cranfield, Beds.

High Post

Vickers-Armstrongs Ltd: High Post airfield was established in 1931 and used as a Supermarine test airfield from March 1944. High Post replaced Worthy Down, the move being dictated partly by the need for more space to accommodate Spitfire F.21 operations, and partly due to difficulties with intense airfield traffic at Worthy Down. The Spiteful pre-prototype NN660 (a Spitfire XIV with a wholly new wing design) first flew here on 30 June 1944, followed by the first true Spiteful NN664 on 8 January 1945. A total of three prototypes and seventeen production Spiteful were built, although not all of the production aircraft were actually flown.

The Seafang was also flown at High Post; production comprised one (RB520) converted from a Spiteful, plus two purpose-built prototypes and sixteen production aircraft. The E.10/44 prototype, TS409, was built at Hursley Park and assembled at High Post, making its first flight at Boscombe Down on 27 July 1946. The E.10/44 was developed into the Type 398 Attacker naval fighter. The airfield closed in January 1947.

RAF Hullavington

Clive Du Cros' full-size wooden replica (G-BRDV) of the Spitfire prototype K5054 was test flown for the first time from RAF Hullavington on 7 June 1991.

RAF Keevil

Vickers-Armstrongs Ltd: Supermarine Spitfire aircraft constructed by the Trowbridge area dispersed organisation were erected and test flown from Keevil.

John Fairey's Spitfire Trainer 8, seen here at Andover, was first flown at Vickers-Armstrongs' airfield at High Post. (Via Author)

VALKYRIE
MONOPLANES.

THREE TYPES.   40–80 MILES AN HOUR.   FROM £280.

ALL BRANCHES OF AERONAUTICAL ENGINEERING.
DESIGNING AND CONSTRUCTION.
ALL STANDARD TYPES OF AEROPLANES.   PROPELLERS A SPECIALITY.

TUITION FREE TO PURCHASERS.   *PARTICULARS ON REQUEST.*
THE AERONAUTICAL SYNDICATE, LTD.,
ESTABLISHED MARCH, 1909,
COLLINDALE AVENUE :: WEST HENDON, LONDON, N.W.
Telegrams—"AEROVALKY, LONDON."   Telephone—KINGSBURY 14.

Right: (Copyright: BAE SYSTEMS plc)

Below: *The British & Colonial Aeroplane Co. sheds still stand at Larkhill, being among Britain's earliest (and least heralded) aviation heritage sites.* (Author)

HIGH PERFORMANCE FIGHTER AIRCRAFT

SEAFANG
SPITEFUL
SEAFIRE
SPITFIRE

DESIGNED AND CONSTRUCTED BY
VICKERS-ARMSTRONGS LIMITED
AIRCRAFT SECTION
SUPERMARINE WORKS

Larkhill

The Aeronautical Syndicate Ltd was formed in March 1909 by Horatio Barber. Its main design was the Valkyrie canard pusher monoplane, which was initially tested at Durrington Down, close to Larkhill. In September 1910, the Aeronautical Syndicate moved its operations to Hendon. Three Valkyrie variants were built as the Valkyrie A, B and C.

The **British & Colonial Aeroplane Co. Ltd** had a works and flying school at Larkhill from June 1910. The school used early Bristol aircraft, most of which were designed by E.C. Gordon England. Seven Bristol BR7 were in use here in 1913. The site extended to 2,284 acres and lay to the north and east of Stonehenge. The Bristol Boxkite was first

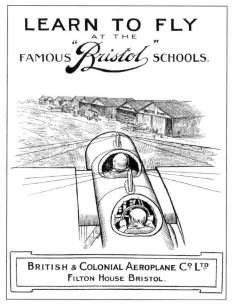

Above and left: (Copyright: BAE SYSTEMS plc)

Below: *This 1912 photograph shows a Gordon England-designed Bristol GE3 biplane, a Prier training monoplane and a Coanda military monoplane. The open aspect of this busy site is in complete contrast to the trees and houses of the present day. The wording on the front of the sheds was prominently featured in contemporary advertising by the company.* (BAE SYSTEMS plc via Duncan Greenman)

flown here on 30 July 1910. Sir George White erected three large sheds at Larkhill, where they remain to this day, albeit surrounded by trees and buildings. A plinth in Wood Road, Larkhill in front of the British & Colonial sheds records:

> *On this site the first aerodrome for the Army was founded in 1910 by Capt. J. Fulton RFA and Mr G.B. Cockburn. The British and Colonial Aeroplane Company, forerunners of the Bristol Aeroplane Company, established their Flying School here in 1910. In September 1910 experiments were conducted using a Bristol machine which were successful in establishing one way radio communication from an aeroplane in flight. The first military air trials were held here in 1912.*

The British & Colonial Schools at Larkhill and Brooklands were undoubtedly the most important and successful flying schools in the years prior to the First World War. In 1911, they taught fifty-six pilots to fly, virtually half the total for the whole UK. Up to the outbreak of the First World War, the Bristol Schools had trained 309 pilots out of a UK total of 664, continuing this excellent record.

In November 1911, the company was advertising that 'The Bristol Flying Schools at Salisbury Plain and Brooklands have trained nearly 1/3rd of England's aviators...a greater percentage than any other school in the country. Average time occupied in tuition – 3 weeks.' The Bristol School at Larkhill closed on 14 May 1914, transferring to Brooklands. One of the last British & Colonial types to be flown at Larkhill was the Bristol Scout A, which was first flown on 23 February 1914.

British Aircraft before the Great War lists two other early types to have been flown at Larkhill: the **Carter** biplane of 1911 and the **Cockburn** biplane of 1912. The Carter machine was a fairly crude-looking single-seat biplane, with wings of unequal span. It was reported to have made short straight flights in January 1911, but does not appear to have been successful. The Cockburn machine (the responsibility of the G.B. Cockburn mentioned on the commemorative plaque in Wood Road) was similarly briefly reported in January 1912. The machine was reported by *The Aeroplane* to be 'a miniature Farman', and was therefore presumably of 'Boxkite' configuration.

For the purpose of the 1912 Military Trials, twelve temporary hangars were established next to the British & Colonial Aeroplane Co. sheds. On 23 August 1912, whilst flying in the Military Trials, Wilfred Parke, flying the Avro Type G biplane, accidentally entered a spin, recovered successfully and described the control actions that produced recovery. This major contribution to flight safety was known as 'Parke's Dive'. Recovery was achieved at very low level immediately in front of the Bristol sheds. After the completion of the Trials, the Type G was flown at Shoreham and at Brooklands.

Old Sarum

Aircraft manufacture at Old Sarum has been associated with the production, by a series of companies, of the Edgley Optica and Norman Fieldmaster. These production activities are described chronologically below.

Edgley Aircraft Co. Ltd, which was formed in 1974, chose Old Sarum as a production site for the Optica observation aircraft. The first production aircraft, G-BLFC, flew on 4 August 1984. The company ran into financial problems and production was halted when the company entered receivership in October 1985. **Optica Industries Ltd** took over Optica production from Edgley, restarting production in January 1986, only for the production line to be destroyed as a result of arson on the night of 16/17 January 1987.

Brooklands Aircraft Co. Ltd: Optica Industries became the Brooklands Aircraft Co. Ltd (later Brooklands Aerospace Ltd) on 14 April 1987, after the hangar fire. Brooklands continued Optica production and took over production of the Fieldmaster from **Norman Aeroplane Co. Ltd** (NAC) when NAC, previously **NDN Aircraft Ltd**, entered receivership in mid-1988.

The Fieldmaster project was sold to **Croplease Ltd** in April 1989. Brooklands developed a fire-fighting variant, the Firemaster 65, under contract from Croplease, the prototype of which (modified from Fieldmaster G-NACL) first flew at Old Sarum on 28 October 1989. Brooklands Aircraft Co. Ltd entered administration on 23 March 1990, following which the Optica project was taken up by **FLS Lovaux**. Optica production comprises the initial prototype, fifteen aircraft built by Optica Industries, five built as the Scoutmaster by Brooklands Aerospace and two OA7-300 constructed by FLS/Lovaux.

Salisbury

Vickers-Armstrongs Ltd: Supermarine Spitfire production was dispersed following the bombing of the Southampton factories in late 1940. Salisbury became a production centre, with fuselages built at Wessex Motors; wings at the Wilts & Dorset Bus Garage; fuselage assembly, engine installation, leading edge manufacture and wing assembly at Castle Road works; and final assembly and test at Chattis Hill training gallops, which were also used for powerplant overhaul. Salisbury production included the Spitfire Marks V, IX, XII, XIV and Seafire. The nearby airfield at High Post later became the experimental flight test centre.

South Marston

Phillips & Powis Aircraft Ltd: South Marston was used as a shadow factory for the production of the Miles Master, some 900 Master II and III being built here. Construction of the factory (by Spears of London & Glasgow Ltd) was started at the beginning of 1940, with full production being achieved by the end of that year, the first aircraft being delivered on 13 March 1941.

The site was used by **Short Brothers (Rochester & Bedford) Ltd** for dispersed production of the Short Stirling, together with associated factories in nearby Blunsdon and Highworth, after the closure of the Rochester factory due to enemy action. The Short Stirling and Miles Master were produced contemporaneously, the two assembly lines being on opposite sides of the site.

Above: *Supermarine Type 525 VX138 was the precursor to the Type 545 Scimitar, and one of a series of prototypes and development aircraft flown between 1946 and 1957.* (Via Author)

Right: (Copyright: BAE SYSTEMS plc)

Opposite: *The first production Optica G-BLFC flies past The Needles.* (Ken Ellis Collection)

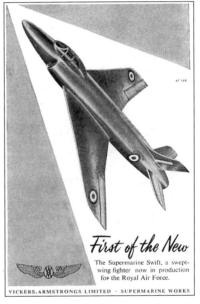

First of the New

The Supermarine Swift, a swept-wing fighter now in production for the Royal Air Force.

VICKERS-ARMSTRONGS LIMITED · SUPERMARINE WORKS

Subsequent to its use for Stirling production, South Marston became the province of **Vickers-Armstrongs Ltd (Supermarine Division)**, and was operated as an off-shoot of the Castle Bromwich shadow factory. The main production types were late model Spitfire (F. Mk 21, 22, 24) and Seafire (F. Mk 45, 46, 47). Subsequent production included the Attacker, Swift and Scimitar.

Thirty-six Attacker aircraft were delivered by air to Pakistan from South Marston, these non-naval aircraft being used for land-based operations. Including prototypes, a total of 184 were built (three prototypes, 145 for the Fleet Air Arm and thirty-six for Pakistan).

The first production Swift F. Mk 1 WK194 was flown on 25 August 1952, to be followed by the first production Swift F. Mk 4 WK198 on 27 May 1953. WK 198 was used to break the world speed record on 25 September 1953, attaining a speed of 737.7mph. Including the final prototypes (see Chilbolton), production comprised: two Type 541; twenty F. Mk 1; sixteen F. Mk 2; twenty-five F. Mk 3; thirty-nine F. Mk 4 (most converted to FR. Mk 5); fifty-nine FR. Mk 5 (plus cancelled orders for a further 108 aircraft); one PR. Mk 6 XF780; one prototype (XF774); and twelve production F. Mk 7. Total production was, therefore, 175 aircraft.

Attacker WA486 is prominent in this mixed formation, in the company of a Sea Hawk, a Sea Vampire F.20 and two Gloster Meteors. (Via Nick Blackman)

The Type 545 Scimitar was developed from the Supermarine 525 VX138, via three Supermarine 544 development aircraft, the first of which (WT854) was flown on 19 January 1956 (some sources state 20 January). The first production Scimitar, XD212, was flown on 11 January 1957 and was followed by an additional seventy-five production machines. The last aircraft left South Marston during December 1960. The Scimitar was, perhaps, never the most glamorous type, but it was well liked by its pilots as a solid machine endowed with excellent handling qualities. After 1957 South Marston replaced Hursley Park as the location of the Vickers-Armstrongs design office.

The site is now split between Honda (whose facility extends over a significant portion of the airfield) and a group of factory units on the northern side of the site. Spitfire F. Mk 21, LA226, was preserved here from 1968 until 1984. One group of buildings remains in use by Vickers Property as offices, and some of the hangars are used for furniture storage and by a timberyard. As one leaves the industrial park, one passes the Supermarine Sports Club, the only direct evidence now available of the site's history.

Sutton Benger

The **Angus** Aquila G-ABIK was designed and built by Mr Arthur Angus of Sutton Benger in 1931 and was flown briefly at Hanworth before being destroyed in a fatal accident.

Trowbridge

John Greenland has painstakingly built a **Comper** Swift to the original drawings, the aircraft flying for the first time on 7 August 1993, registered as G-LCGL. The aircraft was constructed at Blackacre Farm, Holt, near Trowbridge.

Vickers-Armstrongs Ltd: Trowbridge was the location of one of the dispersed Supermarine Spitfire production centres. Fuselage manufacture and wing assembly were carried out at Bradley Road and aircraft erection and flight test took place at Keevil. There were a number of other facilities in Trowbridge and Westbury contributing to this effort. Trowbridge production included the Spitfire Mk V, IX and XIV.

Bibliography

50 Golden Years of Achievement, Hamble 1936-1986 (British Aerospace, 1986)

75 Years of Aviation in Kingston, 1913-1988 (British Aerospace, 1988)

Andrews, C.F. and Morgan, E.B., *Vickers Aircraft since 1908* (Putnam, second edition, 1988)

Aspin, Chris, *Dizzy Heights – The Story of Lancashire's First Flying Men* (Helmshore Local History Society, 1988)

Babington Smith, Constance, *Testing Time* (Cassell & Co. Ltd, 1961)

BAe Corporate Communications, *British Aerospace – The Facts* (British Aerospace, 1992 and 1996)

Banks, Air Cdr F.R., *I Kept No Diary* (Airlife, 1978)

Baring, Maurice, *Flying Corps Headquarters 1914-1918* (Buchan & Enright Ltd, (reprint) 1985)

Barnes, C.H., *Bristol Aircraft since 1910* (Putnam, 1964)

— *Shorts Aircraft since 1900* (Putnam, 1989)

Blackmore, L.K., *Hawker – A biography of Harry Hawker* (Airlife, 1993)

Boot, Roy, *From Spitfire to Eurofighter* (Airlife, 1990)

Borlase-Matthews, R., *The Aviation Pocket-Book 1919-1920* (Crosby, Lockwood & Son, seventh edition, 1919)

Boughton, Terence, *The Story of the British Light Aeroplane* (John Murray, 1963)

Boulton Paul Association, *Boulton Paul Aircraft* (Chalford Publishing, 1996)

Bramson, Alan, *Pure Luck – The Authorized Biography of Sir Thomas Sopwith 1888-1989* (Patrick Stephens Ltd, 1990)

Brett, R. Dallas, *History of British Aviation 1908-1914* (Air Research Publications & Kristall Productions. Eightieth Anniversary Edition, 1988)

Brew, Alec, *Staffordshire and Black Country Airfields* (Chalford Publishing, 1997)

— *The History of Black Country Aviation* (Alan Sutton, 1993)

Bruce, J.M., *British Aeroplanes, 1914-1918* (Putnam, 1962)

Burnet, Charles, *Three Centuries to Concorde* (Mechanical Engineering Publications Ltd, 1979)

Campbell, Peter G. ed., *Tails of the Fifties* (Cirrus Associates (SW), 1997)

— *More Tails of the Fifties* (Cirrus Associates (SW), 1998)

Catchpole, Brian, *Balloons to Buccaneers – Yorkshire's Role in Aviation since 1785* (Maxiprint, 1994)

Clouston, A.E., *The Dangerous Skies* (Pan Books, 1956)

Cluett, Douglas, ed.; Learmonth, Bob and Nash, Joanna, *The First Croydon Airport 1915-1928* (Sutton Libraries and Arts Services, 1977)

Cobham, Sir Alan, *A Time to Fly* (Shepheard-Walwyn, 1978)

Cooper, H.J. and Thetford, O.G., *Aircraft of the Fighting Powers, Volumes 1-5* (Harborough Publishing, 1940-1944)

Cooper, P.J., *Forever Farnborough – Flying the Limits 1904-1996* (Hikoki Publications, 1996)

Coulson, Phil, *Proud Heritage – A Pictorial History of British Aerospace Aircraft* (Royal Air Force Benevolent Fund, 1995)

Curtis, Lettice, *The Forgotten Pilots* (Nelson Saunders, third edition, 1985)

Dowsett, Alan, *Handley Page* (Tempus Publishing, 1999)

Duke, Nevil, *Test Pilot* (Allan Wingate, 1953)

Duval, G.R., *British Floatplanes* (D. Bradford Barton, 1976)

East, R.A. and Cheeseman, I.C., *Forty Years of the Spitfire – Proceedings of the Mitchell Memorial Symposium* (Royal Aeronautical Society, Southampton Branch, 1976)

Ellis, Ken, *British Homebuilt Aircraft since 1920* (Merseyside Aviation Society, second edition, 1979)

Ellis, Paul, *Aircraft of the RAF, a pictorial record 1918-1978* (Macdonald and Jane's, 1978)

— *British Commercial Aircraft – Sixty Years in Pictures* (Jane's Publishing, 1980)

Endres, Günter, *British Aircraft Manufacturers since 1908* (Ian Allan Publishing, 1995)

Falconer, Jonathan, *Stirling Wings – The Short Stirling goes to War* (Budding Books, 1995)

Fletcher, Lt-Com. R., 'Britain's Air Strength', *The Air Defence of Great Britain* (Penguin, 1938)

Foxworth, Thomas G., *The Speed Seekers,* (Macdonald and Jane's, 1975)

Gardner, Jean, *Aviation Landmarks* (Battle of Britain Prints International, 1990)

Georgano, Nick; Baldwin, Nick; Clausager, Anders and Wood, Jonathan, *Britain's Motor Industry – The First Hundred Years* (G.T. Foulis & Co., 1995)

Gingell, G.N.M., *Supermarine Spitfire – 40 Years On* (Royal Aeronautical Society, Southampton Branch, 1976)

Goodall, Michael H. and Tagg, Albert E., *British Aircraft before the Great War* (Schiffer Publishing Ltd, 2001)

Green, William and Cross, Roy, *The Jet Aircraft of the World* (Macdonald, 1955)

Green, William and Pollinger, Gerard, *The Aircraft of the World* (Macdonald, 1953)
— *The Aircraft of the World* (Macdonald, 1955)
Green, William, *The Aircraft of the World* (Macdonald, 1965)
Gunston, Bill, *Fighters of the Fifties* (Patrick Stephens Ltd, 1981)
— *Plane Speaking* (Patrick Stephens Ltd, 1991)
— *World Encyclopaedia of Aircraft Manufacturers* (Patrick Stephens Ltd, 1993)
Hall, Malcolm, *Filton and the Flying Machine* (Chalford Publishing, 1995)
Hallam, Sqn Ldr T.D., *The Spider Web* (Arms & Armour Press, (reprint) 1979)
Hamlin, J.F., *Peaceful Fields... Volume 1: The South* (GMS Enterprises, 1996)
Henshaw, Alex, *The Flight of the Mew Gull* (John Murray, 1980)
Holmes, Harry, *Avro* (Chalford Publishing, 1996)
— *AVRO: The History of an Aircraft Company* (Airlife, 1994)
Hooker, Sir Stanley, *Not much of an Engineer* (Airlife, 1984)
Jack Webster *The Flying Scots – A Century of Aviation in Scotland* (The Glasgow Royal Concert Hall, 1994)
Jackson, A.J., *Avro Aircraft since 1908* (Putnam, 1965)
— *British Civil Aircraft since 1919* (Putnam, second edition, Vol. 1 1973, Vol. 2 1973, Vol. 3 1974)
James, Derek N., *Spirit of Hamble – Folland Aircraft* (Tempus Publishing, 2000)
— *Westland Aircraft since 1919* (Putnam, 1991)
Jarram, A. P., *Brush Aircraft production at Loughborough* (Midland Counties Publications, 1978)
King, Peter, *Knights of the Air* (Constable & Co. Ltd, 1989)
Lambermont, Paul and Pirie, Anthony, *Helicopters and Autogyros of the World* (Cassell, 1958)
Lane, John, *The Redwing Story* (Mrs Phyllis Lane, 1992)
Lewis, Peter, *British Aircraft, 1809-1914* (Putnam, 1962)
— *British Racing and Record Breaking Aircraft* (Putnam, 1970)
Lithgow, Mike, *Mach One* (Allan Wingate, 1954)
— *Vapour Trails* (Allan Wingate, 1956)
Marshall, Sir Arthur, *The Marshall Story* (Patrick Stephens Ltd, 1994)
Mason, F.K., *Hawker Aircraft since 1920* (Putnam, 1961)
— *The British Bomber since 1914* (Putnam, 1994)
— *The British Fighter since 1912* (Putnam, 1992)
Mason, Tim, *British Flight Testing: Martlesham Heath 1920-1939* (Putnam, 1993)
— *The Cold War Years – Flight Testing at Boscombe Down 1945-1975* (Hikoki Publications Ltd, 2001)
McMahon, Lou, and Partridge, Michael, *A History of the Eastbourne Aviation Company 1911-1924* (Eastbourne Local History Society, 2000)
Middleton, Don, *Test Pilots – The story of British Test Flying 1903-1984* (Willow Books, 1985)
Mondey, David, *British Aircraft of World War II* (Chancellor Press, 1994 edition)
— *The Schneider Trophy* (Robert Hale, 1975)
Negus, Geoffrey and Staddon, Tommy, *Aviation in Birmingham* (Midland Counties Publications, 1984)
Nockholds, Harold, *The Magic of a Name* (G.T. Foulis & Co. Ltd, 1949)
Oliver, David, *Hendon Aerodrome – A History* (Airlife, 1994)
Ord-Hume, Arthur W.J.G., *British Light Aeroplanes – Their Evolution, Development and Perfection 1920-1940* (GMS Enterprises, 2000)
Oughton, James D., *Bristol: An Aircraft Album* (Ian Allan, 1973)
Pearcy, Arthur, *Lend-Lease Aircraft of World War II* (Motorbooks International, 1996)
Pegg, A.J., *Sent Flying* (Macdonald, 1959)
Penrose, Harald, *Adventure with Fate* (Airlife, 1984)
— *British Aviation – Ominous Skies* (HMSO, 1980)
— *British Aviation – The Adventuring Years* (Putnam, 1973)
— *British Aviation – The Pioneer Years* (Cassell Ltd, revised edition 1980)
— *British Aviation – Widening Horizons* (HMSO, 1979)
Powell, Wing Cdr H.P., *Men with Wings* (Allan Wingate, 1957)
Price, Alfred, *The Spitfire Story* (Arms & Armour Press, second edition, 1995)
Quill, J.K., *Spitfire – A Test Pilot's Story* (John Murray, 1983)
Ransom, S. and Fairclough, R., *English Electric Aircraft and their Predecessors* (Putnam, 1987)
Riding, Richard, *Ultralights – The Early British Classics* (Patrick Stephens Ltd, 1987)
Ritchie, Sebastian, *Industry and Air Power: The Expansion of British Aircraft Production, 1935-1941* (Frank Cass, 1997)
Robertson, Alan, *Lion Rampant and Winged* (Alan Robertson, 1986)
Robertson, Bruce, *Aviation Archaeology* (Patrick Stephens Ltd, second edition, 1983)
— *British Military Aircraft Serials 1878-1987* (Midland Counties Publications, 1987)
— *Sopwith – The Man and His Aircraft* (Air Review Ltd, 1970)
Robinson, Brian R., *Aviation in Manchester* (Royal Aeronautical Society, Manchester Branch, 1977)
Saunders, Hilary St George, *Per Ardua – The Rise of British Air Power 1911-1939* (Oxford University Press, 1944)
Shaw, Paul, *Discover Aviation Trails* (Midland Publishing, 1996)

Shute, Nevil, *Slide Rule* (Readers Union, 1956)
Simpson, R.W., *Airlife's General Aviation* (Airlife, 1991)
Slade, Brian, *Leysdown – The Cradle of Flight* (Santa-Maria Publications, 1990)
Smithies, Edward, *War in the Air* (Penguin, 1992)
Sturtivant, Ray, *British Prototype Aircraft* (The Promotional Reprint Co. Ltd, 1995)
Swanborough, Gordon, *British Aircraft at War 1939-45* (HPC Publishing, 1997)
Tapper, Oliver, *Armstrong Whitworth Aircraft since 1913* (Putnam, 1973)
Taylor, H.A., *Fairey Aircraft since 1915* (Putnam, 1974)
Taylor, J.W.R. and Allward, Maurice F., *Westland 50* (Ian Allan, 1965)
Taylor, J.W.R., *Fairey Aviation* (Chalford Publishing, 1997)
Taylor, Michael J.H., *The Aerospace Chronology* (Tri-Service Press, 1989)
Taylor, Michael, *Brassey's World Aircraft & Systems Directory* (Brassey's (UK) Ltd, 1996)
Temple, Julian C., *Wings over Woodley – The Story of Miles Aircraft and the Adwest Group* (Aston
    Publications, 1987)
The Aeroplane Directory of British Aviation (Staff of *The Aeroplane*, Temple Press Ltd, 1953)
The Story of Acton Aerodrome and the Alliance Factory (London Borough of Ealing Library Service,
    second edition, 1978)
Thetford, O.G. and Maycock, C.B., *Aircraft of the Fighting Powers, Volume 6* (Harborough Publishing,
    1945)
Thetford, O.G. and Riding, E.J., *Aircraft of the Fighting Powers, Volume 7* (Harborough Publishing, 1946)
Merriam, F. Warren, *First through the Clouds* (B.T. Batsford Ltd, 1954)
Waterton, W.A., *The Quick and The Dead* (Frederick Muller Ltd, 1956)
Webb, T.M.A. and Bird, Dennis L., *Shoreham Airport, Sussex* (Cirrus Associates (SW), 1996)
Wheeler, Air Cdr A.H., *That Nothing Failed Them* (G.T. Foulis & Co. Ltd, 1963)
Wixey, Ken, *Gloucestershire Aviation – A History* (Alan Sutton, 1995)
 — *Parnall's Aircraft* (Tempus Publishing, 1998)

Magazines and other publications:

Flight, numerous editions of 'The First Aero Weekly in the World – A Journal Devoted to the Interests,
    Practice and Progress of Aerial Locomotion and Transport. Official Organ of The Royal Aero Club of
    the United Kingdom'
Grey, C.G. and James, Thurstan, eds, *The Aeroplane* (Temple Press Ltd)
Aeroplane Monthly (IPC Magazines Ltd)
The Aeroplane Spotter July 1941-December 1945 (Temple Press Ltd)
Jane's All the Worlds Aircraft, various editions from 1909 to date (Samson Low, Jane's Information Group,
    and (reprints) David & Charles Ltd, Collins & Jane's)
Popular Flying (The Magazine of the Popular Flying Association)
Royal Air Force Flying Review, 1954-55, 1957-58, 1961-62 (Mercury House)

Index

Visit our website and discover thousands of other History Press books.

www.thehistorypress.co.uk